BE CIVIL!

BE CIVIL!

a guide to learning civil
litigation and evidence

VIRGINIA DUNN

Worth Publishing

First published 2011 by Worth Publishing Ltd
www.worthpublishing.com

Printed and bound in Great Britain by Good News Digital Books Ltd

British Library Cataloguing in Publication Data
A catalogue record for this book is available from the British Library

ISBN 9781903269206

Cover and text design by Anna Murphy

For Ray and Rosie

About the author

Virginia V Dunn, BA, MA, Barrister began practice in civil and family law and spent most of the last 25 years teaching students training for the Bar at the Inns of Court School of Law, now the City Law School. She taught a range of subjects there, including litigation and evidence. For much of the time, she co-ordinated the civil litigation course, and has first-hand knowledge of how the subject is taught and assessed. She is currently a Visiting Lecturer there. She contributes to several of the City Law School's Bar Manuals supporting training for the Bar, and has written for the Institute of Legal Executives. This book is the culmination of many years helping students to enjoy learning the subject with her popular revision notes.

Preface

If you are reading this, my guess is you are getting ready to sit a professional examination. Whether you are at the beginning or end of your course or, having already qualified, are embarking on a change of direction in early practice, this book is intended to help. Its purpose is to make civil litigation easier and more fun to understand, so that when the time comes, you really know what you are talking about.

My experience of teaching has shown me that most students look upon civil procedure, not so much as a Cinderella subject, but as one of the ugly step-sisters. It often seems to them like an avalanche of apparently disjointed rules and regulations, so that what is covered in class one week is forgotten the next. And anyway (they think) crime is *so* much more fun. This attitude makes it hard to get to grips with the subject. My approach is intended as an antidote.

The key to learning civil litigation is to see the big picture. If, for example, you are putting together a jigsaw puzzle, it is much more difficult if you do not know what it should look like when it is completed. That is what I hope to provide. You have been (or are about) to look at all the individual pieces of the civil litigation puzzle in some detail on your course. This book is the picture on the box.

It is intended to augment, not replace, your own learning. It can assist with classroom preparation, by allowing you to focus intelligently on the subject matter, research more knowledgeably and contribute intelligently to discussions, rather than merely writing down everything you see and hear. It should be especially helpful as you prepare for examinations by reinforcing the bigger picture while reviewing the essential individual concepts. I also offer many revision tips. This book should also remind you of the value of common sense (an under-rated commodity) in learning how to think about and understand any aspect of the law, including civil procedure and evidence.

This book is the product of many years of helping students to learn and enjoy its subject. In particular it is an elaboration of the revision notes they had access to when I taught full-time at the Inns of Court School of Law/City Law School. I am grateful to all of my students – past and present – for teaching me to teach them better. Many colleagues at City Law School were also very supportive of this enterprise, in particular: Lisa Laurenti (who keeps me teaching and learning), Catherine Hill (who keeps me in touch with my roots), Ros Carne (who tried, with limited success, to curb my enthusiasm for exclamation marks), Robert McPeake (whose library extended to *Hart's Rules*) and especially Stuart Sime, who spent time he did not have to make some very useful editorial suggestions. My most grateful thanks, however, go to Ronnie Lachkovic (who runs the BPTC Civil Litigation course at City Law School) and Sir Peter Coulson, who kindly wrote the Foreword. Ronnie (who doubles as Lady Coulson) not only took a personal interest in the book (and its author), but also the time to read virtually all of the manuscript, which is very much improved as a result. Neither she, nor anyone else of course, should be held accountable for any of its content, and any errors which remain are mine alone.

I should also thank my supportive daughters, Eden, Kate and Rachael Sanders, who have become adept at making their own or ready-meals (which they sometimes like better than mine, if the truth be told) while I was chained to my desk. Finally, I should like to pay tribute to Martin Wood and Andrea Perry at Worth Publishing for their help in producing this book. It took patience, professionalism and good humour, which they have in abundance.

The dedication is to two people very close to my heart, always: my husband Ray Sanders, a social security appeal judge, who died in 2002, and Rosie Samwell-Smith, former BVC course director at the ICSL, who died in 2010. How I wish they were here to see this.

VVD
London
March 2011

Foreword

One of the principal aims of the Woolf reforms and the Civil Procedure Rules was to streamline civil litigation, and make it simpler and more straightforward. It might be said that, with the White Book running to two fat volumes, we have yet to fully achieve that ambition. And although there can be little doubt that the situation has improved considerably since my early days in practice, it is also undeniable that a student confronting the CPR for the first time needs a sensible place to start the process of assimilation.

That is where this useful book comes in. 'Be Civil!' presents a convenient, short guide to the basic rules of civil practice and procedure, expressed in clear and direct language. It will be an admirable companion for those wrestling with the subject for the first time. And it even manages the difficult feat of making its subject matter both interesting and fun. I have no doubt that it will be very popular with students and new practitioners.

The Hon Sir Peter Coulson
Member of the Civil Procedure Rules Committee

Glossary of terms

Affidavit This is a written, sworn statement containing evidence. It was at one time commonly used to support interim applications, so will still be referred to in older cases. Affidavits are still used for freezing and search orders, but most interim applications nowadays present their supporting evidence by means of witness statements.

Alternative Dispute Resolution (ADR) This is a collective description for methods of resolving disputes otherwise than through the normal litigation process.

Civil Procedure Rules (CPR) One of the primary sources of procedural law in England and Wales. It was brought in as a new procedural code in 1999.

Cross-examination *(compare with examination-in-chief)* Questioning of a witness by a party other than the party who called the witness.

Damages A sum of money awarded by the court as compensation to the claimant. 'Additional' damages punish a defendant's objectionable behaviour and 'exemplary' damages compensate a claimant for it.

Evidence-in-Chief The evidence given by a witness for the party who called him.

Examination-in-Chief The questioning process by which a party's evidence-in-chief is elicited orally.

Joint liability *(see also several liability)* Parties who are jointly liable share a single liability and each party can be held liable for the whole of it.

Overriding Objective The principal aspiration of the CPR, which is to deal with cases justly.

Obiter Judicial observation in a case which is not strictly binding, as it is not the point to be decided in the case.

Part 36 Offer A formal offer of settlement under the CPR.

Plaintiff   Pre-CPR description for a Claimant.

Pleadings   This is an old-fashioned way of referring to statements of case.

Practice Form   Form to be used for a particular purpose, as specified by a practice direction.

Privilege   The right of a party to refuse to disclose or produce a document or to answer questions on the ground of some special interest recognised by law.

Set aside   Cancelling a judgment or order or step taken by a party in the proceedings.

Several liability   A person who is severally liable with others may remain liable
(see also joint liability) for the whole claim even where judgment has been obtained against others.

Stay   A stay imposes a halt on proceedings, apart from taking any steps allowed by the rules or the terms of the stay. Proceedings can continue if, but only if the stay is lifted.

Tort   A civil wrong, other than breach of contract, which is compensated by damages.

Westlaw   An online legal resource.

Without Prejudice   Negotiations with a view to settlement are normally conducted 'without prejudice'. This means that the circumstances in which the content of those negotiations may be revealed to the court are very limited.

Abbreviations and references

ADR	Alternative Dispute Resolution
ATE	After-the-event
BCP	Blackstone's Civil Practice
BPTC	Bar Professional Training Course
BVC	Bar Vocation Course (before re-named BPTC)
CFA	Conditional Fee Agreement
CH	Chancery Division (of the High Court)
CLS	Community Legal Service
CPR	Civil Procedure Rules
CRU	Compensation Recovery Unit
ECHR	European Court of Human Rights
ECJ	European Court of Justice
GLO	Group Litigation Order
LEI	Legal Expenses Insurance
LSC	Legal Services Commission
MIB	Motor Insurance Bureau
MR	Master of the Roles
para/s.	paragraph/s in CPR and BCP and WB etc
PD	Practice Direction
PI	Personal Injuries
PSLA	Pain, suffering, loss of amenity element of personal injuries damages
r/rr.	rule/s
RSC	Rules of Supreme Court (predecessor to CPR)
RTA	Road traffic accident
SATs	Standard Achievement Tests (school assessments)
s/ss.	section/s
TCC	Technology and Construction Court
WB	The White Book (Civil Procedure)
WFO	Worldwide freezing order

Case References

AC	Appeal Court
All ER	All England Law Reports
CPLR	Civil Procedure Law Reports (Westlaw)
EWCA	Neutral case citation for Court of Appeal case
EWHC	Neutral case citation for High Court case
FSR	Fleet Street Reports
KB	Kings Bench (Older Law Report Citation)
LSG	Law Society Gazette
NLJ	New Law Journal
QB	Queen's Bench Division of the High Court
RPC	Reports of Patent, Design and Trade Mark cases
UKHL	Neutral case citation for House of Lords case
UKPC	Neutral case citation for Privy Council case
WLR	Weekly Law Reports
[ ]	Indicates para/section of judgment

Statute References

AJA 199	Access to Justice Act 1999
CEA 1995	Civil Evidence Act 1995
CJJA 1982	Civil Judgments and Jurisdiction Act 1982
HRA 1998	Human Rights Act 1998
LA 1980	Limitation Act 1980
SCA 1981	Senior Courts (formerly Supreme Court) Act 1981
SoGA 1979	Sale of Goods Act 1979

Contents

BE CIVIL!

Introduction

This book sets out the nuts and bolts of the way in which disputes are resolved in the civil courts of England and Wales. It is written primarily for students on the Bar Professional Training Course ('BPTC'), but will also be of use to solicitors and other practitioners. It can be used as an overview, as your course progresses, or more particularly as a revision guide, as you prepare for your professional examinations or experience early practice. What it is not is a substitute for your own learning. This book can do a lot for you, but it cannot do everything.

So there are some ground rules. *The first is that you must learn your way around the accepted practitioner texts.* If you are on the BPTC, you will have been given what is known in the trade (for obvious reasons if you are looking at a copy) as the 'White Book'.[1] This is still the favoured reference book of most judges, so you must familiarise yourself with it, and know how to use it. But take it gradually – you do not need to go all the way on the first date!

The White Book comes in two volumes. The first contains the relevant rules and other primary source material, accompanied by explanatory notes as appropriate. This commentary is, of course, a secondary source of information, although it will lead you to relevant case law. One of the nice things about this lay-out is that the primary and secondary source materials appear side-by-side, and

---

1 There is also a 'Green Book' (yes, it is green). There was a time when this was used only for procedure in the County Court, and the White Book only for that in the High Court, but because the rules are now essentially the same for both jurisdictions, this division of labour no longer exists (although County Court practitioners may be a little more apt to use the Green Book). Both books are set out in similar ways, so if you can use the one, you can use the other.

are easily distinguished one from the other,[2] so it is easy to move from one to the other. Volume II contains procedural legislation (more primary source material), specialist information, and some very useful general guidance in Sections 11 to 15. Have a look inside the cover to each volume for a guide to its contents. When I refer to the White Book in my footnotes, I will use the abbreviation 'WB'.

You may also have been given Blackstone's Civil Practice ('BCP'). This is the newer kid on the block. It performs a similar function to the White Book in that it contains the same sort of primary and secondary source material, but the presentation is different. BCP is rather more of a cross between a textbook and a practitioner reference work, and for this reason tends to be more helpful to students. It comes in one volume, the first half of which is complete commentary. All of the primary source material is in the second half. This allows you to read the commentary in coherent chapters, but it does mean you have to flip back and forth between the explanatory text and the relevant rules, which can be a little frustrating at times. However, it covers some areas of interest which the White Book does not (for example, guidance on drafting statements of case), includes useful tables and examples, and beginners may find its procedural checklists easier to follow than the White Book's. Again, look at the contents summary for a quick guide to what is inside.

In short, both works have strengths and drawbacks. I will thus make what I hope is even-handed reference to both throughout this book[3], bearing in mind the needs of the novice. Both are published annually and produce supplements when between editions. Both contain print which is getting so vanishingly small (although I think the White Book wins the prize here) that at times you will wish you had a magnifying glass (I am sure I have seen 'terms and conditions' in a bigger font!). Similarly, both are printed on paper which you may fear will dissolve

---

2 For example, the rules are all in bold, and the font size is different when you move to the commentary.

3 References will be to the most up-to-date editions available at the time of writing, namely WB 2010 and BCP 2011.

in your hands, but it won't. It is surprisingly resilient! You just need to be patient and in the right frame of mind when you use these books. Take it slowly and do not rush.

To the extent that you are not provided with copies by your course, they will be in any decent law library. Consult them there – do not feel you must purchase them! You may, at first, find BCP more accessible, certainly in terms of learning the subject, but even so you *must also* become *confident at navigating the White Book.* Let's be honest – no-one reads these books for pleasure. They are reference works for practitioners who understand the subject and need to keep up-to-date. Their primary purpose is to inform, not teach. So, you do not have to love them, but you do need to know *how to use* them. The more you understand the subject, the easier it will become. But when your pupil supervisor turns to you in court and asks you to look up something for her quickly in the White Book, she needs a fast result, not a blank stare. Judges will not like it either if the practitioner source they prefer is the one whose cover you have never opened.

The second ground rule is that you must read some cases. By that I do not mean the headnotes or summaries or a précis or an analysis in a textbook (although read those too if you wish) – I mean *actual judgments given by actual judges*! This, of course, is another primary source of the law. For some reason students tend to come to their professional training courses, if not with an aversion to reading cases, then with a very strong desire to find a way to avoid doing so. I do not know whether this is because they were made to read *Re Diplock*[4] when they were five years old or what, but such an attitude is completely and utterly counter-productive. There is *no better way to learn* about the law than to see it in operation, and that is just what the cases do. A well-written judgment, which sets out the facts and relevant law clearly, and explains why the case has been decided the way that it has, will teach

---

4   A very old, and very long
    case!

you a whole lot more about the rules and principles involved than any secondary source – and it is usually much more interesting to read.[5]

To encourage you in this endeavour, at the end of most chapters I have suggested you read one judgment[6] in (usually) one case. They are all accessible through Westlaw.[7] It will not necessarily be the leading case in the subject, nor the most recent, nor the most talked-about[8] – I have tried to choose cases which are particularly well written, or fun to read, or even a bit bizarre, so that you can see how useful they are. All of them will tell you a lot about civil litigation and should show you that, contrary to the popular belief of many students, *cases are your friends.*

So if you do your part, I will do mine. This book will boost your understanding of civil litigation and evidence, principally by showing you how the various pieces of the 'procedural puzzle' fit together. This is the key to understanding the subject. If you can see the big picture clearly, the smaller detail will fall into place.

You must never try and learn rules in an intellectual vacuum. Think of all the games you know. Football. Monopoly. Even Snakes and Ladders has rules. As a general proposition, such rules will always be based on consistency, predictability, fairness and the purpose of the game. Those governing civil litigation are not really very different. To help you understand these rules, I use a thematic approach, which might be a little different from the way in which you have been taught. I hope this will help reinforce what you have been learning and give you further insight into the subject. Similarly, this book may well cover areas which are not on your particular examination syllabus, but naturally the focus throughout is litigation.[9] There are some study tips at the end of most chapters, and I close the book with a brief guide to approaching revision and the different sorts of examination questions which you may encounter.

---

5 Practitioner secondary sources are often updated in such a piecemeal way as to make them less rather than more readable over time (at least until they are completely re-written).

6 And I mean the judgment - you can skip all the preliminaries and go straight there. Some reports set out the legal argument as well, which can be interesting too, but I want you to focus on what the judge says.

7 An online legal resouce service, provided by most teaching institutions for their law students. There are others.

8 These will be referred to in the relevant chapters themselves, so feel free to read them too.

9 Remedies, as such, are not covered in detail.

The main rules of the civil litigation game are, of course, the Civil Procedure Rules ('CPR'), which came into force in 1999 (additional detail about implementation is set out in Practice Directions ('PD'), which immediately follow the rules to which they relate). These embody what became known as the Woolf reforms, named for the judge whose task it was to devise this completely new and modern system. The principal impetus behind the CPR was a desire to take the pace and direction of litigation out of the hands of the parties (for which read 'the lawyers') and place them firmly in the hands of the court. This was a radical departure at the time.[10] The idea[11] was that litigation (where this is, as a last resort, necessary) should become:

- more efficient, both in terms of costs and time, because it proceeds more quickly and only real contests get to trial;
- more accessible, to the extent it is less legalistic and easier to understand;
- more proportionate, so that cases proceed in a manner and at a pace commensurate with their complexity;

and so ...

- more just overall than was the case before the CPR.

These aspirations are manifested and expressed in the *'overriding objective'* of the rules, which is to enable the court 'to deal with cases justly'. What this means in practical terms is explained in CPR, r 1.1(2). It is worth setting this out in full.

'Dealing with a case justly includes,[12] so far as is practicable:

(a) ensuring the parties are on an equal footing;

(b) saving expense;

---

10 The vocabulary of litigation was also updated. For example, 'plaintffs' became 'claiments', 'claim forms' replaced 'writs' which started proceedings in the High Court and so on. So be prepared when reading older cases. For the sake of consistency, I shall use the modern vocabulary in this book, even when referring to events which occurred before the CPR.

11 The reality has not always lived up to the ideal. The overall cost of litigation is still a problem. See, for example, Jackson LJ's review of the subject for the profession (noted in Ch. 18).

12 Note the use in this rule of the word 'includes'. The list is not exhaustive.

     (c) dealing with the case in ways which are proportionate –

         i) to the amount of money involved

         ii) to the importance of the case

         iii) to the complexity of the issues

         iv) to the financial position of each party;

     (d) ensuring that it is dealt with expeditiously and fairly;

and

     (e) alloting to it an appropriate share of the court's resources, while taking into account the need to allot resources to other cases.'

Tape a copy of CPR, r 1.1 to your fridge or bathroom mirror, because the overriding objective and its constituents are of *primary importance* to understanding civil litigation. *They give the rules purpose and also dominate their content. It is essential always to bear them in mind.* Everyone, the parties as well as the court actively managing cases, is under a duty to comply with the overriding objective.[13] So CPR can also stand for –

C ourt Control ...

P roportionality ...

R esolution by efficient means.

If you begin by eating, sleeping and dreaming about the overriding objective (within reason), then you will have made a good start.

Civil jurisdiction is exercised mainly by the County Courts (which are located all over the country) and the High Court, which has some regional outposts, but is based at the Royal Courts of Justice in London. The High Court, along with the

---

13 CPR, r 1.2 and 1.3

Crown Court (a criminal court) and the Court of Appeal used to be known together as the Supreme Court of England and Wales, but when the House of Lords (the highest appellate court in the land) was re-branded 'The Supreme Court', this meant that suddenly there were too many chiefs. So the High Court, Crown Court and the Court of Appeal became the Senior Courts.[14]

The High Court, which deals with the more complex civil cases, is itself divided into three divisions:

(i)   The Chancery Division ('CH'), which deals with land, trust, probate and such cases;

(ii) Family Division, where matrimonial and related cases are assigned;

(iii) The Queen's Bench Division ('QBD'), which deals with admiralty, judicial review and commercial cases. Most tort and contract cases appropriate for the High Court are started here.

There are also some specialist courts in the High Court, including the Commercial Court and the Companies Court,[15] but this book concentrates on mainstream litigation, which will tend to proceed either in a County Court or the Queen's Bench (or Chancery Division) of the High Court.

So off we go. But before we start, there is one *final ground rule*, and that is: *you should have fun* reading this book. And if, by the end of it, you have *understood* what you have read, both in principle and in application (as opposed to merely memorising or 'learning' it), and if you have also abided by my ground rules, then you should be well able to meet the challenge that awaits you.

---

14 And the Supreme Court Act 1981, which is the primary source of their procedural powers, became the Senior Courts Act 1981.

15 These tend to have their own special ways of doing things. For further information on these specialist courts see BCP, para.2.15ff.

PART ONE
getting started

CHAPTER 2

Litigation lite:
pre-action behaviour

Courtroom drama may make good television, but by and large it is a costly, time-consuming and forbidding way to resolve disputes. Parties who can settle their differences on sensible and agreed terms will retain ownership of, and faith in, the outcome. For that reason, it has always been a matter of common sense as well as good practice that litigation should be seen as a last and not a first resort.

An important innovation of the CPR was the introduction of a formalised system for the early exchange of information about legal disputes, which is intended to increase the opportunities for an informed settlement without proceedings ever having to be issued. This manifests itself in the various pre-action protocols, which exist for, and are tailored to the needs of certain specific types of disputes,[1] including personal injuries claims which would litigate on the fast track.[2] In addition, there is an overarching Practice Direction which gives guidance about pre-action conduct generally, and in particular for those cases not covered by a specific protocol.[3] I shall refer to these last two as the 'PI protocol' and the 'pre-action PD', respectively.

Pre-action conduct tends to be the expertise of solicitors, who are there on the front line from the beginning. After all, the idea is to avoid, not incur legal costs! Nevertheless, it is important for barristers to have a clear grasp of the fundamentals

---

1 For example, building disputes, construction and engineering disputes, clinical negligence cases, mortgage possession claims, defamation cases.

2 The Pre-Action Protocol for Personal Injury Claims. There is a brand new Pre-Action Protocol for Low Value Personal Injury Claims in Road Traffic Accidents occurring after 31 April 2010 ('the RTA Protocol'). As to track allocation, see below at Ch. 8.

3 Practice Direction – Pre-action Conduct.

because compliance (or lack of compliance) with proper pre-action behaviour can have serious consequences down the line, especially where case management[4] and costs orders[5] are concerned.

You can find the various Protocols set out in all practitioner texts.[6] Although you should be aware of the existence of the other published protocols, for examination purposes the BPTC,[7] like this chapter, focuses on the generic pre-action PD and the general PI protocol referred to above.[8] BCP also includes a helpful procedural cheklist for both of these.[9]

It is important to grasp the essential framework and function of the protocols. The necessary detail will fall into place so long as you understand the two main objectives of appropriate pre-action conduct:

(1) to empower the parties to resolve their dispute fairly without having to litigate if possible;

and

(2) in cases where going to court cannot be avoided, to ensure that the case proceeds as quickly and efficiently as possible when it gets there.[10]

The PI protocol was a trailblazer. It was one of the first to be published and provided a prototype for those which followed.[11] It contains four essential elements.

---

4   See Ch. 13
5   See Ch. 18
6   At the moment, details of the newest protocol is only found in the supplements to BCP 2011 and the 2010 White Book (para.C13A).
7   For year 2010-2011

8   But be aware that the new RTA protocol now applies to a sub-group of personal injuries actions, that is to say claims worth no more than £10,000 (excluding interest) arising only out of road traffic accidents.

9   Procedural checklists 1 and 2
10 See pre-action PD , para.1.1
11 The new RTA protocol, however, marks a significant procedural departure from the others, incorporating as it does its own versions of certain court procedures.

1. A STANDARD 'LETTER BEFORE CLAIM' DETAILING THE NATURE OF THE CLAIM

Until recently this used to be called a letter *of* claim, but it sounded too much like the real deal and so the name was changed to make the pre-action context clearer. Previous correspondence between the parties may well have made the prospective claimant's intentions clear, but it is this specific letter which starts off the formal pre-action process. Two copies should be sent to the defendant[12] (or one to the defendant and one to the relevant insurers, if known). The letter should be concise but include sufficient detail so the defendant can understand and investigate the issues raised without having to ask for more information. It should contain, and seek from the defendant, any relevant documents.[13] The letter should be professional, not spiteful in tone and should contain relevant funding information.[14] A fill-in-the-blanks example is appended to the protocol.[15] Most solicitors would have something similar on their template data base.

2. PROMPT IDENTIFICATION OF ISSUES

Defendants should acknowledge receipt of a 'letter before claim' within 21 days, naming any relevant insurer (if not already known). Having done that they then have three months to investigate the claim. A defendant should provide the claimant with the documentary evidence and/or other clear explanation for any denial of liability. A counter-allegation of, say, contributory negligence should be clearly set out and met with an equally detailed response by the claimant.[16] The idea is that there is *early* identification of the *real* nature of the dispute. As soon as possible,

---

12 Although strictly speaking no-one is being sued yet, it is now common to refer to the parties as 'claimant' and 'defendant' once the pre-action protocol process has got underway.

13 See the list of documents suitable in various types of personal injuries action at PI Protocol, Annex B.

14 E.g. whether claimant is publicly funded or has the benefit of a conditional fee arrangement (although precise details of the latter need not be disclosed).

See further, Ch. 18

15 At PI Protocol, Annex A.

16 A counterclaim would require the defendant, in effect, to send his own letter before claim. As to counterclaims generally, see Ch. 5

the claimant should provide the defendant with a schedule of special damage and *both* sides should consider whether the claimant has needs which could be met by *rehabilitation* treatment or other measures.[17] The earlier rehabilitation is factored into the equation (and indeed begun), the better for everyone.

3. EARLY EXCHANGE OF RELEVANT EVIDENCE, INCLUDING EXPERT EVIDENCE

Relevant documents are exchanged almost from the outset. Different types of personal injuries cases call for the disclosure of different kinds of documentary evidence.[18] For example, a current MOT certificate might be relevant to a road traffic accident claim,[19] but not in a workplace accident case, where health and safety compliance documents would be more to the point.

The hope is that very early on, both sides should be in a position to assess the strength (or weakness) of their respective cases – and negotiate accordingly. Expert evidence[20] can be a crucial component of this picture. In personal injuries cases, this usually takes the form of medical reports, but other expertise (e.g. from an engineer, or car mechanic) may also be relevant.

There are several ways in which expert evidence can be exchanged and/ or presented, both before and after proceedings are issued in civil cases. The pre-action PD merely requires the parties to 'consider how best to minimise the expense'[21] and sets out various ways this might be done in its Annex C. One important way expense is saved is by the use of a *single* expert on an issue (rather than one for each party), which can come about in a number of ways. Put generally, a single expert can be:

---

17 para.4.1 and PI Protocol, Annex D.

18 See PI Protocol, Annex B.

19 Bear in mind that for the most minor road traffic accidents, occurring after 30 April 2010, the new RTA Protocol will apply.

20 See below Ch. 17 on the nature of expert evidence generally in civil litigation.

21 para. 9.4

22 *Carlson v Townsend* [2001] CPLR 405, and see generally below in Ch. 17

23 See generally Ch. 17. The terminology distinguishing joint selection from joint instruction can be confusing. 'Single joint expert' is not particularly descriptive but in the context of litigation refers to the expert whom both sides select and instruct: CPR, r 35.1(2). The pre-action protocols are a little less precise in their vocabulary. The important thing is to be clear what you mean in your

- jointly selected or agreed (where both sides participate in the selection of, and can put questions to the expert, but only one side pays for and gives instructions to the expert, calls the evidence and retains legal professional privilege in the evidence, unless and until it is disclosed to the other side[22]);

or

- jointly instructed (where both parties participate in the selection of, *and* also instruct the expert who will send each side a copy of the report. Generally the costs of such reports are shared. This is the norm in fast track cases which litigate[23]);

or

- one party could get expert evidence independently and hope its use can be agreed and sanctioned by the court.

The PI protocol shows a distinct preference for the first of these. The notes of guidance say that the protocol encourages 'joint selection of, and access to, experts'[24] and the body of the protocol sets out a process resulting in joint selection, but not joint instruction of an agreed single expert in the pre-action period.[25]

So far as *medical* evidence is concerned, however, the guidance notes to the PI protocol also recognise that a patient may well seek, or have already obtained, a medical opinion from his or her own doctor in the process of formulating a cause of action. It therefore anticipates, indeed 'promotes'[26] the practice of a claimant, having obtained an informal medical report, disclosing this to the defendant, who can then query the report and/or agree it without the need for obtaining his own or selecting another expert. Such an expert would, again, remain the claimant's expert. This is a cheap and cheerful option, but is probably only viable when the

---

own mind (and writing).

24 para. 2.14

25 Joint selection works like this: the claimant sends a list of possible experts to the defendant, who then indicates whether he objects to any of them. The claimant is free to choose and instruct any remaining on the list. If the defendant objects to them all, the claimant is still free to instruct one from the list, but both he and the defendant may have to explain their list, choice and objections to the court who can, if necessary, decide who has and who has not acted unreasonably.

Similarly, explanations would be necessary if both decided to instruct separate experts. See para. 3.15-3.21

26 para. 2.14

medical evidence is relatively uncontroversial. Even at this stage, a defendant may not find the claimant's doctor to be completely free of bias.

A claimant wanting to use his own (i.e. the treating) doctor as the single expert *at trial*, however, may well find that the defendant and/or the court would consider this expert insufficiently objective for those purposes, resulting in the evidence being excluded. Care should thus be taken from the outset, since, even if the claimant wins, the costs for such (unusable) reports may not ultimately be recoverable.

4. REALITY CHECKS, FURTHER NEGOTIATIONS OR ADR BEFORE LITIGATING

The protocols and pre-action PD all reinforce the message that litigation should be a last resort and stress the importance of 'reality checks' and serious thought being given to whether there might be some other, alternative, way to resolve the dispute. Both sides may be required to provide evidence that ADR has been considered and it would certainly be frowned upon if proceedings were started while negotiations were on-going, unless the limitation period was about to expire.[27] It is important to note, however, that the duty is to *consider* ADR, not necessarily engage in it.[28] Not all cases are suitable for ADR.[29]

To an extent, the pre-action protocols and pre-action PD[30] create a system of pre-litigation litigation, but without the wigs and gowns, expense and bad tempers that flare when the bureaucracy bears down and parties begin to lose control over the outcome. You might think of it as 'litigation-lite'. Certainly if, despite everything, proceedings are issued, the groundwork will have been laid for the expeditious conduct and progress of proceedings. Many of the steps of the litigation

---

27 See generally, Ch. 10

28 The protocol makes this point in emphatic font at para.2.19.

29 For a good example, see *Halsey v Milton Keynes General NHS* [2004] 1 WLR 3002.

30 This operates to require the same essential pre-action behaviour as discussed above in cases not covered by a specific protocol, but adapted to the circumstances of the particular case. For example, the time given to a defendant to respond to a letter before claim should be 'reasonable' and would vary depending on the complexity of the claim: pre-action PD para.7.2.

process, especially where disclosure and exchange of evidence is concerned, will already have taken place.

Compliance with proper pre-action behaviour is a cornerstone of the CPR and is viewed very seriously. The court will not look kindly on someone who approaches the protocol in the wrong spirit,[31] and it has an armoury of effective penalties for wilful non-compliance.[32] In particular, it will not be pre-disposed to assist a party seeking a helpful direction or extension of time who has failed, in some fundamental and inexcusable way, to engage with the ethos of the protocols. Adverse costs orders are another important sanction. Having said that, the court will not concern itself with minor or technical infractions. Sometimes, circumstances will justify a departure from the protocol, especially if mediation is in progress or being attempted.[33] Moreover, any punishment for non-compliance should always fit the crime.

---

31 See e.g. *King v Telegraph Group Ltd*, [2004] EWCA Civ 613, [2005] 1 WLR 2282 where the court penalised the claimant by putting a cap on the costs which the defendant might have to pay because the letter before claim was written 'in a vituperative tone calculated to raise the temperature and inflate the parties' costs'.

32 And see generally case management at Ch. 13

33 As in *Roundstone Nurseries Ltd v Stephenson Holdings Ltd* [2009] EWHC 1431 (TCC)

revision tips

- Be aware that if the accident occurred after 30 April 2010, low value personal injury claims arising from road traffic accidents now come under the RTA protocol and not the more general PI protocol. So to test knowledge of the latter, the examination scenario will involve personal injuries caused by something other than a road traffic accident, and/or an accident which occurred before May 2010 and/or injuries worth more than £10,000.

- Review the BCP checklist for both the PI protocol and the pre-action PD.

- Always double check your examination syllabus to ensure you have a good understanding of the relevant protocols. Solicitor's examinations, for example, may well test a wider knowledge of the pre-action protocols than the BTPC.

It is worth reading ...

Lightman J's judgment in *Hurst v Leeming* [2002] EWHC 1051 (Ch); [2003] 1 Lloyd's Rep 379. This is something of a cautionary tale, I suppose, given that the claimant is a solicitor and the defendant, a barrister, but don't let that put you off. It is short and to the point and a precursor of sorts to the (more important) *Halsey* case. Too bad we could not have been there for the 'frank exchange of views' between the judge and the defendant on the merits of the latter's utterly hopeless case. Counselling might have been more appropriate than mediation!

CHAPTER 3

Proceedings and parties

If a dispute does not settle in the pre-action phase, then it will become necessary, if the case is to be pursued, to commence proceedings. This involves questions of where and how to start an action, and against whom. This is also a convenient chapter for discussing special rules about joining parties to proceedings.

1. WHERE TO START?

An important effect of the CPR was to end, generally speaking, the distinction between High Court and County Court procedure. The latter had been created in the image of the former, and so, despite some significant differences, there were always many similarities.[1] There is now a unitary code of practice, which applies to all civil courts, although some specialist areas, such as family law (which has its own CPR-like procedure), are specifically excluded.

Where a party brings a civil action will depend both on rules about *jurisdiction* (which court is capable of dealing with the claim) and about *commencement* (where to start off a claim). It is important not to confuse the two concepts.

There are certain types of cases where only the High Court has jurisdiction.

---

1   The County Courts are entirely the creature of statute, the County Courts Act 1984. The High Court has a longer pedigree and an inherent juristiction, but its procedures are governed primarily by what is now called the Senior Courts Act 1981.

These include libel, judicial review, certain human rights claims, and equity cases exceeding £30,000. There are even a very few cases where only a County Court has jurisdiction, for example certain possession and lower value consumer credit claims. But in the *general run* of contract and tort cases, the High Court and County Courts have *concurrent* jurisdiction, which is to say that either has the power to deal with such cases.

Although jurisdiction is concurrent in such cases, there are, nevertheless, *important* rules about *commencement* which dictate where certain actions must be started. In particular:

1. In *personal injuries and fatal accident* cases: claims of *less than £50,000, must* be commenced *in a County Court.*[2]
   Remember that some aspects of a case (e.g. costs, interest, contributory negligence) are to be disregarded when calculating the claim *for these purposes.*[3]

2. Generally, as regards all *other types of money claims*: those which *do not exceed £25,000 must* be commenced *in a County Court.*[4]

Bear in mind that these are fundamentally rules about *commencement, not jurisdiction.* Their purpose is to force litigants to begin 'smaller' claims in a County Court, where they will most likely be tried (if the case gets that far). Note, too, the possible sanctions for non-compliance with these commencement rules. Deliberate flouting can result in the claim being struck out. More usually, there will be a penalty in costs, either at the end of the trial, assuming the case litigated all the way in the High Court when it should have been brought in a County Court[5] – or when the case is transferred from the High Court to the County Court where it belongs.[6]

---

2 CPR, PD 7, para.2.2. The actual wording is 'proceedings which include a claim for damages for personal injuries', so the latter need not be the only claim being made for the rule to be applicable.

3 ibid and Art 9 High Court and County Courts Jurisdiction Order, 1991 (SI 1991/1724 as amended).

4 CPR, PD 7 para.2.1. This threshold figure was fairly recently raised (from £15,000 to £25,000), so beware older reference or text books.

5 A winner's costs could be reduced by up to 25% to reflect the fact that the case could have litigated more cheaply in a County Court. See Senior Courts Act 1981, s 51(8),(9).

6 ibid, s 51. This is the most typical outcome. See also *Restick v Crickmore* [1994] 1 WLR 420, CA.

Further, it is important to understand that it does *not* follow from these rules that claims crossing the relevant thresholds must be started in the High Court. Such actions *may* also be commenced in a County Court, although where the claimant believes that the High Court could better deal with the claim because of its complexity or its public importance, then the case should be started there.[7]

Equally, the court, for the same sorts of reasons, can transfer cases from the High Court to the relevant County Court (and vice versa!) as part of its extensive case management powers, either on its own initiative or on application by any party. Pretty routinely, relatively high value claims (for example, those between £50,000 and £100,000), although quite properly started off in the High Court, will be sent 'down' to a County Court for trial.

2. HOW TO START?

Civil proceedings involving run of the mill factual disputes (e.g. negligence, breach of contract, breach of trust) are started by means of the issue of a Part 7 claim form, which comes in one standard form (to be adapted as necessary). The claim form is issued by the court at the request of the claimant, whether 'in person' or, more usually, acting through his or her solicitor. The claim form is the lead document in what are known generically as statements of case.[8] The claim form kicks off the proceedings, although it need not set out in detail the specifics of the case against the defendant. This is done in the particulars of claim,[9] which can either be on the claim form itself, come as a separate document with the claim form, or follow within 14 days of service of the claim form (and in any event while the claim form is still valid for service).[10]

---

7   CPR, PD 7 para. 2.4
8   See generally CPR, Part 16, para.4. As to validity of the claims form, see Ch.12

9   The particulars of claim should set out in detail the cause of action, the facts relied upon by the claimant and the remedy sought (CPR, r 16.4). In personal injuries claims, a medical report and schedule of past and future loss and expense ought to accompany the particulars of claim: PD 16.

10   CPR r 7.4(1)(a) and (b)

Where practicable the particulars of claim should be set out on the claim form itself (typically where it is short) or accompany the claim form. However, where neither is possible (for example because the draft is long or complicated or time is a factor), the claim form itself must give concise details of the nature of the claim, remedy sought and contain a statement of value (i.e. less than £5,000; £5,000 – £25,000; more than £25,000; or don't know). These values, as you can probably tell, are for track allocation purposes.[11]

If commenced in the High Court, the claim form must state that the relevant threshold has been crossed, or that it is a specialist High Court case. If the particulars of claim are not actually contained on the claim form, the latter must state whether they are 'attached' to (i.e. included with) the claim form or will follow later. It must also contain a statement of truth. If served separately, a copy and certificate of service of the particulars of claim must be filed with the court.[12]

Not all disputes are fact-based. Those which are essentially about legal questions or issues are initiated by using a Part 8 claim form. Typically such actions ask the court to construe a document such as a Will or a deed. In such cases, the so-called 'weapons of litigation',[13] which are pertinent to contentious disputes of fact, are not generally deployed. Written evidence is served with the claim form (as opposed to particulars of claim) and any trial will essentially involve legal submissions on the basis of that evidence rather than cross-examination of witnesses of fact.

So, for example, *compare*:

- claim for breach of contract (Part 7) versus asking the court to answer the legal question "What does this contractual term mean?" (Part 8)
- claim for breach of trust (Part 7) versus asking the court to construe a Will so the trustees know to whom to give the estate's money (Part 8)

---

11 CPR, r 16.3 and see generally Ch. 8
12 CPR, r 7.4(3)

13 Especially orders for disclosure of documents, and testing of oral evidence at trial.

Specialist proceedings and certain procedural applications also use Part 8 claim forms as required by relevant rules, statutes and practice directions.[14] In the main, these will only be of interest if you practise in these areas,[15] but you should be aware of the existence of this alternative procedure.

3. WHOM TO SUE: PARTIES AND JOINDER

A. PARTIES

When starting proceedings, one needs to make clear who is suing whom[16] – and for what. This is often fairly obvious, but thought must be given to the rules regarding special types of parties, as well as to what happens when there is more than one party on each side.

As regards the first of these, the following merit special mention, if only because they commonly feature in litigation and regularly crop up in examinations.

(a) Children

An individual attains full age at 18. Until then, a person is, legally speaking, considered to be 'acting under a disability'.[17] In the past (and in older cases) such people have been referred to variously as minors or infants, but the CPR now uses the more modern description 'child' or 'children'.

Children must sue and defend by their '*litigation friend*', although the court may order that a child is able to conduct proceedings on his or her own behalf.[18] Remember that the child is the party (e.g. claimant or defendant), but he or she must litigate by means of a litigation friend. The title of the proceedings would reflect this in the following way:

---

14 For example, the approval of children's settlements per CPR, r 21.10(2). See also list in PD 8, Section B.

15 Although it is worth noting that the new RTA protocol makes use of a 'modified' Part 8 procedure.

16 This needs to be made clear on the statements of case.

The full name of each party must be given, including an individual's full and proper title. See PD 16, para.2.6. BCP also gives a helpful summary at Table 14.1 of how various types of parties are named in proceedings.

17 As are persons lacking mental capacity to conduct

proceedings, who are now called 'protected parties' in accordance with the Mental Capacity Act 2005. Similar rules apply to them as to children, when suing or being sued. See generally CPR, part 21.

18 CPR, r 21.2 (2) and (3). This is uncommon, but might be

Miss WENDY DARLING   Claimant

(a child by **MR GEORGE DARLING**   her litigation friend)

A person assuming the role of litigation friend usually does so voluntarily and so *without* any court order. Typically such a person would be the child's parent or guardian, but in any case it must be someone with no conflicting interests, who is capable of acting fairly and competently and who, if the child is a claimant, will undertake to pay any costs ordered against the child.[19] The litigation friend must file a certificate of suitability with the court.[20] In the rare instances where no appropriate person steps forward to be a child's litigation friend, the court can make an order that one is appointed.[21]

It is important to note that settlements of claims made by a child require *special* attention. There are two principal reasons for this: children need protection from exploitative or disadvantageous settlements, and defendants need to be confident that the settlement made is in effect final.[22] The court can also give directions to ensure the money is used and applied properly.

The procedure varies depending on whether the offer of settlement is made before or after proceedings have started. Thus –

(i)   *If no action has yet been commenced* in respect of a child's claim, a Part 8 claim form is the mechanism used for seeking the court's approval for the settlement.[23] It should set out the details of the claim and the terms of the proposed compromise. Seeking court approval for a pre-action compromise is always advisable, if not actually required by the rules, because without it the settlement could unravel.

---

appropriate for an older child in certain circumstances.

19 CPR, r 21.4(3)
20 CPR, r 21.5
21 CPR, r 21.6

22 At common law a child will not be bound by an out-of-court settlement unless made for his benefit. Court approval of the settlement gives the defendant a valid discharge from liability.
23 CPR, r 21.10(2)

(ii) *Once proceedings have been commenced,* the rules specifically state that any settlement, to be valid, must be approved by the court.[24] In such cases, a Part 7 claim form will already have been issued and so the application for approval of the child settlement is, like all interim applications, made under CPR part 23.[25]

It is easier, of course, to make things compulsory once the courts have been seized of the case. If no action has been started, the rules can do little else but provide a mechanism for seeking court approval. The critical point is that in either case, until a proposed children's settlement is approved by the court, there is no binding agreement, and either party can resile from it.[26]

(b) Partnerships and sole traders

A partnership is the association of two or more persons who co-own a business for profit. A partnership typically trades under a firm name.[27] Generally speaking, it is 'one for all and all for one' in partnerships; in most situations each partner, who was a partner at the relevant time, will be bound by acts done on behalf of the firm and liable in respect of them.[28]

Unless it is inappropriate to do so, claims by or against a firm must use the *name* under which the *partnership carried on business* at the time the cause of action arose.[29] There was a time when this was merely an alternative to suing in the name of all of the individual partners (which could be very tiresome if there were a lot of them), but it was so routinely preferred that it seemed sensible to make it the rule, rather than a matter of choice. As to when it might be 'inappropriate' to sue or be sued in the name of a firm, your guess is as good as mine – like the proverbial elephant, it might be difficult to describe, but you will probably know it when you see it.

---

24 CPR, r 21.10(1)
25 See generally Ch. 4

26 *Drinkall v Whitwood* [2004] 1 WLR 462
27 Note that just because a business calls itself 'Jones and Co' does not make it a registered company.

28 See generally Partnership Act 1890
29 Assuming it has a name. See PD 7A, para.5A.3

In the title to proceedings, the fact that a partnership is named is signified by putting the words 'a firm' in brackets after the name, as in *Warner v Penningtons (a firm).*[30]

Compare the rules about naming partnerships in proceedings (whether as claimant or defendant) with the rule about suing a sole trader. The latter is merely an individual carrying on business whether in his own or another name. Such individuals if not trading in their own name[31] may be sued in their 'business name as if it were the name of a partnership.'[32] This option helps the claimant who might not know the name of the person behind the business name. A sole trader bringing a claim presumably knows his own name, so it is unnecessary to give him this option. Whether the individual's name is known or not, the title would reflect the status of sole trader. Thus the defendant might be described as 'BITS 'N' BOBS (a trading name)' or (if both names are known) 'MR ROBERT SMITH t/a BITS 'N' BOBS'.

(c) Companies

Limited Companies registered under the Companies Act 2006 (or a predecessor) must sue and be sued using the full, registered company name.[33] If the company does not end its name with the traditional 'Ltd' or 'plc', then its name should be followed by an accurate description of how its liability is limited.

The essential difference between a partnership and a limited company, technically speaking, is that the latter is a legal artifice, created so as to limit its owners' liability.[34] It is capable of suing and being sued.[35] A partnership is, in a sense, the sum of its human parts, whereas a registered company has its own legal personality, which is distinct from the human individuals through which it must act. One sues in the name of a firm because it is convenient (and the rules

---

30 [2010] EWHC 1753 (Admin). See suggested reading in Ch. 17

31 PD 7A, para.5C.1

32 PD 7A, para.5C.2

33 If the company is in liquidation, then the words '(in liquidation)' should indicate this.

34 This is why 'limited' is part of the description!

35 Compare this with the status of unincorporated associations (e.g. many charities, trades unions) which have no separate legal personality, and so generally cannot sue or be sued in their names. Where a charity is unincorporated proceedings may be brought against it by suing an officer of the charity 'on behalf of' the (named) charity. Alternatively, the trustees of the charity may be named as parties. See generally BCP para.14.35-14.41.

say so); one sues in the name of a limited company because there could be no alternative.

(d) Bankrupts, trusts and deceased persons

When a person becomes bankrupt, generally speaking, all causes of action (other than for personal injuries and defamation) vest in the 'trustee in bankruptcy', whose offical name appears, for example, as 'the trustee of the estate of Mr JUSTIN PENNY a Bankrupt'.[36] If a claimant becomes bankrupt in the course of proceedings, the trustee in bankruptcy may carry on with it, if the court agrees to substitute the name of the trustee for the bankrupt's name.[37] If, on the other hand, it is the defendant who goes bankrupt, this is obviously very bad news for the claimant. Whether the case proceeds really depends on the circumstances,[38] but if there is no money to be had from the defendant, a claimant would have to be very wary of throwing good money after bad.

Claims involving trust property generally may be brought by or against the trustees without joining the beneficiaries, and any judgment will bind the latter unless the court orders otherwise.[39]

A claim will ony cease upon the death of a claimant if the cause of action is personal, such as a libel action. Otherwise the executors or administrators of the estate can take over the claim. Again, this would necessitate an order to substitute the one party for the other. Similarly, on the death of a defendant, a claimant may apply for an order to continue the action against his personal representatives.[40]

B. JOINDER OF PARTIES AND CAUSES OF ACTION

If you, as a claimant, want to sue one person or one firm or one company in respect of one cause of action, that is straightforward enough. But what if you have more

---

36 The trustees in bankruptcy do not have to disclose their own names: Insolvency Act 1986, s 305 (4).

37 This is a good example of the use of the court's powers under CPR, r 19.2. See below at Ch. 11

38 It could be 'stayed' or could continue on conditions. See Insolvency Act 1986, s 285.

39 CPR, r 19.7A

40 CPR, r 19.2

than one person you want to sue … or there is more than one of you who wants to sue … or you have more than one cause of action in respect of which you want to sue? The CPR give claimants very wide latitude to combine – or 'join', as it is called – causes of action or parties into one claim without seeking permission, although the court will always have the last case management word on which claims will be heard together and which will not. Common sense will very much dictate decisions on this, taking account of the overriding objective, especially the need to save expense and deal with cases expeditiously and fairly.

It is useful to distinguish between joining causes of action and joining parties to proceedings, especially since these two things may be happening simultaneously! It also helps to differentiate between what claimants and defendants can do in this context.

(a) Joining causes of action

(i) By claimant

A claimant may use a single claim form to start *all* claims which can be 'conveniently disposed of' in the same proceedings.[41] No permission of the court is necessary. This is a nice, simple rule, ostensibly giving the claimant wide scope for making common sense decisions about combining causes of action in one claim form.[42] Although there need not be any special connection between the actions, the wording of the rule suggests some link between them: even if it might seem 'convenient' to a claimant to use only one form to bring various, possibly disparate, claims against a single defendant, the wording of the rule refers to how convenient it would be to 'dispose' of the actions together. The court will focus on this too – ultimately it will be the one to decide whether to hear cases together or separately.[43]

---

41 CPR, r 7.3

42 A typical example might be where the claimant's case against the defendant can be formulated in alternative ways, for example negligence and occupier's liability.

43 See below

(ii) By defendant

A defendant with a claim against the claimant can raise it by way of a counterclaim.[44] Thus, a defendant can join a cause of action to the one(s) brought against him by 'countering' with his own claim against the claimant, no matter what the cause of action or remedy sought. No permission is relevant if the counterclaim is against the claimant alone and is filed at the same time as the defence, at the end of which it typically appears.[45] No connection between the claim and counterclaim is required, although if they are completely unrelated, the court may well separate the two in due course.

(b) Joining parties

(i) By claimant

CPR, r 19.1 says that 'any number of claimants or defendants may be joined as parties to a claim.' In conjunction with CPR, r 7.3, referred to above, this gives the claimant the freedom,[46] when starting all claims which can be 'conveniently disposed of' on the one claim form, to join as many parties to those claims as are relevant so to dispose of them. Again, as a matter of common sense, it follows that 'convenience' will require, when deciding whether to join various claimants or defendants to one or more causes of action, a degree of interrelationship between the parties and the claim(s).[47] Suppose, for example, a claimant had building work done which went badly wrong, both because of poor workmanship on the part of the builders, but also because of the lack of supervision of those builders by the architects overseeing the work. It would make sense to sue both the builders and the architects in the one claim because, even though there are two separate contracts or causes of action, the allegation is that both parties, in their own ways, were responsible for the loss and damage.

---

44 This is one possible 'additional' claim described in Part 20, discussed further below.

45 CPR, r 20.4(2), 20.5(1). Where permission is required, a Part 20 claim form will be required: CPR, r 20.7

46 This freedom is limited where claimants are jointly entitled to a remedy, when the rules make joining them all as co-claimants obligatory, rather than optional. See CPR, r 19.3

47 The current rules do not require this, as the old rules did, but it seems logical as a matter of common sense when adding defendants to a claim.

CPR, r 7.3 and 19.1 are very open-ended and together give the claimant a great deal of latitude as regards joinder at this early stage.[48]

(ii) By defendant

Defendants can bring parties into proceedings in two ways. First, if a defendant is counterclaiming, he can join co-defendants to that counterclaim *with the permission of the court*.[49] Secondly, defendants can bring in parties by way of Third Party proceedings, another form of 'additional claim', which is discussed in detail below.

It is always important to remember that what the parties have joined together, perfectly appropriately under the rules, the court can always put asunder. The court, as part of its case management mandate, will be the ultimate arbiter of what is and is not 'convenient' to be disposed of together and will *sever* causes of action and order separate trials whenever it believes that this will further the overriding objective. To a great extent, of course, both solicitors and barristers should anticipate when this might happen – and act accordingly.

Equally, where two actions have been started separately, the court has the power to order that they be *consolidated* into one action, if this would further the overriding objective.[50] In one sense consolidation is the mirror image of severance. But do not confuse consolidation with Representative Actions[51] or Group Litigation.[52]

Finally, *once litigation has started*, the court has equally wide powers to put right situations where, say, a potential party was not joined at the outset or one party needs to be replaced by another.[53] Thus the court has a wide discretion to remove, add or substitute parties after the action has started. Again, common sense considerations apply, so that the court may order that a new party be added

---

48 We are discussing the rules about deciding whose names to put on the claim form, and in respect of which claims, when commencing proceedings. Usually no permission of the court is needed. Adding parties or causes of action at a later stage almost always requires the permission of the court. See generally at Ch. 11.

49 CPR, r 20.5. For example, suppose a claimant brings an action against a defendant for payment for (lawful) services rendered. This defendant is in fact owed money by the claimant and his brother (which may explain the lack of payment). The defendant will no doubt want to counterclaim in respect of the debt, but if he wants to claim from both debtors, he will need permission to 'join' the brother to the counterclaim against the

to proceedings, or indeed removed, if doing so helps the court 'resolve' all matters in dispute.[54] The court can do this on its own initiative or on application, but remember that the permission of the court is *always* required to add or substitute parties once the claim form has been served. Note too that this area of litigation also impinges on matters of limitation and amendment, discussed below.[55]

4. THIRD PARTY PROCEDURE AND OTHER ADDITIONAL CLAIMS

A. THIRD PARTY CLAIMS

A defendant in an action can make certain linked claims against a person *not yet a party* to the action brought against him. Such have historically been called third party claims and the party brought into the action, a 'third party'. The CPR lumps these sorts of claims in with counterclaims, and claims between existing defendants – referring to them globally as 'Additional Claims'.[56]

The expression 'third party', however, continues to be used in law reports and advocacy, and indeed the title of proceedings (if not the official Part 20 claim form), to distinguish third party claims from the other types of additional claims. I will use it here. Before recent amendments, the rules had contrived to create the most complex and confusing titles for what were previously referred to as 'Part 20 claims', but mercifully these have now been simplified (actually, re-simplified) so as to return to straightforward titles of Claimant v Defendant v Third Party.[57] The previous descriptions need not concern you for examination purposes, but you may come across some left-over examples of it for a while in early practice. They need to be seen to be believed!

Let's start with a given set of facts:

existing claimant. It might be quite straightforward, but still requires permission (and some consequential direction) because so far the brother has apparently had nothing to do with the ongoing litigation.

50 CPR, r 3.1(2)(g)

51 These are relatively rare these days, but may be a convenient way of litigating a dispute where otherwise a large number of persons would need to be named as parties (either as claimants or defendants), which would be inefficient both in terms of time and expense. If all the people

to be represented have the same interest in the outcome, then one or more persons can bring (or be allowed to continue to pursue or defend the action) as representatives of all the others. See CPR, r 19.6(1). 'Same interest' is interpreted pretty strictly. See, for

> *C is injured in an accident while a passenger in D's car. C sues D.*
> *Let's call the driver of the other car involved in the accident T.*

Before the introduction of the CPR, there were only four types of claim which a defendant could initiate against a third party:

(a) A 'contribution' claim

This is a claim that the third party is wholly or partly to blame for the claimant's loss.[58] Thus, in our example, D could bring in T as a third party claiming that T (who, like D, owed C a duty of care) was wholly or partly to blame for the accident through his poor driving, and seeking a 'contribution' (commensurate with T's actual contribution to the accident) to anything that D may have to pay C in the main action.

(b) An 'indemnity' claim.

This is a claim that the third party is under an *obligation* to the defendant, usually arising in contract, to reimburse the defendant for some or all of what the defendant may be ordered to pay to the claimant. Note that this is *not* an allegation that the third party caused or helped to cause, or is to blame for the claimant's loss. It is a different animal from a contribution claim and the two should not be confused. The most common example of an indemnity claim involves insurance companies. Remember that they rarely pay out on the whole of a claim, since there is usually an 'excess' to be paid by the policy holder or not all losses are covered by the policy, so it is a little dangerous to think of an indemnity as always equivalent to a 100% contribution! But so-called indemnity clauses are common in building contracts, where a total indemnity will be more

---

example, *Smith v Cardiff Corporation* [1954] QB 210.

52 This is rather like the class action in the USA and is a relatively recent addition to our system. Group Litigation Orders (and an order of the court is required) are intended to assist in multi-party claims where there are common questions of law or fact, and other existing procedures are incapable of providing a cost effective and expeditious way of dealing with action. They are typically used in cases where a large number of people have been affected (albeit in different ways) by a disaster of some kind, e.g. industrial accident, investment mis-selling, damaging side-effects of drugs). Funding of such cases can be very problematic.

53 CPR, r 19.2

54 See CPR, r 19.2(2)-(4)

common. It all depends on the extent of the obligation!

In our example, if the defendant's insurance company denied their obligations to him under his insurance policy with them, he could join the company as a third party and claim an indemnity from them. In effect, the defendant would be saying to the third party: "Under our contract of insurance, you promised you would pay if I was found liable in these circumstances, so if I have to pay anything in damages to the claimant in respect of this accident, I want you to meet your obligation to me about that".

It may be useful to think of these two third party claims as *defensive* in nature because they are dependent on the claimant succeeding against the defendant. If the main action settles, with the defendant agreeing to pay something to the claimant, there will still be a question of what, if anything, the third party should pay to the defendant.[59] *But if the defendant is not liable to pay anything to the claimant in the action, there is nothing to contribute to or in respect of which to indemnify.*

(c) A claim for the defendant's own remedy

A defendant can also claim his own remedy or relief against a third party so long as it is the same or similar to that claimed by the claimant and it arises out of the same or similar facts. So, in our example, D, having sought a contribution from T, might also go on to say, in effect: "... and by the way, T, while you were injuring C, you also injured me in that accident, and I want damages from you for my own injuries and losses caused by your negligent driving".

This type of claim might usefully be thought of as *offensive* in nature because it is *not* dependent on the claimant's claim succeeding against the defendant. Although it commonly goes hand-in-hand with a contribution claim, regardless of what happens to the main action, this claim for the defendant's own remedy

---

55 See Chs. 10 & 11

56 See generally CPR, Part 20 and WB editorial introduction at 20.0.2.

57 If a defendant needs to bring in more than one new party against whom he has separate claims they will be called 'Fourth Party', 'Fifth Party', and

so on. If an identical claim were to be made against two new parties they would be referred to as the 'First Named Third Party' and the 'Second Named Third Party': PD 20 para.7.

58 A right to a contribution arises where liability is joint and several, i.e. where two

or more persons are liable to the same claimant for the 'same damage.' If a third party is not capable of being liable to the claimant, there can be no claim for a contribution *Cooperative Retail Services Ltd v Taylor Young Partnership Ltd* [2002] 1 WLR 1419 (HL) can continue in its own right, just as if it had been brought separately. *This is an important distinction, which is often tested in assessments.*

(d) A connected question of law or fact

Finally, there has traditionally been a 'safety net' category of third party claims, which caters for situations where there are questions or issues needing adjudication which are common to both the main claim (C v D) and the third party claim (D v T). Such may not fall neatly into categories 1 to 3 above, but the original and third party claims are so inter-related that it would be silly not to deal with them together.

Suppose, for example, I was sued by someone who claims ownership of the White Book which I use and think is mine. The cause of action against me would be the tort of conversion or trespass to property (the civil law's answer to the theft, in effect). As the defendant, I bring in the person who sold me the disputed White Book as a third party because if the claimant were to succeed against me, it would mean that I paid money for something that belongs to someone else. My cause of action against the third party would be breach of contract. The issue or question common to both claims is "Who has good title?". It obviously makes sense to deal with the two cases together, because the answer to that question will determine the outcome of both cases. Otherwise I might be running up and down the hallway giving evidence in two cases in different rooms with two different judges, but telling both courts the same thing. And what would happen if one judge decided the book was mine, but the other decided it wasn't?

The purpose of third party proceedings has always been to avoid this sort of multiplicity of action and the risk of different results where the logical connection between the main action and third party claim dictates that the two matters be

---

59 See *Stott v West Yorkshire Road Car Ltd* [1972] 2 QB 651. There might even be an issue as to whether the settlement is legitimate. This is why, when people are insured against claims, the insurance company (who will be picking up most of the tab) wants to be in charge of how the case is handled, and in particular whether to settle or not (and for how much).

heard together. This is still the purpose of Part 20 procedure under the CPR, which is stated as being to enable additional claims 'to be managed in the most convenient and effective manner.' But because Part 20 is not simply about third party claims, one gets to essentially the same destination as under the old rules, but by a slightly different route.

The old rules mandated that only claims **(a)** − **(d)** mentioned above were capable of getting off the ground as third party claims. The CPR specifically refers only to types **(a)** and **(b)** (contribution and indemnity claims) as viable third party claims, but not to types **(c)** and **(d)** as such. Instead it gives a defendant free rein to claim any 'other remedy' from the third party.[60] It then leaves it to the court, in the exercise of its discretion and case management powers, to *detach*, as it were, those which it decides should not be heard together with the main action. CPR, r 20.9 specifically uses the language of the old rules in describing the 'matters to which the court should have regard' in deciding whether a third party claim should be 'dealt with separately' from the main claim, including (but not limited to) references to whether the defendant is seeking from the third party 'substantially the same remedy' as the claimant (as in type **(c)** above) or whether there is a 'question connected with the subject matter' to be determined (as in type **(d)** above).[61]

In effect, as regards third party claims type **(c)** and **(d)** as described above, these are now simply factors which the court will look at when deciding whether or not to let the claim continue as a third party claim. Practitioners, of course, ought to be able to predict when a claim by a defendant would appropriately be tried with the main action as a third party claim, but ultimately it is for the court to decide this.[62] In the normal course of events, both common sense and the overriding objective would dictate that claims falling within categories **(c)** and **(d)** mentioned above ought to be heard together with the main action as third party claims.

---

60 CPR, r 20.2(1)(b). No permission is required if made early enough. See below.

61 CPR, r 20.9(2). In addition it adds a more generic consideration, i.e. the degree of 'connection' between the main and third party claim, thus opening up possibilities and giving the court a bit more discretion than it had under the old rules.

62 We have noted that under CPR, r 19.2 the court may add, substitute etc a party to ongoing litigation if this would help determine all of the issues in dispute or there is some other relevant connection between the claim against the party to be added and the ongoing litigation. *Do not confuse this* with a defendant's ability to make (or seek permission to make) third party claims under Part 20.

When bringing in a third party, a Part 20 claim form must be issued and served on the other parties (including the one to be added!).[63] If the third party claim is issued *before or at the same time as* the defence is filed, no permission of the court is needed.[64] Otherwise, permission is required and in such cases, the matters set out at CPR, r 20.9, referred to above, will be relevant. It is because the defence and the third party claim interact with one another [65] that the filing of the defence is the procedural point around which the question of permission turns. If, for example, a defence has already been filed and served, and the defendant later seeks to add a third party to the proceedings, the defence document which is in the hands of any existing party/ies will, in effect, need to be 'recalled' to be amended and re-served to incorporate the third party.

B.   ADDITIONAL CLAIMS AGAINST CO-DEFENDANTS

So far, two types of 'additional claim' under Part 20 have been discussed: counterclaims and third party claims. There is one more that needs mentioning. Where two or more defendants have been sued by a claimant, so that they are *already parties* to the action, they can make the same sorts of claims against one another that a defendant can make when bringing in a third party (who until then is *not* a party to the action).

At this point the jargon can get confusing because practitioners still persist in using the old-fashioned term 'contribution notice' to describe the mechanism by which such a claim is made (even when the claim is not a contribution claim!).[66] Moreover, if a co-defendant, who is not otherwise in a hostile relationship with his other co-defendants, merely wants to ask the judge to use his existing powers to apportion liability in a particular way, even though this is a contribution claim of sorts, no formal notice need be issued, thereby saving unnecessary expense.[67]

---

63 CPR, r 20.7(2)
64 CPR, r 20.7(3)
65 For example, the name of the third party will need to be added to the title of the proceedings.
66 The rules do not use this expression, but some commentators and practicioners still do.

67 Where there is joint and several liability, a judge has power to apportion liability amongst defendants whether they ask him to or not: Civil Liability (Contribution) Act 1978. If all a co-defendant wants to do is argue for a 30:70 split in his favour (as opposed to, say, 50:50) then only unofficial notice to the other defendant(s) is required. A defendant serving formal notice when not necessary to do so may not recover the costs.

If, however, there is some other issue or claim being made between co-defendants (an order for disclosure of documents, perhaps, or a claim for an indemnity or damages for some other remedy or relief), a Part 20 claim form must be issued and served.

These kinds of additional claims might be (and sometimes are) more accurately described as 'party and party claims' to distinguish them from third party claims.

revision tips

- If the main action folds or is otherwise *unsuccessful*, whether the third party proceedings can continue independently essentially depends on whether the third party claim is 'defensive' or not. If it is 'defensive', it will die a death with the main claim. To the extent that it is 'offensive' in nature, or there is otherwise a live issue to be determined between the parties, then the third party claim can carry on independently. With claims involving 'connected questions' of law or fact, you will need in each case to look at the relationship between the main action and third party claim – they often stand or fall together.

- Remember that, subject to the court's case management powers, *only claimants* decide who the defendants will be. And *only defendants* bring in third parties

- *Remember too that a claimant cannot obtain judgment against a third party.* If a claimant suspects that the third party might conceivably be the *entire* villain, then that claimant should turn the third party into a defendant!! He can do that by amendment (see Ch. 11).

It is worth reading ...

The judgment of Lord Denning MR in *Stott v West Yorkshire Road Car Ltd* [1972] 2 QB 651. It is short and explains the factual background. The relevant legislation has changed, and so too some of the descriptions used (claimants were called plaintiffs and District Judges were called registrars back then). But it is a good example of a typical third party scenario. Anyway, if you have never read a Denning judgment, then you are in for a treat. They are models of clarity.

CHAPTER 4

Interim applications and service

1. MAKING INTERIM APPLICATIONS

The issuing of the claim form begins the *interim* (sometimes called interlocutory) phase of the proceedings which, despite sounding rather temporary, in effect covers all the preparatory stage(s) through which a case passes until trial or settlement is reached.[1] Interim applications are thus applications for orders or directions from the court made prior to the substantive trial of the action. It has always been true that most cases settle and never get to trial, which is why the focus of any civil litigation course is on what does (or does not) go on in this interim period between issue (sometimes pre-issue) and trial. The CPR rules are designed to control this aspect of litigation to such an extent that even fewer cases get to trial than did before, and that those which do, get there much more quickly.

CPR Part 23 sets out the general rules about interim applications, to which reference is often made in other parts of the rules.

In High Court cases, *most* interim applications are made to the *'Master'*, who is essentially a procedural judge, with no significant trial jurisdiction.[2] There are *some* interim applications, however, which must be made to a High Court *judge*, most notably most *injunctions*.[3]

---

1   If you think of litigation as a linear continuum, with commencement of proceedings at one end, and trial at the other, everything in between (and sometimes even pre-action) is the interim phase.

2   'Master' is a curiously archaic judicial title which survived the modernising ethos of the CPR. The Masters sit in London at the Royal Courts of Justice in London. Their out-of-London equivalent is the more prosaically titled High Court District Judge.

3   See below Ch. 6

In the County Courts, the equivalent of the Master is the *District Judge*.[4] It is thus to a District Judge that *most* interim applications requiring a hearing in the County Courts are made. Those applications with which the District Judge cannot deal are made to the Circuit Judge. *Unlike Masters*, County Court District Judges have a certain amount of trial jurisdiction; they can try cases where the claim does *not exceed* £25,000[5] and so also grant injunctions in such cases. Otherwise, it is the Circuit Judge who tries cases in the County Courts, and who has the general power to grant injunctions there.

Most interim applications are made by giving the other side *notice* ('inter partes' in the old jargon).[6] This is because, where the matter is of any importance, all interested parties are entitled to have their say and be heard on the matter. Similarly, most applications are to be made *in writing* by using a standard form *notice of application*.[7]

Exceptionally, interim applications are made without giving the other side notice ('ex parte' in the old jargon). Sometimes this happens out of necessity, for example when there is no defendant on record or the matter does not essentially concern the defendant at the time.[8] Otherwise, applications are made without notice either because the matter is so *urgent* that there is *no time* to give notice or where *secrecy* is vital.[9] It is very important to note that where applications are made without giving the other side notice, the applicant comes under a *duty* to make what is known as 'full and frank disclosure' of all material facts, including those adverse to the application. This is exactly what it sounds like, and amounts to an obligation, in effect, to *compensate* for the other side's absence, *not to exploit it*. It is a crucial and continuing duty in any application made without notice, and sanctions for a failure to meet this obligation can be severe.

Most interim applications must be supported by *written* evidence. The rules

---

4   Out of London, it is not uncommon for one person to act as both a High Court and County Court District Judge, as the cases arise.

5   In other words, small claims or fast track cases. They can also hear certain possession actions and hearings to assess damages in the County Court.

6   CPR, r 23.4

7   CPR, r 23.3. Do not get confused, as well you might, between an application made *by* notice of application (referring to the document used) and an application made *on* or with notice (letting the other side know about the application by serving on them the application notice).

8   Applications to extend the validity of the claim form (see Ch. 12). Such applications are made by means of an application notice, but without sending a copy to the other side.

allow such to be provided in several ways. It can either be:

(i)   included on the notice of application itself, if it contains a statement of truth;

(ii) found in any statement of case served in the proceedings, which should already contain a statement of truth;

(iii) contained in a witness statement (i.e. statement of evidence of a relevant person), containing a statement of truth, to be served with the notice of application;

or

(iv) contained in an affidavit (i.e. a sworn statement) to be served with the notice of application.

Because affidavits cost rather more than witness statements (due to the costs of being 'sworn'), a litigant will not generally recover the costs of making an affidavit. The 'statement of truth' now performs much the same function as swearing to the truth of an affidavit, but more cheaply. Thus, most interim applications are supported by witness statements, except where affidavits are specifically required by the rules.[10]

The rules seek to encourage dealing with interim applications 'on the papers', that is to say without the need for parties to attend a (costly) hearing. This furthers the overriding objective by saving time and money. Thus, the court may determine an interim application without a hearing either if the parties agree or the court considers that a hearing would be unnecessary.[11] A party who is not happy about the latter may apply to have that decision set aside, varied or stayed.[12]

The court's case management powers are extensive.[13] They even include making interim orders when no-one has asked for one![14] Again, an unhappy

---

9   Typical examples of the latter are applications for freezing and search orders. See generally Ch. 7

10 For example when applying for freezing and search orders – see Ch. 7. But watch out when reading older cases. At one time all interim applications were supported by affidavit evidence.

11 CPR, r 23.8

12 CPR, r 3.3(5)(a)

13 CPR, r 3.1(2) sets out some of the typical orders the court might make on interim applications. And see Ch. 13

14 This is known as the court 'acting on its own initiative', and is an important part of the court's ability to control proceedings before it. See CPR, r 3.3

party can trigger a hearing by applying to set aside the order.

The person making the application is called the 'applicant' and the person responding is called the 'respondent.' These terms might be used interchangeably with claimant and defendant, where the claimant is also the applicant. But sometimes the defendant in the main action is the one applying for the interim order, so you must be careful with your terminology – both in your own mind and for the benefit of the judge.

There are the obvious exceptions, but generally speaking hearings on interim applications are heard in public. Most are pretty mundane, however, and would not be apt to draw in the crowds. The more complicated the matter, the more apt one would be to instruct counsel, file and exchange skeleton arguments[15] and so forth. Disputes of *fact* on interim applications raise the question of how the court should deal with these, given the lack of oral testimony and opportunity to test the evidence, which after all is just set out on pieces of paper.[16] It is generally thought that such questions are decided by asking whether the applicant has established a 'good arguable case' on the matter – a middling sort of standard, which in essence amounts to saying that the court should be as satisfied as it can be in the circumstances, given the limitations inherent in hearings based on written evidence but at the same time wanting to avoid mini-trials of matters raised on interim applications.[17]

2. SERVICE

A. SERVICE OF THE CLAIM FORM (AND OTHER DOCUMENTS)

Service of the claim form is the next procedural step after issuing proceedings. A claim form issued for service inside the jurisdiction remains valid for four months.[18]

---

15 Skeleton arguments are usually required for applications before County Court or High Court judges, unless the matter is very simple or time is short. These provide a concise summary of the party's submissions and give the opportunity for pre-reading. They are, in their own way, a piece of written advocacy, but they are not a substitute for oral argument. See WB, Vol 2 and guidance in Chancery Guide (at Section 1 paras 7.18 – 7.38)

16 It is always worth remembering that it is *not* the advocate's role to give evidence. His or her job is to get the court to view the available evidence in a particular way.

17 See e.g. *WWP Holdings Italy SRL v Bennett* [2007] 1 WLR 2316

18 The claim form is valid for service *outside* the jurisdiction for *6 months*:

It must be served during this time, unless an extension is granted.[19]

The service rules include considerations of how, where and by whom service is to be effected. The first thing to remember is that generally, any document prepared or issued by the court, which includes the claim form, will be served by the court.[20] This is the most stress-free form of service. But there are times when this does not happen.[21] One is the rare occasion when the rules or the court require personal service by the claimant.[22] Another, much more commonly invoked, is where a claimant notifies the court of a desire to serve the claim form himself.[23] In such circumstances, there are a host of alternatives.

Personal service
This is effected by leaving the claim form with the relevant person;

Leaving the claim form at an address
The claim form is left at an address given for service or the usual or last known residence/place of business, the claimant having taken reasonable steps to ascertain the correct current address;

Next business day: first class post, document exchange (DX) etc
The claim form is sent to an appropriate address by first class post, DX or other method, which provides for delivery on the next business day (again the claimant having taken reasonable steps to ascertain the correct, current address);

Fax or email
Before service is permitted by fax or other electronic means, the party who is to be served, or his legal representative, must have expressly indicated in writing a

---

CPR, r 7.5(1)

19 See generally Ch. 12

20 Usually by first class post, although it is for the court to choose. See CPR, r 6.4 and 6APD.8. The court will equally serve other documents which it has prepared, although if such documents are prepared by the parties themselves, they are responsible for service unless the court orders otherwise. See CPR, r 6.21

21 CPR, r 6.4(1)

22 CPR, r 6.5(1). An example is a claim form relating to committal proceedings.

23 CPR, r 6.4(1)(b). A certificate of service must be filed within 21 days, unless all defendants have acknowledged service by that time: CPR, r 6.17(2)

willingness to be served in this way and provided a fax-number, email address or other electronic identification as appropriate. Agreement to be served in one of these ways can be expressed by including (i) a fax number on the legal representative's writing paper or (ii) an email address on the legal advisor's writing paper, plus a statement that this can be used for service or (iii) a fax number, email address etc on a statement of case or response to a claim filed with the court.

All of these service options requires the claimant to take a certain step ('the required step'), as set out in CPR, r 7.3(1).[24] Having chosen a method, it is important that service is made *to the right person or place*. One important rule is that where the defendant's *solicitor* is authorised to accept service on the defendant's behalf and the claimant has been given written notice both of this fact and the relevant address, then the claim form *must* be served at that address.[25] Otherwise, service should be effected at the address given for service[26] (which, again, could be the address of the defendant's solicitors). Failing that, the appropriate address for service will be the defendant's 'usual or last known address.' This could be the defendant's last *known* address, even if the claimant knows the defendant no longer lives there, so long as the claimant took reasonable steps to discover a current address (or serve in some other way).[27]

When did service occur?

Once service has been effected on the right person and in an appropriate way, the next question is *when* service will have occurred. Previously this was calculated on a rather piecemeal basis, depending on the service option selected. Now it is dealt with by a strict, but generic and uniform rule, which says that service of the claim form takes effect on the second business day after completion of the required step.[28] This even applies to personal service, which in real time is instantaneously! So *regardless* of

---

24 See also PD 6A for more detail on each step.

25 CPR, r 6.7

26 CPR, r 6.8

27 CPR, r 6.9 and *Mersey Property Holdings v Kilgour* [2004] EWHC 1638 (TCC). As to alternative service, read on.

28 CPR, r 6.14

what step is required, and *regardless* of when or indeed whether the claim form might actually have been received, service of the claim form is *deemed* to have taken place on the second *business* day after the relevant step was taken. Watch out for holidays and weekends – they are not business days![29]

The effect of deeming provisions

It is important to understand the effect of such deeming provisions. Where they apply, service takes effect on the deemed date *and no other*. They create, in effect, an irrebuttable presumption of law[30] and no evidence is admissible to prove that the claim form arrived on some other date, or even not at all. This may sound severe, but the deeming provisions inject some predictability into this aspect of litigation, and only very rarely does the outcome of a case turn on service of the claim form.[31]

The advantage of letting the court serve the claim form is obvious – the claimant does not need to provide a certificate of service or otherwise prove, or worry about being responsible for service, as is the case when a DIY option is chosen.[32] The latter, however, can give the litigant some control over when and how service is effected and for that reason some claimants choose to do it themselves.

Claim form versus other documents

You will notice that CPR, Part 6 is divided into distinct sections, so that there is, in effect, one set of rules for service of the claim form (Part II) and another second set for service of documents *other than* the claim form (Part III). There are many similarities between the two, and often the same or similar wording is used.[33] For example, when any party is acting through solicitors, and their business address has been provided, *all* documents in a case should be served on that address.[34] But there are also some discrepancies.[35] For example, notice the somewhat subtle difference

---

29 CPR, r 6.2(b). So, if the relevant step is taken on a Friday, service is deemed to occur on the following Tuesday (assuming Monday is not a Bank Holiday).
30 See generally below at Ch. 17

31 But where limitation is at issue, the date of service can suddenly become very important. See generally, Ch. 10.
32 CPR, r 6.17(2)

33 This is partly because only the rules about serving the claim form were overhauled in 2008, and not the rules about service of other documents.
34 CPR, r 6.23
35 CPR, r 6.26

in the deeming provisions as regards service by post of documents other than the claim form ('second day after posting if that day is a business day; or if not, the next business day after that day'). But, as the method of serving other documents becomes more instantaneous, service is equally deemed to occur more quickly (e.g. service by email or indeed personal service). Normally, service of other documents is even less controversial than service of the claim form in the general run of the case, but you still want to be aware of the fact (and basic detail) of the difference. It can crop up in exams.

Special cases

Finally, be aware of special rules about serving claim forms on particular types of parties[36] and what to do if none of the sanctioned methods of serving the claim form seem to work. Pay attention, in particular, to the following.

Serving children

Where the defendant is a child (who is not also a protected party), the claim form must be served on one the child's parents or guardians, or if no such person exists, on an adult with whom the child resides or in whose care the child is.[37] These are the sorts of persons who would typically assume the role of 'litigation friend' once proceedings are brought. Once the litigation friend is identified, then service of all subsequent documents would be on that person.[38]

Serving partnerships

As discussed above, partnerships should generally be sued in the name of the firm. Special refinements to the service rules thus become necessary, because a firm is not an individual or legal entity and so poses some service quandaries. A firm is not a

---

36 As discussed in Ch. 3

37 CPR, r 6.13(1). Analogous provisions apply to protected parties: CPR, r 6.13(2)

38 CPR, r 6.25(2)

person, so how, for example, would you serve a firm 'personally'?

If the court effects service on a partnership, it will normally do so by first class post to the firm's address (or other address given for service). If the claimant wishes to serve the claim form himself the possibilities are as follows:

(i) If the claimant has been notified of solicitors who are authorised to accept service on the firm's behalf, the claimant must serve the defendant firm at this address. This can be effected by post, leaving the claim form, DX or other electronic means as appropriate.

(ii) The partnership can be served *'personally'* by leaving the claim form with any of the partners or leaving it with a person having, at the time of service, the control or management of the partnership business at the principal place of business of the partnership.[39]

(iii) Service can also be effected by post, leaving, faxing etc the claim form at the principal or last known place of business of the firm or other address provided by the defendant.

Note that a proprietor of a business, even if a sole trader (and not a firm) can be served either at his own usual or last known residence or the address of his principal or last know place of business.[40]

Serving claim forms on companies

Companies dance to a slightly different drummer. They can be served under the CPR rules, or they can be served at their registered offices under the Companies Act 2006. The former include the 'principal office' or any place of business of the company which has a real connection with the claim, or personal service on

---

39 CPR, r 6.5(3)
40 CPR, r 6.9

a senior person in the company. This provides rather more latitude for place of service, than simply the registered office. Having said that, if serving the claim form by post on the registered office under the Companies Act 2006, it will be deemed to be delivered 'in the ordinary course of posting', unless proved to the contrary. So a rebuttable presumption in that case![41]

Contractually agreed service

The rules also allow for a contractually agreed method of service. If the action is based solely on a contract, one of whose terms specifies the manner of serving a claim form should such a claim arise, then the claim form *may* be served in this way.[42] This option, when applicable, essentially gives the claimant another choice when serving the claim form.

Alternative service

In many ways a claimant is spoiled for choice when serving the claim form; it is not often that at least one of the available methods of service will not work.[43] But it does happen sometimes, especially if a prospective defendant is elusive or actively evading service. So, if the court is persuaded that there is a 'good reason' to authorise service by 'a method or at a place not otherwise permitted' by the rules, it can make an order permitting service by an 'alternative method or at an alternative place.'[44]

The claimant's application to the court for such an order must be supported by written evidence, which would typically explain what attempts to serve have been or would have been made were they not impractical, as well as what method of service is being put forward as more likely to bring the claim form to the defendant's notice. Dealing with cases fairly and efficiently and in keeping with

---

41 See generally Ch. 17
42 CPR, r 6.11
43 This was not always the case.

44 CPR, r 6.15(1). Absence of a bad reason is not necessarily a good one: see *Brown v Innovatorone* [2009] EWHC 1376 (Comm).

45 See e.g. *Albon v Naza Motor Trading Sdn Bhd* (no 2)[2007] EWHC 327(Ch), [2007] 1 All ER (Comm) 813

the overriding objective will also be a relevant consideration for the court.[45] If the court makes an order for alternative service, it should go on to specify not only how service is to be effected, but when such service is deemed to be served and how long the defendant has to respond.[46] Alternatively, the court can order that steps which a claimant has *already* taken to bring the claim to the attention of the defendant, constitutes good service.[47]

It is also worth noting that this a good example of an interim application which, out of necessity, would be made *without* giving the other side notice. If the claimant could serve the defendant for the purposes of the application, it is unlikely he would need the order at all!

Dispensing with service

In exceptional circumstances, the court may dispense altogether with the need to serve the claim form.[48] This might happen where there has been a very minor, technical fault with service, but it is no longer possible to try again to serve properly.[49] But the court will use this power very sparingly; otherwise it would undermine the rules themselves. Service is not that hard to achieve, so it will be rare for the court to excuse a claimant for not managing to do it.

B.   SERVICE OUT OF THE JURISDICTION

Usually proceedings in England and Wales are served on defendants *within* the jurisdiction. But what happens if the claimant is in the jurisdiction, but the defendant is not? Is it possible to bring proceedings here, and if so, how does one go about serving them on a foreign defendant? Answering these questions invites consideration of the rules about service *out* of the jurisdiction.

This, itself, is a complex area of procedure, and what follows is merely an

---

46 CPR, r 6.15(4)

47 CPR, r 6.15(2)

48 CPR, r 6.16(1)

49 As in *Cranfield v Bridgegrove Ltd* [2004] 1 WLR 2441

introduction to the subject. Any practitioner dealing with such a case will simply have to delve into the detail, but will no doubt find this easier to do with a basic understanding of how the system works. At the time of publication, service out of the jurisdiction is *not* included on the BPTC syllabus for the Civil Litigation & Evidence Assessment. However, it remains of particular interest to those training to become solicitors – since it is they who are principally the ones who issue and serve proceedings – and can come in handy for the pupil barrister.

Before the coming into force of the Civil Jurisdiction and Judgments Act 1982 ('CJJA 1982'), permission of the court was always required when a claimant wanted to commence proceedings in the courts of England and Wales and serve them on a defendant who was out of the jurisdiction. The CJJA 1982 carved out a special system for those extra-jurisdictional cases 'with a European flavour', allowing a claimant to bring certain actions in England against defendants in Europe *without having to ask the court's permission.* The CJJA 1982, which made various international conventions between European states applicable in English law, has since been fine-tuned by later legislation and EC Regulation,[50] but the essential framework remains the same. For the sake of clarity I will refer to the countries who are part of this European system as 'participating states.'[51]

European system: permission not required

If a claimant living here wants to sue a defendant living[52] in another participating state, the European system applies. This essentially says that the defendant *must* be sued in the country of his domicile *unless* the CJJA 1982 confers jurisdiction on the courts of England and Wales[53] either (i) exclusively or (ii) by virtue of an agreement between the parties conferring jurisdiction on our courts or (iii) because the case is one of those specified in the legislation where a person living

---

50 See CPR, r 6.30ff for detail.

51 In the rules they can, somewhat confusingly, be referred to variously as 'Regulation' or 'Member' States. Think in terms of members of the European Union, although the list of countries is actually a bit wider than this.

52 Strictly, the test is 'domicile', but that can be a technical subject in itself. Domicile is wider than, but includes habitual residence. See e.g. CJJA 1989, ss 41-46.

53 Being another participating state. I am describing the system from the point of view of an English claimant, but it is actually formulated generically and not in terms of specific countries.

in another participating state *may* be sued here, as an alternative to being sued in his own country.

This last category includes cases, for example, where a tort or other 'harmful event' is committed (or damage is suffered) here; the contract (or the principle obligation under the contract) was to be performed here; the trust property which is the subject of the dispute is situated here.[54] What the specified cases have in common is they all describe situations where there would be sufficient *connection* with England and Wales to make it sensible to confer jurisdiction on it. It is important to note that with category (iii), suing the defendant here is an *alternative to suing him in his own country.* This is usually more convenient for a claimant living here; but assuming the conditions are met, it is the claimant's option. But a choice *must* be made: to bring the action here, there must be *no other pending proceedings* in respect of the action.[55]

The important thing to remember is that where a claimant brings an action in England and Wales against a European defendant by virtue of these rules, the claim form may be issued and served on the defendant in his own country without the need for the permission of the court. The claimant must file and serve a notice with the claim form stating the basis on which the courts of England and Wales assume jurisdiction.[56] Translations will be necessary.

Outside the European system: service only with permission

Where the defendant does *not* live within a participating European state, then the old principles apply and a claimant needs the *permission* of the court to issue and serve on a defendant outside the jurisdiction. The application is made without notice and must be supported by written evidence setting out the grounds of the application. There are three matters which the claimant must establish:

---

54 Art 5, Jurisdiction and
  Judgments Regulation.
55 CPR, r 6.33(2)(a)

56 CPR, r 6.34

(i) There must be a 'good arguable case' that the court can assume jurisdiction within one of the 20 grounds set out in PD6B, para.3.1. Again, these grounds involve cases where there is sufficient nexus between the cause of action and the English jurisdiction (or English law) to make it sensible for the courts here to assume jurisdiction.

(ii) There must be a reasonable prospect of success on the merits. This essentially means that trying the case is not a waste of time.[57]

(iii) The court must be satisfied that England and Wales is the proper place to try the case. This again is a common sense consideration, requiring the court to ask itself where justice can be dispensed most fairly, efficiently and expeditiously. This involves looking at things like where the evidence is, the availability of witnesses, and generally the pros and cons of trying the case elsewhere.[58]

So, if the claimant lives within the jurisdiction, but the defendant does not, the first and essential question is: where does the *defendant* live? If the defendant is resident in Europe, think – the CJJA/European system. If the English courts must or may assume jurisdiction, no permission to issue and serve proceedings is necessary. If the defendant does *not* live in Europe, the CJJA/European system is not relevant, permission will always be necessary and different considerations apply. Where examined, professional assessments will test a basic understanding of this distinction, using obvious countries, like France v Mexico (sounds like the World Cup!). In practice, or in a take-home assessment, if you are not sure whether a country is covered by the CJJA or not, you will just have to look it up. But an unseen examination will not try and trick you by putting the defendant in the Channel Islands and leaving you to fret over whether they are part of the

---

57 See *Seaconsar Far East Ltd v Bank Marrkazi Jomhouri Iran* [1994] 1 AC 438

58 See e.g. *Spiliada Maritime Corp v Cansulex Ltd* [1986] AC 460

European system or not (they are not).

Note that where the claim form is to be served out of the jurisdiction, *whether in Europe or not*, it is valid for *six months* as opposed to the usual four. Service will be effected by reference to relevant international conventions and diplomatic channels. Basically, the more remote a defendant is from the English jurisdiction, the longer that defendant is given to respond to the particulars of claim.[59] A claimant who does not require permission to issue and serve proceedings out of the jurisdiction will, on the other hand, need permission to enter judgment in default, should that become relevant.[60]

continues .../

59 See table set out at PD6B
 para.8
60 See generally below, Ch. 5

revision tips

- Do not let the minutiae of the service rules overwhelm your essential understanding of the system. Get a grasp of the basics, and the rest will follow.

- Appreciate that the rules for service of the *claim form* are different from the rules about service of *other* documents. Be confident about the essential differences.

- Be aware of the operation and implications of the deeming provisions.

- Do not confuse the deeming provisions with the more general computation of time rules (CPR, r 2.8/9). As to the latter, know what is meant by 'clear days' and note that when computing *short periods* of time (5 days or less) for *doing an act* (e.g. giving notice), holidays and weekends are *excluded* from the calculation. For example, if an application must be served 3 clear days before a hearing date on Tuesday 14 October the 3 clear days would be the previous Thursday, Friday and Monday (assuming that is not a Bank Holiday), so the last day for service would be Wednesday 8 October. This is *not* the case for *longer* periods.

- Check your syllabus to see if Service out of the Jurisdiction is on it. If it is, just be sure to distinguish between the European system and the non-European system.

It is worth reading ...

Judgment of *Munby J* (as he then was) in *R (Lawer) v Restormel Borough Council* [2007] EWHC 2299 (Admin); [2008] HLR 20. This is not a mainstream case (it involves the Local Authority's obligation to house the homeless), but it is easy to follow the story. At this point it is the judge's comments about the without notice interim application (which was made over the telephone!) which you should take on board.

CHAPTER 5

Early judgment without trial

Most civil cases never get to trial; some never even get to first base. Not only do the rules contain certain carrots to encourage informed negotiation and the early settlement of meritorious cases, they also include several sticks to ensure that cases without merit are thrown out well before the expense of a full trial. The most lethal of these sticks are *striking out*[1] and *summary judgment*.[2] These can be deployed against *both* claims and defences and are draconian but important weapons in the court's armoury for keeping control over its proceedings and achieving the overriding objective. Where claims are defeated, then of course to that extent the defendant wins and the claimant, as the loser, will usually have to pay both side's legal costs.[3]

Claimants have the *additional* procedural stick of obtaining *judgment in default* under CPR Part 12, which in effect penalises defendants who do not make clear their desire to defend a claim.[4] A claimant who succeeds through any one of these methods in defeating the defendant's case will get judgment (almost invariably with costs) without the aggravation and expense of a trial of the action.

Early judgment for the claimant

The two most common procedural devices claimants used to get early judgment without having to go to full trial are *judgment in default* under **CPR Part 12** and *summary judgment*.

---

1 See Ch. 13
2 See below
3 See generally Ch. 18 on costs rules

4 Judgment can be entered in default of compliance with other procedural requirements, but CPR, r 12.3 is the first opportunity for a claimant and is the form of default judgment discussed in this chapter.

1. DEFAULT JUDGMENT

Default judgment applies where a defendant does not want, or does not indicate a desire to contest a claimant's action. Since it would be silly to carry on any further in those circumstances, the claimant may in such cases 'enter' judgment 'in default' of the defendant's manifesting an intention to defend. Where the claim is for *money*, default judgment is usually an *administrative*, not a judicial, process; it is available on request from the relevant court office by merely filling out a form. No application or appearance before a judge is needed. However, *non-money claims* (e.g. injunctions), always require an *application to the court*.

Availability of default judgment

With some limited specialist exceptions (certain consumer credit cases, Part 8 claims, contentious probate cases), a claimant may obtain default judgment in respect of *any sort of claim*.[5]

Meaning of default judgment

It is important in this context to remember that the document to which the defendant must respond is the *particulars of claim*, and *not* the claim form as such.[6] When the particulars of claim are served, they must be accompanied by a 'response pack' containing forms of admission, defence and acknowledgement of service.[7] These give the defendant a range of options for responding to the claim. Silence is not really one of them!

On receipt of these documents, a defendant wanting to defend a claim can manifest this intention in one of two ways:

---

5   CPR, r 12.2/PD 12,
    para.1.2/3
6   CPR, r 9.1(2)

1. by acknowledging service of the particulars of claim within 14 days and then later filing a defence (within 28 days of service of the particulars);

or

2. by skipping the acknowledgment stage altogether and filing a defence from the outset within 14 days of service of the particulars of claim. The rules say that defendants should file a defence at the outset if practicable.[8]

It is worth noting that the time for filing the defence can be extended by a further 28 days with the consent of the parties.[9]

Not surprisingly, default judgment is therefore possible in two basic situations:

(a) where the defendant has failed to file either an acknowledgement of service or defence in time (in effect, where there has been no response at all from the defendant);

or

(b) where, having filed an acknowledgement of service, the defendant has nevertheless failed to go on to file a defence in time.[10]

PROCEDURAL PREREQUISITES

The procedural requirements for entering judgment in default all have to do with ensuring that a defendant who wants to defend an action has had every opportunity, but has nevertheless failed to respond to the claim in an appropriate manner consistent with defending. *First of all*, the court must be satisfied that the defendant has actually been served with the particulars of claim. If the court has not been

---

7   CPR, r 9.2
8   CPR, r 10.3(1); r 15.4
9   CPR, r 15.5
10   CPR, r 12.3

responsible for effecting service, then the claimant will have to prove service by means of a certificate of service. *Secondly*, the time for filing an acknowledgment of service or defence, as the case may be, must have expired; obviously the defendant must be given the *entire* period in which to respond.

Finally, the defendant must have failed to file an acknowledgment of service or defence as the case may be *and* must not have either admitted the claim and asked for time to pay; satisfied the claim; or applied for summary judgment.[11] Obviously it would be rather perverse to give the claimant judgment in default where the defendant was in the process of attempting to satisfy (or indeed had already satisfied) the claim or had made an application to the court saying the claim itself is so groundless that it is the defendant and not the claimant who should get early judgment. In essence, if, in the allotted time, a defendant wanting to defend has failed to respond in a pertinent manner, the claimant may seek to enter judgment in default.

HOW JUDGMENT IS OBTAINED

On request

In money claims only (and this includes claims for delivery of goods where the claimant will accept money instead) default judgment is available 'over the counter', as it were, unless there are exceptional features (e.g. claims against children).[12] In ordinary money cases, therefore, the claimant merely requests judgment on the prescribed form (including how and when payment of a specified amount of money is to be made where payment by instalments is acceptable). There is no hearing and no question of having to persuade a judge to give judgment on the merits of the case; judgment will be 'entered' so long as the prerequisites mentioned above have been met, which only involves checking that documents have[13] or have not reached their relevant destinations.

---

11 CPR, r 12.3/PD 12,
    para.4.1
12 CPR, r 12.4

13 Or been taken to have
    reached: see the deemed
    service rules, discussed in
    Ch. 4

Thus, in standard, everyday claims for *money* (whether for a specified sum or not) and/or claims for delivery of goods where the defendant is given the alternative of paying their value in *money*, entering default judgment is purely an *administrative* act. These account for the overwhelming majority of cases.

Note, however, that although entering judgment in such cases is administrative, it is *not* automatic, so unless and until a claimant enters judgment in default, a defendant can still manifest an intention to defend, even after the initial time for doing so has expired, thereby precluding judgment being entered. Thus a defendant who does not respond appropriately to the particulars of claim within the allotted time is *at risk* of the claimant's entering judgment against him; but the claimant actually has to *do* something to convert the risk into a reality.

On application

In money claims with exceptional features, and where the claimant is seeking a non-money remedy (e.g. equitable relief), an *application* to the court is necessary. The reason for requiring an application in the latter sort of case is that equitable remedies are 'discretionary' and therefore require a judge to exercise his or her judgment on the merits. The view of the person at the front desk is not good enough for this purpose!

Where permission is required, the application is made in writing and usually on notice in accordance with the Part 23 procedure for interim applications.[14] The application must be supported by written evidence relating to the nature of the claim and the meeting of the procedural requirements.[15] Upon application, there will be a hearing and the court will give such judgment 'as it appears the claimant is entitled to on his statement of case'.[16] In other words, the court will consider the merits of the case, at least insofar as it appears on the pleaded case.

14 See generally Ch. 4
15 CPR, r 12.11/PD 12,
    paras 3-5
16 CPR, r 12.11(1)

TYPES OF JUDGMENT IN MONEY CLAIMS

If the claim is for a 'specified' amount of money (plus interest), judgment will be final as to both liability and quantum (including interest).[17] Where the claim is for an 'unspecified' amount of money or 'damages', or the claimant asks the court to decide the quantum or the interest, the judgment will be partial (sometimes called 'interlocutory' judgment).[18] In other words, it will be final as to the defendant's liability to pay damages, but the *amount* to be paid will remain to be determined. The date of future hearings to decide this will be fixed when judgment is entered.[19]

Under the old rules the distinction was made, not between specified and unspecified money claims, but between 'liquidated' and 'unliquidated' claims. A liquidated demand is one which is objectively ascertainable (usually by looking at the contract to which it relates) and not open to argument, although it might involve an element of calculation. Typical examples are debts and the price of goods sold and delivered. If you buy a Twix bar for 50p and find when you get it home that there is something basically wrong with it, in money terms your claim against the shop for a refund is for 50p – no more and no less – because that is what you paid for the Twix bar. It is a liquidated demand.

Unliquidated claims, on the other hand, are open to argument (even if nobody would bother) or require the exercise of judicial discretion in their assessment. Most claims for 'damages' are unliquidated: indeed the words are practically synonymous (although, confusingly, there is such a thing as 'liquidated damages'). Some claims are obviously identifiable as unliquidated, for example claims for pain suffering and loss of amenity or for future financial loss – so-called 'general damages'. But others can fool you. A claim for the amount paid to have a broken watch repaired or to buy a specially adapted car is also an unliquidated claim because the defendant may want to quibble about the amount which was spent. Maybe the claimant did

---

17   CPR, r 12.5(2)
18   CPR, r 12.5(3)
19   CPR, r 12.7

not need a four-wheel drive Mercedes Benz with diamond encrusted wing mirrors. Just because a claimant can put a price tag on a damage claim does not make it liquidated, although in most cases price tags are accepted as fair and accurate.

Of course, to many people the words 'liquidated' and 'unliquidated' do not convey the meaning lawyers ascribe to them. So it is not surprising that in drafting the new rules an attempt was apparently made to update these expressions with more readily understandable vocabulary. But legal concepts and terms can sometimes be difficult to modernise. Possibly the descriptions 'specified' and 'unspecified' were intended to replace (and so translate into) 'liquidated' and 'unliquidated', but this is not what happened given how easy it is to 'specify' the amount of what is strictly speaking an unliquidated claim. The result is to place the burden on defendants to indicate if they take issue with, and seek the court's determination on, the amount of a claim, which although unliquidated is one on which the claimant has put a specific price tag.[20]

SETTING ASIDE DEFAULT JUDGMENT

Because of the non-judicial nature of most default judgments, it is not something which is subject to an appeal, as such. Instead, defendants who have had default judgment entered against them can apply to have it varied or 'set aside'. Such applications are made using the Part 23 procedure for interim applications.

Default judgment will be set aside 'as of right' if it was wrongly entered. That is to say, it *must* be set aside if the court finds there was a procedural defect in obtaining it (for example, if the time for acknowledging service had not expired when judgment was entered).[21]

Otherwise default judgment may, and presumably will only, be set aside if it appears to the court on looking at the evidence in support of the application that

---

20 Even so the distinction between liquidated and unliquidated claims comes up in other contexts, so it is useful to understand it.

21 CPR, r 13.2

'the defendant has a real prospect of successfully defending the claim' or there is some other 'good reason' for letting the case carry on.[22] This is sometimes known as setting aside 'on the merits' of the case. Notice how the rule intentionally invokes the summary judgment test, although in this context the burden of proof is on the defendant.[23] In addition, the court is to have specific regard to whether the application to set aside was made *promptly*.[24]

On the one hand, the court will not let a defendant's case be lost simply because of an isolated failure to comply with the timetable rules. Lord Atkin's sentiments expressed over 50 years ago in *Evans v Bartlam*[25] remain equally valid today:

> The principle obviously is that unless and until the Court has pronounced a judgment on the merits or by consent, it is to have the power to revoke the expression of its coercive power where that has only been obtained by a failure to follow any of the rules of procedure.

Recent cases confirm that the court's primary considerations ought to be, not procedural failings on the part of the defendant, but rather the nature of the defence, prejudice to the claimant and, of course, the justice of the case. See, for example, *Thorn plc v MacDonald*[26], where the Court of Appeal set out the relevant principles in a helpful list. An inadequately explained delay in applying to set aside may be indicative of a weak defence, but should not be taken as decisive.

On the other hand, there has to be some real point in carrying on with the case. It would be a waste of time and money to put the defendant's ship back on course when it would almost immediately – and inevitably – be sunk on the rocks of a successful summary judgment application.

When a court sets aside default judgment on the merits, it may impose conditions.[27] The most common is that the defendant pay the costs 'thrown away', since

---

22 CPR, r 13.3(1)
23 See discussion which
   follows
24 CPR, r 13.3(2)
25 [1937] AC 480, HL
26 [1999] CPLR 660
27 CPR, r 13.1(3)

these will have been incurred as a result of a failure to follow the rules. Additionally, the defendant may be ordered to pay the whole, or some part, of the disputed sum into court before being allowed to continue defending the action. The court should not, however, impose a financial condition which the defendant cannot possibly meet, since this would just be a roundabout way of giving judgment for the claimant.[28]

2. SUMMARY JUDGMENT

SUMMARY JUDGMENT FOR THE CLAIMANT

It is relatively easy to manifest an intention to defend a claim; in the first instance this merely involves ticking a box on a form. Sometimes a defendant will seek to mount a defence – perhaps out of desperation or as a delaying tactic – when there is in reality nothing that can be said that would prevent the claimant succeeding at the end of the day. If this is so, it is really rather pointless to wait until the end of the day.

The rules provide two important means of ensuring that cases without merit are quickly laid to rest. One is the 'striking out' procedure. A defence must be set out with clarity and precision and make clear where issue is being taken. Incoherent or meaningless defences would be liable to be struck out by the court. [29]

Summary judgment is a related, and to some extent overlapping, procedure. It is used for situations where whatever a defendant says, however clearly or logically set out, it is incapable of succeeding as a defence (or is inherently implausible) and there is no other compelling reason why the case should continue on to trial. The point of summary judgment for the claimant, therefore, is to provide early judgment in those cases where the defendant has no realistic hope of success and any defence raised will merely have the effect of delaying the inevitable judgment for the claimant.

28 The onus will be on the defendant to prove the impossibility of any condition. See also discussion of summary judgment below.

29 CPR, r 3.4(1) and see below

Availability of summary judgment

With a very few exceptions (notably certain residential possession proceedings), summary judgment for the claimant may be given in any type of case.[30]

Applying for summary judgment

Unless the court gives permission, the claimant may only apply for summary judgment after the relevant defendant has responded to the particulars of claim by filing an acknowledgement of service or defence (a failure by the defendant to respond to the claim would, of course, mean that the claimant could seek default judgment as discussed above). An application by a claimant who has failed to comply with any relevant pre-action protocol[31] will not normally be entertained until a defence has actually been filed (or the time for filing has expired).

Applications for summary judgment are normally made after the filing of the acknowledgment of service (thus precluding a claimant entering default judgment) but before the filing of the allocation questionnaire.[32] Certainly they should be made as promptly as possible. The idea is to put a hopeless case down before unnecessary time and costs are wasted. Furthermore, a delay in applying, while not necessarily fatal, might show a certain lack of conviction on the part of the applicant.

The application is made in accordance with the rules on making interim applications under CPR 23, with relevant modifications. Thus the application is made in writing. Notice must be given to the respondent(s), although the notice period is at least 14 days before the hearing, rather than the usual 3.[33] The written evidence in support of a claimant's application must identify concisely any point of law or provision relied upon and include a stated belief that there is no defence with a real prospect of success or other reason for a trial of the action.[34] A defendant's evidence in reply, geared to showing why there ought to be a full trial of the claim

---

30 CPR, r 24.3(1)
31 See generally Ch. 2 above
32 PD 26, para.5.3.
    See generally Ch. 8
33 CPR, r 24.4(3)
34 PD 24, para.2

or issue, must be filed at least seven days before the hearing. If the applicant wishes to respond to this, further evidence must be filed within three days of the hearing.[35]

Once the application by the claimant is made, a defendant may, but need not, file a defence before the hearing.[36] If the application is made before the case has been allocated to a case management track, the application will be heard before the allocation is made.[37] If the matter arises at the allocation stage, the question of summary judgment can be dealt with at an allocation hearing.

The hearing

For the claimant to succeed, the court must consider that the defendant 'has no real prospect of successfully defending' the claim (or an issue in the claim) *and* there is no other compelling reason to have a trial.[38]

'No real prospect of success'

The first part of this test ('no real prospect of success') may have been intended as an up-to-date articulation of the previous test, although some think it translates into the court being more robust than in the past about dismissing dubious defences.[39] It still remains the case, however, that it is a serious matter to deprive a defendant of the right to put a defence case at trial and so the 'standard of proof' is a high one. In *Swain v Hillman*,[40] the architect of the CPR, Lord Woolf, confirmed that the words 'no real prospect of success' are self-explanatory – 'real' means realistic, not fanciful; possible, not necessarily probable. He emphasised the need to keep summary judgment applications in proper perspective. They are not, he said, meant to dispense with the need for a trial where there are issues which should be considered and tested there (i.e. what used to be called 'triable issues').

Nor are they mini-trials. They are hearings to determine whether and to

---

35 CPR, r 24.5(2)
36 CPR, r 24.4(2)
37 PD 26, para.5.3(2)
38 CPR, r 24.2

39 See e.g. *E.D.and F. Man Liquid Products Ltd v Patel* [2003] CPLR 384, where Potter LJ at [8] said the current test requires the defendant "to have a case which is more than merely arguable, as was formerly the case under RSC Ord 14."

40 [1999] CPLR 779

what extent there *ought* to be a trial, disposing in the process of cases with no realistic[41] prospect of success or other raison d'être. However it is described, given that justice is an integral part of the overriding objective, before granting summary judgment the court must be clear in its own mind that a trial would be a waste of time and money.

'No compelling reason for a trial.'

Sometimes the court may feel that the defence has little or no prospect of success, but there is some other compelling reason for a trial. This usually arises when the claimant's actions appear discreditable in some way. An infamous example is *Miles v Bull*.[42] In that case a farmer sold his farmhouse to the claimant while his estranged wife was still living in it. The wife had not registered her rights of occupation before the sale and so she was not protected as against the new owner, who wanted her out of the house. The new owner sued the wife for possession and applied for summary judgment. The wife did not really have a defence, but the court held that the husband and new owner had conducted their business in such a secretive, if not underhand, way that the wife ought to have access to all of the weapons of the litigation process to test the new owner's claim. In effect, the court felt that the claimant ought to be put to strict proof of the claim in order for justice to be done.

Burden of proof

CPR, r 24.2, unlike its predecessor, is not explicit about where the burden of proof lies in summary judgment cases. Assuming an application by the claimant,[43] the question is this: is it his job to persuade the court that the defendant's case has no real chance of success; or is it the defendant's job to prove that it does? The old

---

41 In *E.D. and F. Man*, op. cit., Potter LJ at [6] said the terms 'real prospect' and 'realistic prospect' were interchangeable. Cases with a 'real prospect' of success, he added [at 8], would "carry some degree of conviction."

42 [1969] 1 QB 258

43 Defendants can also apply for summary judgment, as discussed below.

rules clearly put the burden on the defendant, presumably because at that time he would have known more about his own case than the claimant. And while it may have been the original intention to replicate this in the new rules, there is not now anything in CPR, r 24.2 or its accompanying PD which succeeds in doing so.

And what do the judges say? The question has never been directly decided, and it does not really keep anyone up at night since cases rarely turn on the point[44], but the weight of judicial observation indicates that the courts now interpret the rules as placing the burden on the applicant *claimant* to show that the defendant's case is not worthy of trial.[45] One logical reason for this is that the claimant is the one asking for early judgment. When the defendant applies to set aside default judgment so that he can put his case at trial, the burden is on him to show his case has a real prospect of success.[46] It would seem to follow that when it is the claimant who is the applicant, then the persuasive burden should be on him.

In any event, the judge will not test or weigh up the respective merits of the cases, which are typically set out in the parties' witness statements and exhibits, except to determine whether there is some point in having a trial. Cases which therefore tend not to be amenable to summary judgment are those where a substantive defence has been pleaded (e.g. frustration), a specific answer to the claim has been raised (e.g. a relevant exclusion clause), a point of law requires protracted argument and/or the relevant facts are disputed.[47] Negligence claims, for example, do not usually lend themselves to summary judgment once liability has been denied and the defendant has set out his disputed version of events. But every case must be looked at individually; in *Dummer v Brown*[48] summary judgment was granted against a coach driver who had previously pleaded guilty to a charge of dangerous driving in respect of the accident giving rise to the claim. Given the difference between the criminal and civil standard of proof, it was inconceivable

---

44 See generally discussion of burden of proof at Ch. 17

45 In *E.D. and F. Man*, op. cit., [at 9] Potter LJ said as much when contrasting the position with setting aside default judgment. Because that case was about the latter, his view was strictly 'obiter', but other cases have taken similar approaches.

46 As discussed above

47 A lot of witness statements going back and forth in response to each other usually indicate a factual dispute worthy of a trial.

48 [1953] 1 QB 710. By way of comparison see *McCauley v Vine* [1999] 1 WLR 1977

in those circumstances that the defendant could escape liability for negligence.[49]

It is important to remember, however, that the court is not liable to take every assertion made at face value; it will reject legal argument which is erroneous or evidence which is inherently implausible, irrelevant, self-contradictory or manifestly inconsistent with other believable facts. In short, the case of the party opposing summary judgment must appear to have a certain degree of credibility, and thus summary judgment applications will often focus on the implausibility (or not) of the parties' allegations. In *Sandhar v Sandhar and Kang Ltd,*[50] for example, a respondent's assertion that he retained a beneficial interest in property was rejected as fanciful. No supporting documentary evidence had been exhibited, nor were the circumstances (including no provision for rental income or how his interest was to be realised) consistent with it. Summary judgment was granted.

POSSIBLE ORDERS ON CLAIMANT'S APPLICATION

At the hearing of the claimant's application for summary judgment, the possible orders of the Master or District Judge are as follows.

Judgment for claimant

This is the appropriate order where no viable or believable defence is raised and/or there is no other reason to have a trial. The claimant will normally get an order for the costs of the application.

Conditional order

This is appropriate where a defence cannot be ruled out altogether but is 'shadowy' or of doubtful credibility; in other words where it appears to the court 'possible that a defence … will succeed, but improbable that it will do so.'[51] This is a safety net for

---

49 See Ch. 17 on admitting previous convictions in a civil case.   50 [2008] EWCA Civ 238, LTL 14/2/2008   51 PD 24, para.4

cases where the judge feels uncomfortable about giving summary judgment, but is only willing to let the defence continue on strict conditions, the most typical of which is that the defendant "put his money where his mouth is" by paying part or often all of the claim into court, failing which the claimant gets judgment. The idea is that defendants should think hard about "throwing good money after bad" if they have no real answer to the claim.[52] The court must not, however, impose a condition unless there is some prospect that the defendant can comply, since this would be tantamount to giving judgment for the claimant.[53] Having said that, the onus is on defendant to establish an inability to meet the condition 'were he really minded to do so.' Both of these principles were established in *Yorke Motors v Edwards*[54] where the appeal court reduced the amount the defendant was ordered to pay into court from over £30,000 to £4,000. The defendant wanted the condition lifted altogether, but the court felt that notwithstanding certain indicators of impecuniosity (including a legal aid certificate), a properly motivated Mr. Edwards (of whose defence the court was very sceptical) could lay his hands on the reduced amount. Requiring a defendant to take a particular step in the litigation may also be a condition.[55]

Dismissal of application

This is appropriate where the defence clearly has a chance of success or there is some other compelling reason to have a trial. The defendant's means are irrelevant here. If there is a real prospect of success at trial, there is clearly a reason for a trial and that is that. Presumably the claimant should have figured that out, so costs of the interim application will normally go to the defendant.

When the claim or any part of it is proceeding to trial (that is, where the claimant's application is dismissed or a conditional order is made), the court will go on to give

---

52 In addition, when money is paid in under such a order, the claimant is a secured creditor for that amount in the event of the defendant's bankruptcy: *Re Ford* [1900] 2 QB 211

53 See e.g. *Chapple v Williams* [1999] CPLR 731, CA

54 [1982] 1 WLR 444

55 The usual order for costs here is 'costs in the case', which means that whoever wins at trial gets the costs of this interim application. See generally Ch. 18

appropriate directions as to the future conduct of the litigation.

EXPANSION OF SUMMARY JUDGMENT

The summary judgment procedure is not limited to use by claimants against defendants. In giving the court effective case management powers, the CPR expanded summary judgment in two important ways.

(a) Defendant's choice

The first is that *defendants* may apply for summary judgment to attack hopelessly weak claims. Thus, summary judgment *for the defendant* will be granted when the court considers that the *claimant* has no real prospect of succeeding on a claim or issue and there is no other reason to have a trial.[56] Defendants' applications for summary judgment are possible in any sort of case and again are a useful adjunct to the power to strike out (which is also available against claimants). In this context, therefore, another possible order to be made by the court in summary judgment proceedings is the striking out or dismissal of the claimant's action. Otherwise, the same principles, procedure and range of possible orders discussed above applies to a defendant's application for summary judgment, adapted as necessary to the circumstances of the reversed roles. *A conditional order*, for example, would be most apt to involve some specified step which *the claimant* is required to make in the litigation before being allowed to proceed.

(b) Court's choice

Secondly, the court can fix a summary judgment hearing *on its own initiative*.[57] Thus, whenever, and as soon as it scents a weak claim or defence (usually at the allocation stage), the court can itself trigger a hearing, having given adequate notice to the

---

56 CPR, r 24.2
57 CPR, r 3.3

parties. This procedure can also be used for the purpose of obtaining a summary determination of certain issues in a case where the court is satisfied that these do not require full investigation, thus reducing the complexity and length of any trial.

COUNTERCLAIMS, SET-OFFS AND SUMMARY JUDGMENT

Often defendants make claims against the claimant in response to the latter's claim against them. When these are included in the same proceedings as the claimant's action they are known as cross-claims or counterclaims. A 'set-off' is a special kind of counterclaim, which historically has had an important impact on summary judgment applications.

All set-offs are counterclaims ...

What makes a set-off special is its ability to operate as a *defence* (to the extent of the set-off). This can be highly relevant to the outcome of a summary judgment application by a claimant. Let us suppose, for example, that a claimant's claim is for £6000 and the defendant pleads nothing else except a (believable) set-off to the value of £4000. There is thus a defence being raised up to £4000, but thereafter there is no answer given to the claim. So on a summary judgment application by the claimant, the proper order would strictly be: summary judgment for the claimant for £2,000 (the part that the set-off couldn't reach, as it were) and dismissal of the claimant's application as regards the £4,000, leaving the defendant free to continue his defence (or even get summary judgment *against* the claimant as regards the £4,000 if there is no real prospect the claimant will win on that issue).

It is important to know whether a cross-claim amounts to a set-off, because the particular magic about a set-off is its *defensive capability*. It is worth remembering that while all set-offs are counterclaims, not all counterclaims are set-offs!

In essence there are three set-off situations:

(i)   *Mutual Debts*

If D owes C £5,000 and C owes D £3,000 (both liquidated demands), then if C sues D for the £5,000, D can set the £3,000 which C owes him off against C's claim. Hence the expression 'set-off'!

(ii)   *Supply contract set-offs*

This applies where goods or services supplied under the contract in respect of which the claimant sues are claimed by the defendant to be defective. So where the claimant sues for the price of goods sold or services supplied (a liquidated demand), the defendant can set-off, in diminution of the price, any claim he has for defects in the quality of those same goods/services supplied (usually an unliquidated claim).[58]

(iii)   *The equitable set-off*

This is a broad and somewhat nebulous category. In essence, a defendant's counterclaim will be treated as an equitable set-off where, even though it is not technically a set-off in law (or other accepted category of set-off), nevertheless it and the claimant's claim arise out of the same contract or transaction or are otherwise so inextricably linked that it would be unfair to uphold the one without taking into account the other. Equity in effect intervenes to treat such a cross-claim as a set-off.

In the leading case of *Hanak v Green*,[59] for example, the claimant sued her builder for breach of contract for failing to complete works at her house. The defendant counterclaimed in respect of extra work done for the claimant by him outside the

---

58 Purists will distinguish between sale of goods cases, where the set-off derives from the Sale of Goods Act 1979, s 53(1), and supply of services cases, where it derives, by analogy, from the case law, but the concept is identical.

59 [1958] 2 QB 9

original contract; secondly, loss sustained as a result of the claimant's refusal to let the defendant's workmen onto the premises; and lastly, trespass to the defendant's tools. All three cross-claims were treated as equitable set-offs.

Another classic example of the equitable set-off arises in landlord and tenant cases. Typically, a tenant who has been sued by his landlord for arrears of rent will be allowed to set off against that claim his counterclaim for damages for breach of the same tenancy agreement (for example, the landlord's failure to repair).[60]

... but not all counterclaims are set-offs

Where the counterclaim is not a set-off (you might think of this as a 'mere' counterclaim), then it can have *no* defensive capability and cannot stop the claimant getting summary judgment. So, assuming the defendant is not raising any other defence, the claimant will get judgment. It may, however, be appropriate to delay, or 'stay' execution of that summary judgment (and make the claimant wait for his money) until after the determination of the counterclaim. On the basis of the pre-CPR case law, this will be appropriate *only* where there is sufficient connection between the claim and the counterclaim, some unresolved issue between the parties and/or some other *compelling* reason to keep the claimant from the immediate fruits of his judgment. In determining whether a defendant's 'mere' counterclaim justifies a stay of execution, the court will have regard to:

(i) the degree of connection between claim and (mere) counterclaim
     (the closer the connection, the stronger the case for a stay)

(ii) the strength of the counterclaim
     (the stronger the counterclaim, the better the case for a stay),

and

---

60 But cf *Bluestorm Ltd v Portvale Holdings Ltd* [2004] EWCA Civ 289, where the tenant's failure to pay rent had the **intended** consequence of impeding the landlord's ability to meet his obligations as landlord.

(iii) the ability of the claimant to satisfy any judgment which the defendant might obtain on the counterclaim (any doubt on this matter strengthens the case for granting a stay).[61]

The outcome of summary judgment applications

It can sometimes be difficult to distinguish between the equitable set-off (which, as a defence, can stop the claimant obtaining summary judgment) and the 'closely connected' counterclaim which does not amount to a set-off, and so, strictly, cannot stop the claimant getting summary judgment, but which justifies a stay of execution of that judgment. You might say that one person's equitable set-off is sometimes another's closely connected counterclaim. Technically, and certainly historically, the outcomes are very different, and for this reason it is important (if only for the sake of argument) to understand how the legal effect of a set-off differs from that of a (closely connected) 'mere' counterclaim. Having said that, the practical result in both cases is much the same since in neither is any money paid over until after the trial (or earlier resolution) of the claim and counterclaim. Often, it is the practical rather than the technical result which matters.

Even predicting when a stay of execution will or will not be granted can be tricky. The Court of Appeal considered the 'lack of overall clarity' which existed under the old rules in *United Overseas Ltd v Peter Robinson Ltd*[62] and concluded that, all things considered it was a good thing because it gave the court useful room for manoeuvre in dispensing justice in individual cases.

This approach, of course, is very much in keeping with the ethos of the CPR, which nevertheless has thrown up a difference of opinion amongst commentators as to the likely outcome of summary judgment applications when counterclaims and/or set-offs are raised. Some are bothered by the fact that the CPR does not duplicate, in

---

61 See generally *Drake and Fletcher v Batchelor* (1986) LSG 1232, per Sir Neil Lawson quoting from the judgments in *AB Contractors Ltd v Flaherty Bros Ltd* (Unreported) 22 February 1978, CA.

62 (unreported), March 26, 1991

the summary judgment section itself, a specific provision for stays of execution where there is a connected counterclaim – and this despite the fact that early drafts of the new rules contained such a provision. They wonder if this means courts will tend not to stay execution of summary judgments.[63] One uncomplicated explanation for this omission, of course, might be that in going through the final drafts and tidying up loose ends, it was thought unnecessary to repeat, in every context in which it might arise, the fact that the court has the power, which it clearly does, to stay execution of judgments.[64] Indeed *The White Book*[65] goes to the other extreme of suggesting it is possible that, under the new rules, the court will stay execution of summary judgments more, not less, readily than before – and that this is an option even in cases where the defence of set-off is raised, when you might suppose judgment should not even be granted in the first place! Legalistic distinctions, the authors say, now give way to the overriding objective. Certainly, where justice demands that no money passes hands until the defendant's cross-claim is resolved, the court can – and presumably will – choose whatever route to that end best accords with the need to dispense justice expeditiously and fairly, even if this means ignoring technical distinctions.

THE CHEQUE RULE

Historically, one important exception to the rule about the defensive capability of set-offs has been the so-called 'cheque rule'. This is summed up in the maxim: "There is no defence to a bad cheque." In effect, when you pay for something by cheque, you promise that the cheque is as good as cash. This is a second and *entirely separate agreement* to the one for the sale or supply of the thing being purchased. The implications of this are important. If you buy something with cash and later discover there is a fault with it, you can try and get your money back but you cannot prevent the money changing hands because the payment will already have been made! You are not

---

63 See e.g. BCP, para.34.36
64 See CPR, r 3.1(2)(f)

65 Para.24.2.6. Do not worry too much about this rather esoteric difference of opinion for exam purposes.

meant to be any better off if you pay by cheque, so that not honouring a cheque which you have written is only very exceptionally treated as excusable by the civil courts.

Thus where a claimant sues not on the original contract of sale/supply (sometimes called the 'underlying' contract), but *on the bad cheque,* then nothing the defendant can say about defects in the thing sold or supplied will be allowed to operate either as a defence or a reason to stay execution of the claimant's judgment on the dishonoured cheque, except in *very* limited circumstances. These involve situations where it is alleged either that the cheque was obtained by fraud or misrepresentation[66] or the underlying contract is void or voidable. If the underlying contract is effectively nullified, then no money should have changed hands in the first instance and the method of payment then becomes irrelevant. Thus allegations of fraud, illegality, invalidity and total failure of consideration can operate, exceptionally, as a defence to an action on a dishonoured cheque.[67]

The cheque rule is a very old one. Of course, writing cheques these days is getting to be as rare as handwritten letters, but the rule applies to any form of promissory note, including direct debit mandates. It has both a legal and commercial rationale. Business people expect to be paid at the end of the period for clearing cheques and so forth and the rule was formulated with the need to promote commercial stability in mind. Legally, its operation is explained by the existence of the two separate agreements. It is precisely because the claimant is suing on the independent contract about payment, to which there is rarely an answer, that counterclaims relating to the underlying contract of sale or supply will be ineffective in preventing summary judgment being given and enforced.

The fact that there is, as a rule, no defence to a bad cheque does not, of course, prevent the defendant complaining about the goods supplied or sold to him under the underlying contract. Indeed, it does not always prevent people stopping

---

66 *Solo Indistries UK Ltd v Canara Bank* [2001] 1 WLR 1800

67 *Nova (Jersey) Knit Ltd v Kammgarn Spinnerei GmbH* [1977] 1 WLR 713, HL. The very limited nature of the exception was highlighted by Sachs LJ in *Cebora SNC v SIP (Industrial Products) Ltd* [1976] 1 Lloyd's Rep at 271 when he said that the court will not 'whittle away [the] rule of practice by introducing unnecessary exceptions to it under influence of sympathy-evoking stories.'

cheques as a bargaining tool when something has gone wrong with such contracts! What it does mean, however, is that such complaints will afford *no defence* to the *claimant's action* on the bad cheque, leaving any claim of defective goods or service to be pursued independently.

revision tips

- Be clear about the distinction – and relationship – between default judgment and summary judgment. The former rarely involves a hearing; the latter always does (as does an application to set aside default judgment). Part 12 default judgment is relevant when a defendant shows no apparent interest in defending a claim; summary judgment against a defendant who *has* shown an interest in defending is appropriate when the claimant shows that the defence has no real prospect of success (and there is no other compelling reason to have a trial).

- A defendant seeking to set aside default judgment will have to convince the court that his defence has a real prospect of success or there is some other compelling reason to have a trial. The test is effectively the same for claimants seeking summary judgment, although in such cases the burden is on the defendant seeking to set aside judgment to do the convincing.

- Know the significance of that special kind of counterclaim known as a set-off. Remember that all set-offs are counterclaims, but not all counterclaims are set-offs. Be able to recognise an obvious set-off and its effect in summary judgment applications.

- Don't forget the 'cheque rule'. Remember the maxim: *There is no defence to a bad cheque.* It will remind you that the principle only operates if the claimant sues on the bad cheque and not the underlying contract

It is worth reading …

Judgment of HH Judge Peter Coulson QC (as he then was) in *Khan v Edgbaston Holdings Limited* [2007] EWHC 2444 (QB). Not every judge guides you so methodically through a judgment – he even gives you a table of contents! What you don't know about default judgment after reading this case, may not be worth knowing. So enjoy!

CHAPTER 6

Remedies without trial:
interim injunctions/payments

An important aspect of any claim is the substantive remedy or relief sought by the claimant. Courts are limited in what they can do to put right wrongs which have occurred. No amount of money can actually replace a missing leg, for example, but this is the remedy which claimants seek, for lack of any other. Another common remedy is an injunction, which is an order that the defendant do, or stop doing, something.[1] Usually it is not until the end of a case, that such remedies are ordered; a judge would have to have heard all the evidence before deciding, finally, who was liable – and for what.

There are occasions, however, when the court will order this sort of relief as an *interim* measure, either where it is obvious the claimant will win at the end of the day and it would be unjust not to grant some part of his ultimate remedy at an earlier, pre-trial stage; or where, without an order pending trial, irreparable damage may be caused to the claimant. Interim injunctions[2] and interim payments are two important forms of this kind of pre-trial order, and it is useful to think of them conceptually as interim versions of the substantive remedy which the claimant ultimately seeks.[3]

---

1   An order to do something is called a 'mandatory' injunction; an order not to do something, a 'prohibitory' injunction.

2   Somewhat confusingly, there are other specialised forms of injunction, which are also granted on interim applications but perform other functions. These are called not by the generic name, but by their more descriptive names, Freezing and Search Orders. See Ch. 7 below.

3   Not all interim remedies mirror the claimant's substantive claim. Most are aimed at assisting the progress of the litigation. But the rules lump them all together in one list at CPR, r 25.1, many of which are discussed in later chapters.

1.   INTERIM INJUNCTIONS (GOING TO SUBSTANTIVE RELIEF)

Interim injunctions are temporary orders granted by the court to regulate the position between the parties to an action pending trial. Because the orders themselves, and the consequences of breach, are very serious, the *general rule* is that applications for interim injunctions are made to a High Court judge or a circuit judge, *not* a Master or District Judge, unless the case is within a County Court District Judge's limited trial jurisdiction[4], or with the consent of the parties.[5]

Application is usually made *on notice*, supported by written evidence. The only justification for applying for interim injunctions of this kind without giving the other side notice is *urgency*.[6] Where the application is made without giving formal notice to the other side, reasonable attempts should be made to tell the other side what is going on. *In the absence of the other side, full and frank disclosure must be made* to the court and the applicant must explain why formal notice could not be given, and set out what was done to give informal notice. To grant an injunction against someone who has not had his day in court is very serious indeed.

It is important to think about what the judge is asked to do when considering whether to grant an interim injunction. Assuming the application is made on notice and both sides are present, the judge is being asked to make a decision on written evidence alone, which is usually conflicting, some of which may be wrong, and which may not tell the whole story. There is no testing of oral evidence, as there would be at a trial. In effect the judge is asked to make a premature decision, on limited and untested written information, about a form of relief which even if temporary may cause one or other side enormous financial or other irreparable damage.

For this reason, the *general rule* is that so long as the action is not frivolous

---

4   Mainly claims under £25,000, on the small claims or fast track

5   There are some other specialist exceptions. See BCP Table 37.2

6   Compare the position here with Search and Freezing Orders.

7   For an amusing case which did not even get over this very low hurdle see *Morning Star Co-operative Society Ltd v Express Newspapers Ltd* [1979] FSR 113.

or vexatious, that is to say, there is a 'serious' (as opposed to a silly) issue to be tried[7], a decision *at this interim stage* is reached by considering the so-called 'balance of convenience': which party would suffer more by not getting what it wants at this stage? This is the well-known test in the leading case of *American Cyanamid v Ethicon*.[8] According to that case, a determination of the merits of the case ought to be left to the trial, where witnesses can be heard and their credibility properly evaluated. Thus, except in the special circumstances set out below, it is only as a *last resort*, to help tip the balance in those rare cases where it does not obviously favour one or other party, that the court at this interim stage should consider the merits of the case[9] and attempt to prejudge the ultimate outcome.[10]

A.   EXCEPTION TO THE GENERAL RULE

It is important to understand, and be able to identify, the situations where the *American Cyanamid* test does *not* apply, either because of an historical exception[11] or the intervention of human rights legislation,[12] or because one or more of the assumptions underlying that case is missing. For example, there are two very different circumstances when the court will decide the interim injunction application 'on the merits'. One is where the facts are not disputed and the law is clear, and applying one to the other is easy. In such cases the court will, quite happily, decide the matter on the merits, because it will be clear whom they favour. The other situation is where it looks as if there will in fact never be a trial because the decision at this interim stage will in effect amount to the final outcome, in which case the courts will again decide the matter on the merits, but much less happily. So that you do not confuse these two, I will refer to them as the 'happy' and 'sad' merits exceptions, respectively.[13]

Let's look at these exceptions in some more detail.

---

8   [1975] AC 396. Balance of 'hardship' might have been a better description. It is more likely to be the case that a mandatory injunction will cause more, and irreparable, hardship than a prohibitory injunction, but there is no underlying difference in principle between interim applications for either kind of injunction: *National Commercial Bank Jamaica Ltd v Olint Corporation Ltd* [2009] UKPC 16, [2009] 1 WLR 1405.

9   Beyond checking that there is a 'serious issue to be tried.'

10   Lord Diplock's judgment in the *American Cyanamid* case sets out in detail how the balance of convenience is to be weighed up and is well worth reading.

11   E.g. defamation cases

12   E.g. s 12(3) Human Rights Act 1998

13   See pp.83-4

(a) Freedom of speech

(i) Defamation cases

The general principle here is that an injunction to restrain an alleged defamation will *not* be granted, or if granted without notice, will be discharged, where the defendant pleads (or intends to plead) justification, unless the alleged libel is obviously untrue.[14] This is an historical exception[15] to protect free speech. It pre-dates *American Cyanamid* and is unaffected by it.[16] In effect, the public interest in freedom of speech takes *absolute* priority over any personal right to protect one's reputation by injunction and the individual is left to his (often not inconsiderable) remedy in damages.

But note that this very strict and stark rule does not extend to trade mark infringement cases, even where the trademark is used in comparative advertising (which might be said to 'bad mouth' the competition), nor to claims for damage to reputation *not* based on defamation. In short, to get the benefit of this defamation exception, the cause of action must be defamation.[17]

Bear in mind, however, that the courts will not protect purveyors of obvious falsehoods and will check to see that the justification plea is not inherently implausible. Otherwise there is no consideration of merits, no consideration of any balance of hardship – if the defendant's plea of justification is a legitimate one, then no injunction will be allowed: end of story. This ancient guardian of freedom of speech in *defamation cases* is thus extremely protective where interim injunctions are sought; even more so than the human rights legislation.

(ii) Other cases

It is with cases *other than* defamation where freedom of speech under Art 10 of the European Convention on Human Rights is at issue, that s 12(3) Human Rights

---

14 See e.g. *Greene v Associated Newspapers Ltd* [2005] QB 972. Allied defences, such as fair comment, can also trigger the rule.

15 Notice the date of the leading case of *Bonnard v Perryman* [1891] 2 Ch. 269

16 As confirmed in the amusing case of *Bestobell Paints Ltd v Bigg* [1975] FSR 421. Obviously it also pre-dates the Human Rights Act 1998.

17 *Boehringer Ingelheim Ltd v Vetplus Ltd* [2007] FSR 29

18 Boehringer, ibid, applying *Cream Holdings Ltd v Banerjee* [2005] 1 AC 253

Act 1998[18] comes into play. This requires the claimant to show a case which will 'probably succeed' at trial before an interim injunction will be granted which interferes with freedom of expression.[19] This clearly involves some consideration of the merits of the case, and so is another exception to *American Cyanamid*.

Applications based on a right to privacy under Art 8 can also present a conflict with Art 10. There is no cause of action for privacy, as such, and this is an evolving field jurisprudentially. Interim injunctions in such cases are determined by applying *American Cyanamid*, but specifically weighing into the balance the public interest element. In other words a court will ask itself, in each case, whether the claim to keep information private ought to yield to the right to free speech under Art 10. In *Douglas v Hello! Ltd*[20] for example, the court would have been a lot more sympathetic to the happy couple's claim that the defendant magazine's desire to publish photographs of their wedding infringed their right to privacy had they not already sold the right to do so to someone else (so in fact privacy was not really the point!).

(b) The common law merits exceptions

(i) 'Happy' merits cases

Where the facts are not disputed and the law clear, it will be straightforward to apply the one to the other. In effect, there is no serious issue to be tried (or no need for a trial) since the outcome is obvious.[21] This is somewhat analogous to a summary judgment situation. Typical sorts of cases falling within this exception include: clear-cut restraint of trade cases, clear-cut restrictive covenant case, clear-cut cases of breach of confidentiality, clear-cut sale of land cases.[22] Note that restraint of trade cases are not an exception *in themselves*, but merely a common example of cases falling under this exception.[23] In these sorts of cases, the court is 'happy' to decide the application on the merits since it is so easy to do so.

---

19 *McKennit v Ash* [2008] QB 73

20 [2001] QB 967

21 *Office Overload v Gunn* [1977] FSR 39, CA

22 And possibly clear-cut cases generally, see e.g *Series 5 Software Ltd v Clarke* [1996] 1 ALL ER 583.

23 *Lawrence David Ltd v Ashton* [1991] 1 ALL ER 385, CA

(ii) 'Sad' merits cases.

Sometimes the outcome at the interim stage would effectively dispose of the action and/or render a future consideration of the issues pointless, at least as far as the injunctive relief is concerned, and as a result there is unlikely to be a later trial. Alternatively, a future trial may come too late to be of any use.[24]   In such cases, the court is unhappy, but feels compelled to decide the application on the merits because if the case never goes to a full trial, it is 'now or never'.[25]

It is important to understand that where the courts, exceptionally, decide the application on the merits under either of these two principles, claimants must have an 'overwhelming' case to get the injunction. There must, in effect, be a compelling reason to deprive the defendant of the chance to put his case at trial.[26] Claimants usually do have a case of this strength in a 'happy' merits scenario, so they are happy too; but they rarely do in a 'sad' merits situation, which makes them feel likewise when they lose the interim application. This does not mean, of course, that they will not win at the end of the day!

The application is much like any other under CPR, r 23. Useful summaries are found in BCP's Checklists 19 and 20. It is especially important to be aware of the relevant *undertakings* which may be necessary when injunctions are ordered or agreed – more will be required if the application is without notice.[27] The undertaking as to damages is the most obvious, but note that PD 25, para.5.1A empowers the court to order that the applicant not only undertakes to compensate the respondent, but also *any other person* who 'may suffer loss as a consequence of the order.' These will no doubt become known as third party undertakings. The draft of the order sought should be in standard form.[28]

---

24 See e.g. *Cream Holdings*, ibid.

25 See e.g. *Cayne v Global National Resources plc* [1984] 1 ALL ER 225, CA.

26 *Per Eveleigh LJ, Cayne v Global*, ibid p.233

27 See generally PD 25A, para.5.1

28 PF 39 CH and PF 40 CH, for pre-action and post-issue applications respectively. A computer disc containing the draft order should also be made available to the court if possible, so it can use it, amended as necessary, for any order it might make.

2. INTERIM PAYMENT (OF DAMAGES)

Interim payments are a means by which claimants can get some of their damages 'on account' as it were, before the trial or assessment of damages. Where:

(i) the defendant has admitted liability;

or

(ii) the claimant has already got early judgment against the defendant, for example default or summary judgment, damages to be assessed;

or

(iii) where the court is *satisfied* that the claimant *would win* substantial damages from a defendant at trial,

then the court can order the defendant to make an interim payment.[29] As to (c) above, it has been said that the claimant must show that he will win on the balance of probabilities, but at the 'upper end' of the scale.[30] However described, the claimant must show a pretty compelling case – up there with summary judgment. The words of the rule really speak for themselves; for the court to be 'satisfied' that the claimant 'would obtain judgment for a substantial sum of money', it would have to be pretty darn sure. The burden is a high one because the court wants to get it right – no one wants the claimant to have to sell his wheelchair because the interim payment made to him needs to be given back.

Thus, in the context of a summary judgment application by a claimant, where the application is dismissed, and the defendant permitted to continue with his defence, it would be inconsistent also to grant the claimant an interim payment award. The court cannot simultaneously be satisfied to the requisite standard

---

29 See CPR, r 25.7

30 *Shearson Lehman Bros Inc v Maclaine Watson and Co Ltd* [1987] 1 WLR 480, CA

that the claimant would succeed at trial for interim payment purposes *and* that the defendant has a real prospect of success at trial. It might, however, be possible to have an interim payment where the summary judgment application has been dealt with by way of a *conditional* order; indeed the making of the interim payment could be the condition.

Interim payments help tide claimants over during what can sometimes be a long period until trial or assessment of damages.[31] They are particularly useful in, *but not limited to*, personal injuries cases. *Stringman v McArdle*[32] (a pre-CPR case) decided that a claimant does not have to show a need for the money to get the order; only that the procedural requirements have been met. On the other hand, the relevant practice direction now specifically requires the claimant to include in the written evidence supporting the application what the money will be used for.[33] *Stringman v McArdle* may still be good law, but later cases stress the undesirability of making an interim payment order which effectively ties the trial judge's hands (or runs the risk of overpaying the claimant). The interim judge will have to be very careful (and conservative) in predicting the sort of order which the trial judge might make. One has to be especially cautious as regards future losses, particularly when these might ultimately be catered for, not with a single sum, but with a periodic payments order.[34] To this extent, therefore, need may be relevant both as to *how much* to order by way of interim payment and, if choices have to be made, *for what aspect* of the claimant's losses.[35]

Multiple defendants

Where there are two or more defendants, if it is clear to the court that a specific defendant will be liable to the claimant, then, assuming the other procedural requirements are met, the court can order an interim payment against that one

---

31 Liability may well be admitted, but calculating damages may be very complex.

32 [1994] 1 WLR 1653

33 PD 25B, para.2.1(2)

34 These are very common with catastrophic injury cases and involve regular payments over what is often a very long time. If a big chunk of money has been expended with an interim payment award (e.g. to buy a specially adapted house), this might mean there is not enough capital left at the end of the day to fund a periodical payment award. In a sense the 'need' for the new house becomes a foregone conclusion by the trial. Coulson J sets out the principles well in *Brewis v Heatherwood & Wrexham Park Hospitals NHS Trust* [2008] EWHC 2526 (QB).

35 See *Cobham Hire Services v Eeles* [2009] EWCA Civ 204

identified defendant, regardless of the fact that there are other defendants named in the proceedings. In other words, even where there are multiple defendants, if the claimant can *clearly* enough put the blame on one of them, the court can make an interim payment order against that one if it sees fit.

Where, however, there are multiple defendants and it is *unclear* against whom the claimant will succeed, then an interim payment can still be ordered, but *only* if it is established that:

- The claimant will succeed against *at least one* of the named defendants, even if it is not clear which;

and

- *all* of the defendants are *either insured, public bodies* or defendants whose liability will be met by, e.g. the Motor Insurance Bureau.[36]

These additional requirements are intended to safeguard the position if the 'wrong' defendant is required to make the interim payment, which could easily happen if it is not clear who will be held liable to the claimant. Where only insurance companies and public bodies are concerned, no great injustice will occur if one of the defendants has to reimburse another at the end of the day. Otherwise, the claimant has to point the finger at the defendant from whom he seeks an interim payment.

Amount of interim payment

It is important that the court does not order an interim payment greater than the amount ultimately awarded at trial. Thus an interim payment must not exceed a 'reasonable proportion of the damages.'[37] The rules are no more specific than this, to allow the courts to exercise their discretion from case to case, although in

---

36 See CPR, r 25.7(1)(e). The Motor Insurance Bureau (MIB) picks up the tab for uninsured drivers.

37 See CPR, r 25.7(4)

practice the amount ordered will be apt to cover the special damage claim, plus (perhaps) some proportion of the general damage claim, taking care not to fetter the trial judge's options.[38] But the wording of the order is left purposely wide. Set-offs and allegations of contributory negligence will obviously have to be taken into account.[39] The idea is that at the end of the day, the claimant recovers *more* by way of damages than was awarded by way of interim payment.[40]

Note that if an interim payment has been ordered, *no mention of it should be made to the trial judge until all matters of liability and quantum are decided*.[41] There is an obvious risk of prejudice if the trial judge knows that an interim judge thought the case so clearly favoured the claimant. This is a *very important rule* which is forgotten at the advocate's peril – it could result in a mis-trial and a personal costs order.

Remember, too, that unlike a Part 36 offer,[42] an interim payment has no costs implications. It is not an offer of settlement in any way. Nor is it a payment into court. Rather it is a court order making a defendant pay out to a claimant *now* some of what the defendant will, or will almost certainly, have to pay out to the claimant at the end of the trial or other assessment of damage.

Procedure

This is a fairly typical Part 23 interim application. It is made on notice, with supporting evidence in writing to include the matters set out at PD 25B, para.2.1, which are specifically geared to the nature of the remedy.[43] A further or second application for an interim payment may be made in appropriate circumstances.[44]

---

38 As discussed above

39 CPR, r 25.7 (4)

40 Though the court has extensive powers to make 'adjustments' if need be, including orders that the claimant reimburse the defendant. See CPR, r 25.8

41 Unless the defendant does not mind, which would be rare. See CPR, r 25.9

42 See below, Ch. 15

43 There is also a useful summary at BCP, Checklist 24.

44 CPR, r 25.6(2)

INTERIM PAYMENTS VERSUS PROVISIONAL DAMAGES

Word of Warning!

Do not confuse interim payments with provisional damages

They sound as if they could be the same thing but they are very different. Interim payments, which can be awarded in any sort of case, are about a claimant getting some of his ultimate damage award *before* the trial of the action. Provisional damage claims are limited to *personal injuries claims only*, and really focus on what happens (or might happen) *after* the trial.[45]

Damages are usually awarded on a one-off, once-and-for-all basis, immediately after liability is established or as soon thereafter as damages can be properly assessed. This is not well suited to situations where, at the time of assessing loss and damage, there is merely a *chance* that some deterioration in health will occur in future.[46] If that chance is assessed on a once-and-for-all basis, it can only be calculated in percentage terms. This can result in the claimant either being over-compensated, if the disease or deterioration never happens, or (more problematically) under-compensated, when it does happen, because the damages awarded earlier reflected merely the possibility, not the actuality. The problem is particularly pronounced in cases where there is a relatively small chance of some dreadful disease occurring.

To remedy this situation, the courts are given the power to make awards of what are known as 'provisional damages.' They work like this: in assessing immediate damages on a once-and-for-all basis, it is assumed that the disease or deterioration in question will not happen, and so is *left out of account altogether*. But if it does occur within a specified time, the claimant[47] can come back to court and have that aspect of his losses accurately assessed.[48]

There are essentially four conditions:

---

45 Or settlement

46 And for which the defendant is responsible.

47 Or his dependents if the claimant has died. See Fatal Accidents Act 1976, s 3.

48 See, Senior Courts Act 1981, s 32A; County Courts Act 1984, s 51

(a) Condition 1

The claim for provisional damages must be set out in the *particulars of claim*.[49]

(b) Condition 2

The possible future disease must be *'serious'* in nature. To be serious, the condition must be something beyond ordinary wear and tear. Conditions like osteoarthritis pose problems because we all are apt to suffer them with age.[50]

(c) Condition 3

It must be *'proved or admitted'* that there is a *'chance'* of the future development or deterioration. In other words, it is only *how* the loss is to be compensated which is at issue, not the nature of the loss, nor the defendant's responsibility for it. The chance of deterioration is usually fairly straightforwardly established by the medical evidence.

(d) Condition 4

The future development or deterioration must be of the claimant's *'physical or mental condition.'* So, provisional damages are limited to this one, albeit important, aspect of a personal injuries claim. It does *not* apply to the chance that a claimant might lose his job or his house or his carer in future – if causally connected, these sorts of loss continue to be assessed on a once-and-for-all basis.

Even if these conditions are all met, it is still a matter of the court's *discretion* whether to make a provisional, rather than a conventional, damage award. Common sense considerations apply, including which form of judgment would dispense better justice and how easily it will be to know when and whether a

---

49 CPR, r 41.2(1)

50 See e.g. *Willson v Ministry of Defence* [1991] 1 ALL ER 638

serious deterioration has in fact occurred.[51]

If an order for provisional damages is made, it should specify both the nature of the disease or deterioration in question *and* how long a period the claimant has to make a future application to the court should the worst happen.[52] Provisional damages are hard enough on a defendant, without the time-frame being completely open ended. Having said that, the period can be expressed to last for the claimant's life, in appropriate circumstances. A claimant making an application for the further assessment of damages must give the defendant or the defendant's insurers at least 28 days notice. Many years might have passed since the original order and it may take some time to find the files. Subsequent procedure is much like that for an interim payment, which conveniently brings me back to my initial warning: be sure you know the difference between interim payments and provisional damages!

continues .../

---

51 *Willson v Ministry of Defence*, ibid

52 See generally CPR, r 41.2(2) and PD 41A, para.2.1. An example of a provisional damage award is given at the annex to PD41A.

revision tips

- The interim remedies discussed in this chapter mirror the claimant's substantive claim. Others are aimed at assisting the litigation process. CPR, r 25.1 lumps them all together in one list but it helps to make the distinction.

- You must be able to recognise both the test in, and the name of, the *American Cyanamid* case. It is worth reading the judgment.

- You should have a basic understanding of situations where the rule in *American Cyanamid* does *not* apply – and *why*.

- Be clear about the *distinction* between interim payments and provisional damages. They sound similar, but they are very different.

It is worth reading …

Lord Hoffmann's judgment in *National Commercial Bank Jamaica Ltd v Olint Corporation Ltd* [2009] UKPC 16, [2009] 1 WLR 1405. This is a Privy Council case, which might just get you feeling sorry for banks (if that is possible)! Lord Hoffmann's judgments are a pleasure to read – this one is short, and to the point, but no less enlightening for that. Note in particular what he has to say about without notice applications and the court's approach to granting (interim) mandatory injunctions. You should be getting the message now that the courts do not much favour applicants who do not give notice to the other side when (as is usually the case) they should.

CHAPTER 7

Making litigation meaningful:
freezing and search orders

There are some forms of interim injunction which are not geared to the claimant's ultimate remedy or relief, but which aim to make the litigation meaningful, either by ensuring the there are funds to enforce against if the claimant wins, or by preserving crucial evidence. These are known, respectively, as *Freezing* and *Search* orders, although the older case law will refer to them by their pre-CPR names of Mareva Injunction and Anton Piller Order.[1] It is important both to distinguish them from the more 'bog standard' type of interim injunction discussed in the last chapter, and also to appreciate just how draconian these forms of order are.

1. FREEZING ORDERS

Freezing orders are designed to stop defendants (or potential defendants) from wilfully turning themselves into paupers or hiding assets so as to thwart a claimant's ability, if he wins the case, to get his hands on them. If there are no assets, there will be no way to execute judgment[2] and the claimant will get no money! Freezing orders make litigation meaningful for a claimant because a 'paper' judgment is of little use.[3]

---

1   Named after the leading cases of *Mareva Compania Naviera SA v International Bulk Carriers SA* [1980] 1ALL ER 213 and *Anton Piller KG v Manufacturing Processes Ltd* [1976] Ch. 55. They were given more modern and descriptive names under the new rules.

2   As to execution generally, see below at Ch. 19

3   It is usually claimants who seek freezing orders, but anyone in a 'claimant-like' position can apply, e.g. a counterclaiming defendant or defendant against a third party.

Freezing orders thus restrain defendants from 'disposing of' or 'dissipating' or even 'dealing with' certain of their assets so as to frustrate the enforcement of any judgment the claimant may obtain against them. The amount 'frozen' should not normally exceed the value of the claim. It is, of course, very serious to stop people using their own money before they have been judged liable to pay some of it to another person, so such orders are not granted lightly. After all, maybe it will be the defendant who wins the case! So, although the granting of such orders, like all injunctions, is discretionary,[4] the conditions for obtaining freezing injunctions are very strict. They are as follows:

(a) Jurisdiction

The applicant/claimant must show a substantive cause of action over which the court has jurisdiction (or in respect of which it can act). An injunction is a remedy, and thus needs a cause of action to which it relates. The order cannot 'simply be made in the air.'[5] As a general rule, therefore, an applicant must be able to point to proceedings underway or about to be commenced, so as to show where and on what basis he expects to get judgment against the defendant. It is no longer strictly necessary to show that the substantive action is to be brought in the English courts,[6] although this will usually be the case.

(b) Strength of case

The applicant/claimant must show he has a 'good arguable case'. This is a middling standard; higher than that required for an *American Cyanamid* type of injunction (which is about as low as it gets), but not as high as, say, interim payment or summary judgment applications.

---

4   S 37(1) Senior Courts Act 1981 enables the court to grant interim injunctions where it appears 'just and convenient' to do so, and 'on such terms and conditions' as it thinks just.

5   Per Lord Mustill in *Mercedes-Benz A.G. v Leiduck* [1995] 3 All ER, PC, at 929

6   See CJJA 19882, s 25 and *Fourie v Le Roux* [2007] 1 WLR 320, HL

(c) Assets

The applicant/claimant must show that the defendant has assets in (or exceptionally out of) the jurisdiction. Assets come in all shapes and sizes: money, land, valuable things, like cars and jewellery. So long as the asset belongs to the defendant, or he can get his hands on it, then it can be the subject of an order. Normally, the assets must be in the jurisdiction, but in exceptional circumstances, the court will make a 'worldwide' order affecting assets both here and/or abroad.[7] The relevant assets must be identified with some degree of precision, so the court can make the order. Normally an order would freeze named assets up to a maximum value, not to exceed the most that the claimant might win in the case.

(d) Risk of dissipation

The applicant/claimant must show that there is a real risk of the dissipation or disposal of those assets so as to render judgment of no value. This is the critical requirement, and the most difficult to establish, in part because there is rarely direct evidence of such a risk. It is usually to be inferred from some conduct or attitude of the defendant's, but an expression of general apprehension on the part of the claimant will not be enough.[8] The ease with which a defendant could dispose of assets will be an obvious consideration, but the claimant's ability to enforce judgment is also key. Remember, too, that it is not the job of a freezing order to provide security for the claim;[9] its purpose is to obviate the risk that a defendant's actions might render him 'judgment proof.' A useful list of factors relating to this aspect of freezing orders is set out at BCP, para.38.13.

Have a look at the standard form of freezing injunction annexed to PD 25, which includes a version for both domestic and worldwide orders, to get a feel for what the order typically sounds like.

---

7   These will only be ordered, effectively, when it is shown that there are no or insufficient assets in the jurisdiction and that there are identifiable assets out of the jurisdiction. See e.g. *Derby v Weldon (No 1)* [1990] Ch. 48. CA

8   See e.g. *O'Regan v Iambic Productions* [1989] 139 NLJ (Sir Peter Pain)

9   The order does not put the claimant in any better position than any other creditor. But note that the fact that a defendant has a dubious credit history does not in itself justify the making of an order: *Mobile Cerro Negro Ltd. V Petroleos de Venezuela SA* [2008] 1 Lloyd's Rep 684 (Walker J at para.36).

2. SEARCH ORDERS

Search orders are about preserving things of vital evidential value to the claimant's case, in circumstances where there is a *real risk* that the defendant might try to destroy or tamper with them, if the evidence were exchanged or sought in the normal way. They make litigation meaningful because a claimant may not be able to prove his case at trial without this evidence. This form of injunction, which is a bit like a civil search and seizure order, allows a claimant, without warning,[10] to enter the defendant's premises to look for, and keep safe until trial, certain named pieces or types of evidence. This obviously involves a very serious invasion of the defendant's personal (or business) space and will not be ordered lightly.

Like any other injunctive relief, whether the court grants a search order is a matter of discretion. *At a minimum,* however, the following are essential requirements:

(a) Strength of case

The claimant must have an *extremely strong prima facie case* on the merits. This is a noticeably higher standard even than the freezing order. Not as high as for summary judgment or interim payments, perhaps, but getting there. If the case were just middling in strength, presumably the defendant's motivation to tamper or destroy evidence would not be very high either.

(b) Harm

The defendant's activities must be shown to cause *very serious actual or potential harm* to the claimant. This is often not difficult to establish as such. Search orders tend to be applied for in cases involving fraud, big money divorces and infringement of

---

10 But with safeguards, see
    below.

intellectual property rights, where either the continued conduct of the defendant or the vanishing evidence is pretty obviously harmful.

(c) Evidence of possession

There must be *clear evidence* that the incriminating evidence is in the possession of the defendant.

(d) Risk of tampering

It must be shown that there is a *real possibility* that the items of evidence will be tampered with or destroyed before (or if) the application were made on notice. As with the freezing order, this requirement goes to the *heart* of the application. Evidence is exchanged in the normal course of litigation, by a standard direction[11] or by an order of the court following a contested hearing, with both sides present. It is assumed that most people will comply with such orders, however reluctantly. Thus, to get the search order there must be a cogent reason for believing that the defendant would disobey a request or injunction to preserve the evidence in question. Again, the court is usually asked to infer such a risk from the defendant's conduct, although it will be wary of 'the extravagant fears which seem to afflict claimants who have complaints of breach of confidence, breach of copyright and passing-off.'[12]

In the exercise of its discretion, the court will also ask itself whether granting the order is proportionate in the circumstances. This will be particularly important if the evidence would significantly harm the defendant or benefit the claimant over and above its preservation for trial.

There was a time when Anton Piller Orders (as search orders used to be called) were given out like sweets, but those days are long gone.[13] Before embarking

---

11 See Ch. 9
12 Per Dillon LJ in *Booker McConnell v Plascow Plc* [1985] R.P.C. 425, at 441

13 See e.g. the court's stern words in *Columbia Pictures Industries Inc v Robinson* [1987] Ch. 28

on an application for a search order, it is always incumbent on a claimant to have considered whether some less draconian measure would suffice.[14]

In any case, remember that a search order is *not* a search warrant. It is directed to a named person, not a place. The defendant can refuse entry, and no one should be kicking in doors or otherwise forcing entrance. It is not a police operation! Having said that, a failure to comply with a search order would amount to a contempt of court and itself could be rather damning evidence against the defendant in the upcoming trial to which the order related.

Given the harsh nature of search orders, there are a host of safeguards and rules designed to ensure that they are carried out properly and fairly, and that any property belonging to the defendant is returned as soon as its evidential value has been preserved (for example after photocopying). These are set out very clearly at PD25A, paras 7.2 to 7.11. In addition, an example of a search order is annexed to the practice direction. Take a careful look at these. Note especially the possibility of including what are sometimes called 'ancillary orders' which augment a search order. These typically require the defendant to disclose relevant information, either as regards the evidence in question or the cause of action itself. None of these are unusual in themselves, since they may be required or ordered in the ordinary course of litigation. In the context of a without notice search order, however, they become part and parcel of the draconian nature of the injunction.

As you might appreciate, there is an uncomfortable interface between search orders and an individual's privilege against self-incrimination, i.e. the right to refuse to answer any questions, or produce any document or thing, if to do so would expose that person to criminal sanctions.[15] Although in one sense rather damning to assert this privilege, the consequence of relying on it has been to

---

14 E.g. order to produce or deliver-up documents, order to inspect etc. See generally list at CPR, r 25.1.

15 See e.g. wording of Civil Evidence Act 1968, s 14(1) which is declaratory of the common law: *Rio Tinto Zinc Corpn v Westinghouse Electric Corpn* [1978] AC 547, p. 636.

thwart the execution of many a search order, given the types of cases in which such orders tend to predominate.[16] As a result, the right to rely on the privilege was *removed by statute* in cases involving *intellectual property and passing off,* although any incriminating evidence obtained *cannot be used in any related criminal trial.*[17] In other sorts of cases, the threat or risk of self-incrimination has been successfully removed by the promise, in writing, not to use the evidence obtained in any criminal proceedings – a sort of contractual version of the statutory provision which can, as appropriate, be included in the order.[18]

There are some points to note about both freezing and search orders:

(a) Secrecy

In both cases, the application is almost invariable made *without notice,* because *secrecy* is essential. Given that the claimant is effectively saying to the court "if the defendant knows I am asking for this order he will hide his money or destroy the evidence", then giving notice of the application would defeat its purpose. The situation may also be urgent, but the key is secrecy. Usually applications are made *after issue* of proceedings, but *before* those proceedings have been *served* (because of the secrecy aspect). In urgent cases, the application can be made 'pre-action', i.e. before proceedings have even been commenced.

(b) High Court Judge

In general, these applications are made to a *judge* in the *High Court.* Only rarely is the County Court or an interim judge empowered to grant freezing or search orders. By the time you find yourself dealing with one of these sorts of applications, you will have outgrown this book!

---

16 The right at common law to rely on the privilege was upheld by the House of Lords in *Rank Film Distributors Ltd v Video Information Centre* [1982] AC 380

17 Senior Courts Act 1981, s 72

18 See e.g. *AT and T Istel Ltd v Tully* [1993] AC 45, HL

(c) Full and frank disclosure

The claimant must make *full and frank disclosure* of any facts which militate against the order being given. This is the general rule where without notice applications are concerned, but is particularly important where such severe injunctions are at stake. Any failure to make full and frank disclosure will result in the order being discharged.

(d) Affidavit evidence

Written evidence in support of such applications is made by way of *affidavit, not* witness statement. This is a rare example of where affidavits are mandated by the rules.[19]

(e) Draconian orders

These orders are both very draconian, and you want to be aware of the various principles and *safeguards* which protect defendants as far as appropriate. These are clearly set out in both the White Book and BCP. So far as freezing orders are concerned, be aware of the limitations and *various grounds of variation or discharge*. With search orders, be aware of the safeguards in *execution*.

(f) Undertakings

The various *undertakings* that a claimant gives when such orders are granted are very important. The undertaking as to damages is even more crucial with these sorts of injunction than a 'normal' interim injunction – the more harm the order may cause, the more assurance the court will need that the claimant's undertaking in damages has substance. The various undertakings that might be needed in any given case are set out in the sample orders appended to PD 25.

---

19   CPR, r 3.1

Bear in mind that, however exciting these forms of injunction are, freezing and search orders are to be treated as *exceptional*. Most litigation is able to proceed without them. They are different from the average interim injunction, and different from each other, although they share some common features and both give litigation value to a claimant by preserving evidence for trial or assets for enforcement. The fact that one of these exceptional orders may be appropriate in a case, does not mean that the other will be – but it is not unheard of for both orders to be made against the same, very mad or very bad defendant. [20]

revision tips

- Both the White Book and BCP have some useful procedural summaries to help with revision. BCP's Checklist 19 reviews without notice procedure generally. The WB's procedural guides D 17.1 and 17.2 deal specifically with Freezing and Search orders.

- Be sure you can distinguish between 'normal' interim injunctions and these exceptional forms of order (and that you can distinguish between the freezing and search order).

- Try 'grading' on a scale of 1 to 10 the strength of case required for the various interim applications we have been discussing so far. Assuming 10 to be the highest, summary judgment and interim payments applications would be right up at the top and *American Cyanamid* cases would be right down at the bottom. The rest are somewhere in between – freezing orders might be about a 5; search orders about an 8?

It is worth reading ...

Another Hoffmann J (as he then was) judgment in the case of *Lock International plc v Beswick* [1989] 1 WLR 1268. Well written as always. This was in the days when the search order was called an Anton Pillar order, but what the judge had to say about the strength of case required and the draconian nature of the order still holds true.

[20]   See e.g. *Columbia Pictures v Robinson* op.cit.

PART TWO

on to trial

CHAPTER 8

Track allocation

Once it seems clear that a case will proceed towards a trial, then the court will allocate it to one of three tracks: (1) the small claims track (this is essentially citizen's justice); (2) the fast track (for basic, no-frills litigation) or (3) the multi-track (for more complex trials lasting more than one day).

After the defence is filed, the court will normally transfer the proceedings to the defendant's 'home court' unless the case is already there.[1] *Allocation questionnaires* will be sent to the parties by the court[2], to be returned by a specified date. Once all the questionnaires have been filed, or the time for filing has expired (or the need for them has been dispensed with[3]), the procedural judge will allocate the case.

Not surprisingly, the information on the allocation questionnaires is geared to assisting the court in allocating the case to the appropriate track for that case. The parties should consult on allocation issues, but it is the claimant who pays the allocation fee. Note that allocation will be deferred where a 'stay'[4] has been requested or ordered to allow for early settlement of the action.[5] If the court needs more information than that contained on the returned questionnaires, it will ask for or set an allocation hearing. When the court allocates a claim to a track, it will notify the parties in writing.[6]

The track to which a case is allocated will reflect both its value and case

---

1   It is not obliged to do so if the defendant is not an individual: CPR, r 26.2. Where there are two or more defendants, the court will transfer to the home court of the defendant who is first to file a defence. CPR, r 26.2(5).

2   Unless not, or not yet, needed. See generally CPR, r 26.3(1)

3   This might happen if the question of allocation had been dealt with on an earlier occasion, for example, a summary judgment hearing. See generally PD 26, para.2.4.

4   A temporary halt to the proceedings which can effectively become permanent.

5   CPR, r 26.4

6   CPR, r 26.9

management needs.[7] The overriding objective requires that cases are dealt with expeditiously, fairly and proportionately, and the three track options are designed to facilitate this. A brief summary of the attributes of each is set out below.

1.   THE SMALL CLAIMS TRACK

Broadly, the small claims track is the normal track for claims under £5,000.[8] There are, however, refinements or exceptions in certain kinds of cases, including personal injuries claims where the value of the pain, suffering and loss of amenity element exceeds £1,000, in which case the normal track will be the fast track.[9]

There may, of course, be other reasons why a claim falling within the value range of the small claims track is not allocated there. These might include the complexity of the case, the nature of the allegations or the need to make use of the more standard features of litigation, which are missing from this track.

The *hallmarks* of the small claims track are as follows:

- On allocation, a date for a hearing (and its length) will be fixed and *directions* given, usually in standard form. Directions differ according to type of cases, for example holiday cases, building disputes etc. but common to all are standard directions about exchanging the *documents which each party will by 'relying on'* in the case,[10] bringing original documents to the hearing, and an obligation to inform the court if the case settles.[11]
  If necessary, special directions can be given and/or a preliminary appointment fixed.

---

7   See CPR, r 26.8 for the various discretionary (non-monetary) factors which may be relevant to track allocation.

8   CPR, r 26.6(3)

9   Even though the overall claim does not exceed £5,000. See CPR, r 26.6(1)(a). There are similar provisions for certain landlord and tenant cases: CPR, r 26.6(1)(b) and r 26.7(4).

10   This is more limited than for the other tracks. See generally below Ch. 9.

11   See generally Appendix A and B to PD27

- *Other common features of litigation are missing* (including wholesale orders for disclosure, interim directions of a case management nature, most evidential rules, Part 36 offers, and the traditional approach to the conduct of the proceedings). The hearing is conducted on an *informal* basis, usually in the District Judge's room. If the parties agree (or if space is at a premium), the hearing will be conducted in private. Evidence is not generally given on oath and the court may limit cross-examination.[12] Crucially, *no expert evidence*, either written or oral, may be given without the court's permission.[13]

- The small claims track is designed to be navigated by the lay person, and so the scope for recovering *costs is severely limited*. In particular, the idea is to exclude lawyers, and so the cost allowed for legal assistance is almost non-existent.[14]

  Appeals, however, are now dealt with in the same way as any other case.

2. THE FAST TRACK

The fast track is the 'Easyjet' of the system, providing a no-frills, value-for-money route to justice for relatively inexpensive, straightforward and predictable claims. It steers a middle course between the bare necessities on offer on the small claims track and the complex handling of cases on the multi-track, although it resembles the latter more than the former. Most defended claims falling within the £5,000 to £25,000 monetary band, and whose trial will take no more than one day, will be allocated to the fast track.[15]

---

12 See generally CPR, r 27.8
13 CPR, r27.5

14 If the court felt it was important that a party be legally represented, this would be a good reason to allocate to the fast track.

15 CPR, r 26.6(4) and (5)

Its *hallmarks* are:

- Few or no interim hearings
- Standard directions
- Speedy timetable with a virtually immutable trial date fixed by the court when the case is allocated
- Limited numbers of experts
- Single joint expert evidence (on any one issue) admitted by means of a written report is the norm
- One day trial
- Trial costs are 'fixed'; 'summary assessment' of other costs[16]

On the fast track, the case will be actively managed to a *tight timetable* usually lasting no longer than *thirty weeks.*[17] Case management directions will be given at *two* stages: when the case is *allocated* to the track and upon the parties filing *pre-trial checklists.*[18] As on all the tracks, many directions are predictable and so are given using a standard form,[19] but they are not given on a 'one size fits all' basis. The court will delete or adapt the form as necessary to produce directions which are able to meet the requirements of the case at hand.

Directions on allocation

This first set of directions, which accompanies the allocation notice sent to the parties, will lay down the case management timetable, including setting the trial date or 'window'.[20] Typically the matters to be dealt with in this first instance will include the identification and exchange of various items of evidence: documentary evidence, witness statements, expert evidence.[21] The court's main concern at this point is to equip the parties with the means to identify and narrow the issues.

---

16 See Ch. 18 on costs

17 CPR, r 28.2 (4)

18 These were previously known as listing questionnaires

19 Model form directions are set out in the Appendix to PD 28, the Fast Track Practice Direction.

20 Like any 'window of opportunity', this is a given period of about three weeks during which the trial will take place, the precise date to be determined closer to the time.

21 Usually to be exchanged in that order. See generally PD 28, para.3 (para.3.12 contains the typical timetable).

Pre-trial directions

The second stage for giving directions occurs after pre-trial checklists have been filed, or dispensed with.[22]   Again standard form directions will be tailored to the circumstances of the individual case. At this point the focus is on checking compliance with previous directions which have been given, and on the impending trial. Typical directions at this stage include how evidence is to be received at trial, agreeing and filing bundles of documents and so on. More complex cases may include more sophisticated directions about the time to be allowed for examination and cross-examination of witnesses and so forth – it is, after all, only a one day trial. The parties should seek to agree such directions between themselves, which the court can then endorse (or make a different order) if it sees fit.[23] The claimant must pay a listing fee, in default of which the claim will be struck out. Both parties should file a statement of costs.

In fast track cases, the court will attempt to limit the giving of directions to these two occasions, and so give directions without the need for a hearing. A crucial feature of this track is that the trial date, or 'window', is practically set in stone, so applications must be sought *promptly* if different or other directions are sought.

Strict adherence to the timetable is encouraged. The parties can agree among themselves to do things in a different order or at a different time only so long as none of the following three dates is altered or adversely affected:

(i) the date for returning the allocation questionnaires;

(ii) the date for returning the pre-trial checklists; *or*

(iii) the trial date/window.

---

22 PD 28, para.7
23 PD 28, para.7.2

These three case management events can only be changed with the court's permission.[24] In particular, the court will not allow a failure to comply with directions to lead to the postponement of the trial 'unless the circumstances of the case are exceptional.'[25]

A fast track trial should only last one day. Were it to run over, the judge will normally sit the next day to finish the case off. Remember, too, that the trial judge may depart from the procedural judge's directions as to the conduct of the case. No doubt most witness statements will stand as the evidence-in-chief[26] and, given that the natural or designated time for speeches and cross-examination will be limited, it will be necessary for advocates to be very focused in their questioning.

As regards costs, the normal rule is that on the fast track these will be dealt with summarily at the end of the trial. This means the judge will decide there and then how much the loser will have to pay toward the winner's costs, assisted by the various statement of costs submitted by the parties before the trial. As to the trial costs themselves, these are fixed by reference to the value of the claim.[27]

3.   THE MULTI-TRACK

The multi-track is for the more complex and time-consuming cases, i.e. those exceeding £25,000 and/or cases requiring more complex management or a trial lasting more than one day. Many of the standard directions given in fast track cases are also relevant in multi-track cases, but the time frame may need to be more generous, or special directions may be given in more complicated cases. As with the other tracks, case management directions will be given on allocation,[28] if only to fix a hearing to determine what happens next, and if the court cannot set a trial

---

24 CPR, rr 26.3(6A) and 28.4(2)

25 PD 28, para.5.4(1). An exceptional circumstance might, for example, include unforeseeable problems with the evidence or an unexpected change of solicitors.
See CPR 26.3(6A).

26 See below, Ch. 17

27 See CPR, r 46.2 at below at Ch. 18

28 See PD 29, para.4 for the range of options for allocation directions on the multi-track.

date at this stage then it should do so 'as soon thereafter as is practicable' – a usefully elastic description.[29] Directions will be case sensitive on the multi-track, which must be capable of meeting the needs of claims from £25,000 to £25,000,000.

Thus some multi-track cases will require greater intervention than others. The parties can agree timetable directions among themselves and with the court's approval.[30] These must include the standard directions as a minimum. Where agreement is not possible, or a claim has special needs, there are several opportunities which give scope for the giving of case management or trial timetable directions as required:

(a) Allocation hearing

This may be necessary to determine the case's track destination – for example, if a party fails to file an allocation questionnaire or if the parties are not agreed as to which track is appropriate.

(b) Case management conference(s)

This is the *principal device for keeping the litigation focused and on track*, and can be held immediately upon allocation and thereafter *as necessary* to monitor and further the progress of the case. The purpose of these hearings is to ensure that the real issues are identified and directions given so as to ensure that each case is managed according to its needs.[31] Agreed directions are encouraged; they obviate the need for case management conferences, which saves time and money.[32] If the parties provide insufficient information to allow the court to do its management job, an effective alternative to ordering a case management conference to sort things out is to impose directions setting out a very tight litigation timetable. This puts the ball in the parties' court – they either have to comply or make an

---

29 CPR, r 29.2

30 Known as 'agreed directions'

31 See generally PD 29, para.5

32 CPR, 29.4, PD 29, para.4.5

application to the court for different directions.[33]

(c) Listing hearing[34]

These are not all that common. If there are matters outstanding following the filing of pre-trial checklists, which usually happens after evidence has been exchanged but before the case is set down for trial, a listing hearing may be necessary. These hearings concentrate on matters affecting the trial *date* and are useful where it is proving difficult getting a case ready for trial. The main focus will be setting the trial date.

(d) Pre-trial review

Typically a pre-trial review, if needed, will take place about eight to ten weeks before the trial. This gives the court the opportunity to see that earlier orders have been complied with and make relevant directions as to the *conduct* of the trial – in particular, how the evidence is to be adduced and what time limits will be placed on cross-examination, speeches and so forth.[35]

On the multi-track, again the parties may by mutual consent agree to vary the case timetable *so long as doing so does not make it necessary to change the dates of any of the five following case management events*, namely:

(i) return of allocation questionnaires,

(ii) any case management conference

(iii) any pre-trial review,

(iv) return of pre-trial checklists *and*

(v) the trial date.[36]

---

33 PD 29, para.4.10

34 These are hearings pursuant to CPR, r 29.6(4). Pre-trial check lists used to be called 'listing questionnaires', and so these hearings came to be called 'listing' hearings.

35 CPR, r 29.7

36 On the fast track it is three case management events which may not be varied without the court's permission; the multi-track rule includes these same three, but adds two more multi-track features, making five altogether.

If any of these dates would be affected, the permission of the court must be sought.[37] As you might expect, the court will be very reluctant to vacate these dates, especially if the only excuse is a dilatory litigant!

revision tips

- This mnemonic might help you remember the sorts of case which will be allocated to the Fast Track:

  F ive to twenty-five thousand pounds
  A day only for the trial
  S tandard Directions
  T ight timetable

- Think in terms of the 'big three' (fast track) and 'big five' (multi-track) case management events which may *not* be changed *without the court's permission.* Otherwise parties are free to adapt the timetable as they wish by mutual consent.

It is worth reading ...

The content of the Allocation Questionnaire. This is Court Form 150 (Form 149 is especially for small claims track cases) and it is available on the WB on-line service which you can access through Westlaw. It is only 5 pages long and will tell you a lot about what issues the court needs to deal with as, and after, it allocates a case.

---

37   CPR, r 29.5

CHAPTER 9

Documents and things:
disclosure/inspection/further information

Once a case has been allocated to a track, it is into the second half of the litigation process, which is dominated by disclosure of documents and related processes by which the parties, to the extent that they have not done so already, acquire relevant information about the nature of the case against them. This allows the parties to assess the true strengths and weaknesses of their respective cases and so helps narrow the issues and encourage settlement. Much of this exchange of evidence should in fact now happen during the pre-action protocol phase.

An order for disclosure of documents[1] heads the list of the standard directions given on all of the tracks, unless it is thought to be unnecessary.[2] It is worth noting that on the small claims track disclosure will generally be more limited than on the other tracks.[3]

So, documents come first – but they are not the only things with evidential value. Parties also acquire relevant information by means of orders allowing for relevant things to be preserved, inspected, and examined for the purposes of litigation. It might be the car, whose brakes failed and caused an accident; or the equipment an employee was using when he was injured at work. If it is appropriate

---

1 Not surprisingly, this is known as 'standard disclosure'.

2 Because, for example, disclosure has already taken place. See below and CPR, r 31.5

3 See below and PD 27, para.10

for an expert to look at these things and give an opinion on what went wrong, the expert will need access to them.

Parties can also request straight out *information* from their opponents, if the circumstances warrant it. These used to go by the somewhat sinister name of 'interrogatories' and could stop a case in its tracks by the sheer volume of (often feigned) curiosity; but the CPR now ensures that only legitimate requests will be sanctioned. If used properly, they can be very effective in ferreting out a weak case.

One thing to notice in the discussion which follows is that each of these types of orders is a relatively uneventful part of the normal litigation process. There are times, however, when such orders are made even when there is no relevant litigation going on (yet), or against people not involved in litigation which is. In such cases, special rules apply.

1. DISCLOSURE OF DOCUMENTS

Disclosure of documents is the longest standing, and one of the most important ways in which relevant evidence is exchanged in litigation. Lord Woolf, when he took on the task of re-wiring the country's civil litigation system in the 1990s, recognised the essential value of what then went under the rather nautical name of 'discovery'. But he put much of the blame for the length and costs of litigation on a process which at the time required a very wide range of documents to be disclosed.

Typically, this was the stage where cases 'went to sleep' under the old rules (which were open to tactical exploitation of various kinds). Lord Woolf referred in particular to the 'curse' of the photocopier. Not surprisingly, it was felt that excessive disclosure led to an expensive, unwieldy and time-consuming process, often to little evidential purpose. For this reason, the current rules (on what has been re-branded 'disclosure') are very much aimed at keeping this aspect litigation *focused and proportionate* – and under court control.

Orders for disclosure of documents form part of the normal litigation process. They can also, exceptionally, be ordered against parties who are not (at that moment anyway) being sued. It is important to distinguish between these two situations.

A. IN THE NORMAL COURSE OF LITIGATION

After track allocation, each side must, if it has not already done so, disclose in advance of trial the *existence* of every disclosable *document* which they have, or have had, in their *possession, power or control*. This is usually accomplished by *exchange of disclosure lists*.[4] Further, each side must allow the other side to inspect such of those documents still in their possession which are not privileged or otherwise protected from inspection. There is a right to inspect such documents, which if necessary must be asserted.[5]

It is important to appreciate that this is actually a two-stage process – *first, disclosure* by list, *then inspection* – although typically the word 'disclosure' is used by practitioners to refer globally to both aspects. Orders for disclosure are generally made on allocation or at a case management conference. Compliance is usually straightforward, so applications to the court will not often be necessary. Inspection can take place either by giving a party the opportunity to come and look at the documents, or by sending photocopies to them. There is a right to request the latter, if reasonable copying costs are paid.[6] Inspection can even take place by electronic means. What is sensible varies from case to case and

---

4 CPR, r 31.2

5 CPR, r 31.3/31.15. If a party unreasonably forces the other side to have to apply to the court for an order to inspect, then that party will no doubt pay for their intransigence in the form of the costs of the application.

6 CPR, r 31.15 (c)

essentially depends on how many documents there are and what form they take.

Unless the court orders otherwise, the usual order for disclosure is an order to give *standard disclosure*.[7] This requires[8] a party to disclose only:

(a) the documents on which he *relies*;

and

(b) the documents which could –

(i) *adversely affect his own* case;

(ii) *adversely affect another party's* case;

(iii) *support another party's* case;

and

(c) the documents which he is required to disclose by a relevant practice direction.

In a nutshell, (a) and (b) amount to all documents which either help or hurt[9] your case, or help or hurt another party's case. As regards (c), there is a brand new practice direction governing disclosure of electronic documents.[10] So-called 'train of inquiry' documents,[11] which were the bane of the old system, are *not* part of standard disclosure. It is possible to ask the court for such an extended disclosure order, but it would need some very effective advocacy to be persuaded to make it.[12]

Note that this is the standard direction for disclosure in *fast track and multi-track* cases. In small claims track cases, different rules apply and standard disclosure is even more limited to those documents on which a party *relies* in support of his case at trial, such documents to be exchanged by the parties no later than 14 days before trial.[13]

---

7   CPR, r 31.5

8   CPR, r 31.6

9   Practitioners sometimes have to explain the purpose of these rules to their clients, who may baulk at 'helping' the other side, usually by pointing out that it is a two-way street.

10   See PD 31B, which gives detailed guidance on the maintenance, preservation and exchange of disclosable e-documents. See WB, second cumulative supplement to 2010 edition, para.31.6.5. for details.

11   These are documents not material in themselves, but which might possibly lead to something that might be material.

12   See e.g. discussion at BCP at 48.18

13   CPR, r 27.4(3)

Remember too that standard disclosure can be *limited or dispensed with*, either by the written agreement of the parties or by court order.[14] This would happen, typically, where disclosure has effectively taken place already, usually in the pre-action protocol phase. It is very important to realise, however, that that parties *may not agree* between themselves to *widen* the ambit of disclosure. *Only the court* can order this, which it will only do if absolutely necessary to achieve the overriding objective.[15] Obviously some multi-track cases will be more susceptible to wider orders than others. Fast track cases rarely will be.

'Documents' are not limited to paper, and include 'anything in which information of any description is recorded' – for example discs, audio tapes, video cassettes, computer programmes, electronic data bases and so forth. Only one copy need be disclosed, although copies with significant modifications will be treated as separate documents.

A party's duty to disclose documents is limited to documents which are or have been in that party's *control*, i.e. if –

(a) it is or was in his physical possession;

(b) he has or has had a right to possession of it;

or

(c) he has or has had a right to inspect or take copies of it.[16]

Standard disclosure on the fast and multi-tracks thus requires a narrower, more focused range of documents to be disclosed than used to be the case under the old rules. This puts less of a burden on the disclosing party and ensures that cases do not get bogged down, merely for the sake of it, in the disclosure process. On the other hand, the disclosing party *must make a 'reasonable search' for*

---

14   CPR, r 31.5(2),(3)

15   Disclosure on the fast track or multi-track should always be taken to be 'standard disclosure', unless the court orders otherwise. CPR, r 31.5(1)

16   CPR, r 31.8(2)

all disclosable documents; what is reasonable will depend on common sense factors, the circumstances of the case and the overriding principle of proportionality.[17] A *disclosure statement* must be included on the exchanged list, indicating an understanding of the duty to disclose, and compliance, as well as making clear, where relevant, when and why it has not been reasonable to search for a document. It must be signed by the lay client (*not* the solicitor), the duty to disclose being that of the parties themselves.[18]

The exchanged list sets out disclosable documents in three discrete sections, which effectively tells the other side: (1) these are the documents I still have and which you may see; (2) these are documents which I have but you may not see and (3) these are disclosable documents I used to have but do not have them any more.[19] The second section typically includes *privileged* documents. They go in the list because their existence needs to be disclosed (although usually this is done so in very vague terms), but the other side is not, at this stage anyway,[20] entitled to see them. The most common privilege claim in this context is legal professional privilege.[21]

There are a few additional points to note about disclosure in the normal course of litigation:

(a) Immediate inspection

A party may ask at *any* time to see a document which has been *referred to in a statement of case, witness statement, affidavit or (to some extent) an expert's report*.[22] This is a common sense rule. Obviously, if the document in question has been mentioned in one of these other documents, its existence is known and so there is no need to wait for the exchange of disclosure lists. Inspection can follow immediately.

---

17 See CPR, r 31.7

18 CPR, r 31.10 and 31.7(3)

19 See PD 31, para.s 3,4 and 9 for contents of disclosure list.

20 An expert's report, for example, may be privileged from inspection at this stage, but will ultimately have to be exchanged if it is to be used at trial. See below Ch. 17.

21 See generally Ch. 17

22 CPR, r 31.14

(b) Possible limitations on disclosure

The court can impose terms on the ambit of inspection (for example, limiting inspection of confidential documents to a party's medical and legal advisors) or agree that inspection may be disproportionate to the issues involved and so need not take place.[23] This latter is a novel invention of the CPR, and most practitioners are hard-pressed to give an example of the rule in operation. In theory, one might be where documents of relative insignificance are situated at the North Pole.

(c) Specific disclosure

Sometimes litigants omit to list all pertinent documents in their disclosure list. If a party can identify a document or a class of documents missing from the other side's list, perhaps because it was referred to in one of the other documents that had been disclosed, then an application may be made to the court for disclosure and/or inspection of that particular document(s).[24] This is known as 'specific' disclosure. Such orders are not limited to inadequate disclosure lists; they can come in handy at various stages of the litigation process.[25]

(d) Use of disclosed documents

There has always been an important principle that a party inspects documents on the understanding, express or implied, that they will only be used for the purposes of the litigation in which they are disclosed, and not for a 'collateral purpose'. However, once the documents have found their way into the public domain, for example by being read out in open court, any such undertaking ceases to be of effect, *unless* the court orders otherwise. Further, even if a document has not been made public, the court has power (although it would use it sparingly) to sanction its use for a collateral purpose.[26]

---

23 See CPR, r 31.3(2). It is for the party who does not want to allow inspection to flag up the matter in the disclosure list and apply for the appropriate order if necessary.

24 CPR, r 31.12

25 See e.g. *Dayman v Canyon Holdings Ltd*

(2006) LTL 11/1/2006.

26 See generally CPR, r 31.22. This is a complex area, but the rules attempt to tread a middle ground between ensuring disclosed document are only used for the immediate litigation purpose, thus limiting their negative impact on the disclosing party; and, recognising that, when documents (and the information in them) have become public, it is hard to justify stopping the one party who may most need to use the document from doing so.

(e)   Penalties for non-disclosure

The court will impose penalties on a party who fails to make proper disclosure and/or inspection. One of the most serious would be to order that the party in default *may not* rely on the documentary evidence in question, unless the trial judge gives permission.

B.   EXCEPTIONAL DISCLOSURE ORDERS (AGAINST NON-PARTIES)

Disclosure of documents is a litigation tool and so an *important general rule* has been that it is *only* available against a *party* to litigation. You cannot go wandering up and down your street seeking disclosure of documents from people you are not suing! Nowadays, of course, as early, and indeed pre-action, disclosure is increasingly seen as way of achieving fair settlement of claims without the need to litigate, so the exceptions to this rule have increased. In many ways the exceptions are close to becoming the rule. Nevertheless, it is still helpful to look at them from this perspective.

In one sense, disclosure under the pre-action protocol procedure is clearly an exception to this general rule, since no action will have been officially commenced at that point. Indeed, the whole point of the pre-action protocols is to avoid having to start proceedings. But it is part of a formal pre-action procedural process, so might be viewed as widening the rule (or the notion of litigation) to include not only the act, but also the foreplay.

In addition, there are some important, and more long-standing, exceptions to the rule that disclosure is only available against a party to the litigation to which it relates. It is important not to confuse them – examinations often test the novice's ability to distinguish between them.

---

27   [1974] AC 133, at 175, HL (my emphasis).

28   In its pure form. There have been some extensions at the margins. See discussion at BCP, 48.84

29   The principle was extended in *Murphy v Murphy* [1999] 1 WLR 282 where an order was made against a person who created a discretionary trust to disclose to a potential beneficiary the names of the trustees so that the former could contact the latter to discuss a possible distribution to him. There was no suggestion of wrongdoing, as such, on the part of the trustees, although the applicant might have wanted to challenge their actions with trust property. Some think this a generous interpretation

(a) The rule in *Norwich Pharmacal*

This is a common law exception, which provides a procedure for getting disclosure of the *identity of wrongdoers*, so that a claim can be made against them.

To paraphrase Lord Reid in the leading case of *Norwich Pharmacal Co v Commissioners of Custom & Excise*:

> if, *whether through any fault of his own or not*, a person gets mixed up in the transactions of others so as to *facilitate* their wrongdoing, he comes under a duty to assist the person who has been wronged by giving him full information and disclosing the identity of the wrongdoers.[27]

The key component of the test[28] is that the person who may be required to disclose the information must have *facilitated,* whether unwittingly or not, the *wrongdoing* of others.[29] It is the *identity* of those others which must be disclosed. It is very important to understand that *mere witnesses* to an event come under *no* such duty and *cannot be made* to disclose what they saw before an action has even been commenced.[30] It does not take much involvement to be a facilitator, but being a mere witness is not enough.[31] In addition, the information sought must not be protected by privilege.[32]

Remember, too, that the facilitators need not *necessarily* have done something wrong themselves – in the *Norwich* case itself, the defendants were so-called 'innocent facilitators'. In lots of cases, however, facilitators have also committed wrongs. Applicants must have a legitimate interest in the information, and not merely a wish to satisfy their curiosity. Typically, but not exclusively, that interest will be the desire to bring relevant legal proceedings against the wrongdoer once they find out who they are.

Norwich Pharmacal orders are only available in the High Court because

---

of the principle, but the relief needs to be 'flexible' so that it is 'capable of adaptation to new circumstances': per *Lightman J, Mitsui & Co Ltd v Nexen Petroleum UK Ltd* [2005] EWHC 625.

30 Witnesses, of course, can be compelled to come to trial to give evidence of what they saw, but they come under no duty to disclose information making it possible to commence the proceedings.

31 See e.g. *Harrington v Polytechnic of North London* [1984] 1 WLR 1293

32 See Ch. 17

they derive from its inherent jurisdiction. They are not limited to disclosure of documents, and can include answering questions or providing a 'narration of facts'. The remedy, however, is *discretionary* and even if all the other requirements have been satisfied, the court may refuse the order if, for example, there is some public interest in doing so.[33]

This is a kind of *pre-action* disclosure, because until the name of the wrongdoer is known, no claim can be brought against him. But it is known by the name of the leading case, so be *very careful* not to confuse it with the procedure discussed below. In a nutshell, a *Norwich Pharmacal* application is appropriate when *the applicant knows he has a good case against someone, but does not know who that someone is.* It will be for the 'facilitator' to supply that information. There have been cases extending the ambit of this form of disclosure to include, additionally, information to help the applicant assess the strength of and even the nature of the case against the wrongdoer. If this trend continues, there may be an eventual merging between this form of pre-action disclosure and that discussed in (**b**) below. *But it is important to be able to distinguish between them.*

The procedure for making the application is a little involved since it derives from the common law, and varies depending on whether the facilitator is innocent or not. If the former, the applicant issues a *claim form* against the 'facilitator', claiming disclosure of the identity of the wrongdoer. An interim application on notice is made to the Master, unless urgency or secrecy justifies not giving notice, as where the order is to be annexed to a Freezing or Search Order.[34] Once the identity of the wrongdoer is disclosed, the proceedings against the facilitator have achieved their objective and so come to a natural end – a fresh claim can now be brought against the newly identified wrongdoer. Remember: if you already know the identity of your wrongdoer, you do not need a *Norwich Pharmacal* order!

---

33 See e.g. *Interbrew SA v Financial Times Ltd*, The Times, 4 January 2002 (at first instance)

34 See Ch. 7

If the claimant is also suing the 'facilitator' for his own wrongdoing, as is commonly the case, the application for this special form of disclosure is made as an interim application in that action. Once the (other) wrongdoers are identified, then they can be joined to the action or new proceedings brought against them.

It is the applicant who pays the costs of these applications, but these may be recovered from the wrongdoer at the end of the day.[35]

(b) Statutory pre-action disclosure (from a 'likely' future defendant)

This form of pre-action disclosure is governed by statute and is available in both the High Court and County Courts.[36] Somewhat confusingly for beginners, it is known as 'pre-action disclosure', as if it were the only one, so be sure you are able to distinguish it from the *Norwich Pharmacal* order. Statutory pre-action disclosure is appropriate where the applicant *knows* who the defendant will be, but does not know whether the case is strong enough to make it worth while pursuing the claim.

Over the years this kind of pre-action disclosure has evolved from being very limited in its scope[37] to being generally available in any sort of case, but not often necessary. Before the days of pre-action protocols and access to medical records, a typical situation where such an order was sought might be one where the applicant went into hospital with a minor complaint and came out with a serious medical condition. Until the applicant and his advisors got a look at his notes to find out what went on in the hospital, it was difficult to gauge whether the suspicion that the doctors had been negligent, and so could be successfully sued, was supported by the evidence. This is what the statutory pre-action disclosure allowed him to do. Pre-action protocols now generally serve this purpose, but of course the application may still be required if, for example, the protocol is not complied with. Most cases nowadays involve commercial transactions.

---

35 Assuming the wrongdoer loses. See generally Ch. 18

36 Senior Courts Act 1981 ('SCA 1981), s 33 and County Courts Act 1984 ('CCA 1984'), s 52.

37 For many years it was only available in personal injuries and fatal accident cases.

Thus, the courts have power to make an order for disclosure of material documents against the respondent where both that person and the applicant are 'likely' to be parties to the 'subsequent proceedings'.[38] It is therefore available against a *future* defendant whose identity is known and who is in possession of *material* documents, the early disclosure of which will *save costs or encourage settlement*.[39] The application is made by way of interim application in the anticipated litigation (that sounds weird, I know). Such disclosure is limited to *documents* which would be disclosable in the ordinary course of litigation.[40]

Over the years there has been judicial consideration of what 'likely' means in the context of the rule (the wording of which has changed somewhat over the years).[41] Lord Denning's broad interpretation (of the original wording) that it amounts to being able to say that a claim 'may well' be brought by the applicant against the defendant, depending on the outcome of the disclosure,[42] has come under some threat from time to time.[43] If, however, the applicant has to show too strong a claim at this point, it would defeat the purpose of the remedy, and it now seems clear from *Black v Sumitomo Corporation*[44] that there is no requirement to show that the claim is likely to be brought, as such; just that if it were brought, the applicant and the respondent will be the likely parties, and in this context 'likely' means 'may well' rather than 'more probably than not.' Generally, therefore, the court will not look deeply into the merits at this stage, although if the case is weak on its face, this would militate against an order being made. In any event, such disclosure should not be used as a 'fishing expedition' (or a 'speculative punt' as we now say) or to force disclosure of a document, the need for which is not made out.[45] And, as you would expect, any application will be determined in keeping with the overriding objective. Even if the court has the power to make the order, there is still a discretion to refuse to do so if, for example, it is oppressive or

---

38 I am paraphrasing. See the actual wording of CPR, r 31.16(3)(a) & (b). The applicant cannot really become a party to the subsequent proceedings unless he or she does something to instigate them.

39 CPR, r 31.16(3)(d)

40 CPR, r 31.16(3)(c). So any and all documents sought under this form of pre-action disclosure must be documents which would in due course be subject to standard disclosure: *Hutchison 3G UK Ltd v O$_2$ (UK) Ltd* [2008] EWHC 55 (Comm).

41 Before the CPR the wording included reference to whether a claim was 'likely to be made', but this was dropped from the current rule. There are still lots of 'likely's in CPR, r 31.16, but they refer to parties, not claims. So the pre-CPR cases are not

otherwise not in the public interest.

So this form of pre-action disclosure *differs* from the *Norwich Pharmacal* order in several respects, namely:

- It derives from *statute*.
- It is *limited* to disclosure of *documents* which would be subject to *standard disclosure* in due course.
- It caters for the situation where a (prospective) claimant *knows* who his defendant will be, but he does not know, until he sees the documents, whether the case is worth pursuing.

The costs of applying for these types of pre-action disclosure order are usually borne by the person seeking the order, although if the court takes the view that the respondent forced an application unnecessarily (because it was obvious the court would make the order), it may award costs to the applicant.

(c)   Orders against 'strangers' to on-going litigation

Once a case has commenced, a party may be able to get an order for the production of relevant documents by a 'stranger' to that litigation, i.e. someone who is *not* one of the *parties* to it. This is allowed where the non-party has documents which assist the applicant's case *and* disclosure would help fairly dispose of the action and/or save costs.[46]

This is not a form of pre-action disclosure, but it is an exception to the general rule we started with because the person against whom the disclosure is sought is not a party to the proceedings to which the disclosure relates. If the court did not have this power, the only way a party to litigation could get access to relevant

---

binding, as such, but still give useful guidance. After all, you cannot have parties if you do not have a claim. See discussion in leading case of *Black and others v Sumitomo Corpn and others* [2002] WLR 1562

42   *Dunning v Liverpool Hospital Board* [1973] 1 WLR 586

43   As in *Burns v Shuttlehurst* [1999] 1 WLR 1449, where it was said the applicant had to show a reasonable basis for the claim.

44   Op.cit.

45   See e.g. *Alan Kneale v Barclays Bank plc (trading as Barclaycard)* [2010] EWHC 1900 (Comm).

46   See SCA 1981, s 34/CCA 1984, s 53, which grant the power, and CPR, r 31.17(3)

documents in the hands of a non-party would be to require the latter to attend as a witness at trial, along with the document.[47] Not only would this be a very roundabout and expensive way to achieve disclosure, but it would be far too late for the desired purpose.

As you might expect, the order will not be made just to annoy the non-party or as a speculative venture, and it will be limited as necessary.[48] Again, there may be other ways a litigant can get the information, thus rendering the application unnecessary.[49]

The application is made by way of interim application in the on-going proceedings, on notice and supported by written evidence. The order must specify what documents are to be disclosed and can ask the respondent to indicate where such documents are, if they are no longer in his possession or control.[50]

2. ORDERS FOR THE INSPECTION ETC OF RELEVANT PROPERTY

Like documents (usually, of course, it is what is contained *in* the document which matters), *objects* can provide useful evidential information. Such things are referred to in the rules as 'relevant property'. To get evidential value from such things, one might need to look at them or take samples from them, perform tests on them and so on. To do that, it may be necessary to preserve the property for one or other of these purposes. To that end the courts have power to make orders giving one party (or his advisors) access to relevant things in the possession of another party. Again, the general rule applies – such orders are normally available only against parties to the litigation in question. But, as ever, there are exceptions.

---

47 A person can be required, by means of a witness summons, to attend court to give oral evidence and/or to produce documents. See CPR, rr 32.2-32.7

48 See e.g. Re Howglen Ltd [2001] 1 ALL ER 376 where an *application* made in very general terms for disclosure against a non-party bank for bank records and interview notes resulted in a very specific *order* limited to three interviews identified in the written evidence accompanying the application.

49 E.g. under Data Protection legislation.

50 See CPR, r 31.17(4) and (5)

A.   IN THE NORMAL COURSE OF LITIGATION

Such orders are commonplace in litigation, and unexceptional. If, for example, a claimant sues her employers because she was injured by a machine she was required to operate at work, it may be important to allow those who are qualified to pass judgment on the state of the offending machine a chance to inspect it while in the same condition it was in when the claimant was injured (or near enough). The machine is the 'relevant property' and such an order typically would allow for the 'preservation' of the machine,[51] and access[52] to it so that it can be examined and so forth by a person who knows how such machines are supposed to work.[53]

A related situation arises when seeking orders relating to the claimant in a personal injuries action submitting to a medical examination conducted by the defendant's expert.[54] As the claimant is a human being and not a machine, the court cannot force the claimant to do this – it would be an infringement of personal liberty. However, the court can achieve much the same result by the indirect method of ordering a halt to proceedings if the claimant unreasonably refuses such a medical examination.[55] Whether or not a stay is granted is entirely within the discretion of the court – the facts of the individual case and the parties' reasons for seeking, or resisting, the proposed medical examination, are all matters to be taken into account. There is a balance to be struck between the claimant's human rights and the defendant's litigation rights. A medical examination which might harm the claimant's health would, of course, pose special difficulties, which would need to be weighed in the balance. Sometimes claimants are only willing to submit to a medical examination on conditions. Those which are personal to the claimant (e.g. payment of fares getting to the examination, the presence of a friend,[56] an assurance the doctor will not discuss

---

51   The idea is that the machine is examined before any defects have been put right or repairs effected.

52   It may well be at the defendant's premises.

53   An expert in other words. See CPR, r 25.1(c) and Ch. 17

54   It is fairly typical to have experts on both sides in a personal injuries action of any complexity.

55   *Edmeades v Thames Board Mills Ltd* [1969] 2 QB 67, CA

56   But see *Whitehead v Avon County Council*, The Times, 3 May 1995, CA, where the Court of Appeal upheld a decision that the claimant's action be stayed unless she submitted to a psychiatric examination without a friend or relation being present.

the case with the claimant except insofar as medically necessary, a request for a doctor of a particular gender if the examination is of an intimate nature) will usually be uncontroversial; conditions which amount to attempts to chose the defendant's expert for him (unless there are doubts about the competence or honesty of the choice of doctor) or interfere with the purpose of the examination will be more apt to be considered unreasonable.[57]

Applications for such orders (whether to gain access to inspect things or people) are made on-notice,[58] supported by written evidence which speaks to the need and relevance of the order. They are, however, often rendered unnecessary by the other party's willingness to give access, because it is so obvious that this is precisely what the court would order.

B. EXCEPTIONAL ORDERS (AGAINST NON-PARTIES)

The exceptions to the general rule that orders for the inspection, experimentation etc of relevant property are available only against *parties* to the relevant litigation, mirror those statutory exceptions discussed above relating to disclosure of documents. Indeed, they too are statutory.[59] Thus it is possible, where the object in question may become relevant to the subject matter of *subsequent* proceedings, to get an order for inspection etc of that thing before those proceedings have been started. Similarly, it is also possible to get such orders against a 'stranger' to on-going litigation, where that non-party is in possession of property which is relevant to the subject matter of that litigation.

When such an order is necessary, the application is again generally made on notice, supported by written evidence identifying the property in question and the need for the order. If the order is, exceptionally, made not only pre-action,[60] but also (doubly exceptionally) without notice, it is called a Search

---

57　See also *Starr v National Coal Board* [1977] 1 WLR 63, CA

58　CPR, r 25.3. Typically such orders are sought at the track allocation stage.

59　See SCA 1981, ss 33 and 34/CCA 1984, ss 52 and 53

60　Or pre-service of proceedings.

order.[61] *Thus it is that a 'search order' is really just a dramatic and surprising version of something which is otherwise quite ordinary.*

3.   REQUESTS FOR FURTHER INFORMATION

One can, of course, get evidential information by requesting it. Not surprisingly, perhaps, these are called 'requests for further information'. Sometimes a party might be vague about aspects of his case or something might be mentioned in a witness statement which requires clarification. Before the CPR, the former situation was dealt with by something called 'Further and Better Particulars' (which was limited to asking parties to be more specific about the allegations made in their statements of case); and the latter, by 'Interrogatories' (a request for answers to questions where these would help fairly 'dispose of the action or save costs'). These two old procedures have been rolled into one, so that a request for further information under CPR, r 18.1 can be used to seek clarification of any matter in dispute, or get information about any such matter, whether or not it is contained, or referred to, in a statement of case.

This litigation tool (and it is a litigation tool – no exceptions here) can be very useful in exposing weaknesses in the case against you. It can reveal an inability to make, much less prove a specific allegation. Having said that, requests will only be ordered where they are relevant, necessary, proportionate and concise; they should not be used as a delaying tactic, nor as a hit and miss expedition 'fishing' for factual ammunition.

So, if a party looks at an allegation and thinks "Well, like what?", or "In what way?" or "How exactly?", this is an indication that an early request for

---

61   See Ch. 7

further information about that allegation may well be appropriate.[62] Or the need for clarification may happen further down the litigation road, for example after evidence has been exchanged.[63] The party seeking clarification first serves[64] a written request[65] on the party from whom it is sought, leaving an appropriate time for responding. It is only in the absence of a proper response (or if the respondent objects to the request), that an application to the court will have to be made.[66] Such applications will be determined by reference to the principles of proportionality and in accordance (surprise, surprise!!) with the overriding objective. Responses should mirror the format in which the request was made and must be verified by a statement of truth.[67]

---

62 It is also a good way of testing your own drafting skills to ensure you have been as specific as possible in drafting the statement of case before it is served.

63 See generally Ch. 17 below

64 The rules say the request should be sent by email where practicable: PD 18, para.1.7.

65 The format is very precisely set out in the rules: PD 18, para.1.6.

66 The court can also make an order on its own initiative as part of its duty to be proactive about case management. See below, Ch. 13

67 PD 18, paras 2 and 3. The request itself is just a series of questions and is thus incapable of being true or false. So, it does not need to be verified by a statement of truth, unlike other documents containing answers, allegations and so on.

revision tips

- Be clear that *standard* disclosure is the normal order in litigation. Wider orders are only made in exceptional circumstances.

- Be clear about how disclosure orders against non-parties *differ* from those made in the normal course of litigation.

- Be clear about the distinction between *Norwich Pharmacal* orders and statutory pre-action disclosure of documents. This is typical fodder for examinations.

It is worth reading ...

- The judgment of *Lord Donaldson MR in X Ltd v Morgan-Grampian (Publishers) Ltd* [1991] 1 AC 1, HL. It is an interesting case about disclosure of journalist's sources, and in particular how the Contempt of Court Act 1981, s 10, fits into the *Norwich Pharmacal* equation. As you will see, journalists and judges don't always see eye-to-eye on the public interest.

- The judgment of Flaux J in *Alan Kneale v Barclays Bank plc (trading as Barclaycard)* [2010] EWHC 1900 (Comm). Unlike some such cases, the facts are very straightforward. The applicant was applying for disclosure of a document that it appeared he wanted, rather than needed, which did not motivate the court to make the order. It is a very clear review of the case and there is an interesting couple of paragraphs on the costs of such applications.

PART THREE
efficiency and control

CHAPTER 10

Limitation of action

The courts have never been sympathetic towards dilatory claimants – even less so are they under the CPR. The ethos of the current system is that litigation is to be avoided where possible, through well-informed and efficient pre-action behaviour and, to a lesser extent, costs disincentives. If, however, litigation becomes necessary, actions should be commenced promptly, and in any event within a specified amount of time, known as the 'limitation period.' Once the claim form has been issued, it should be served in good time – negotiations can follow or continue once those two straightforward procedural steps have been taken. Amendments made late in the day can be problematic, and will only exceptionally be allowed once a relevant limitation period has expired. Finally, tight case management by the court will force the pace of litigation, so that once started, cases get to trial efficiently and speedily.

Limitation is the subject of this chapter; the other aspects of court control referred to above will be considered in those immediately following.

The general rule is that actions must be commenced within the relevant limitation period or face (or risk facing) the impregnable defence that the action is statute-barred. The latter is a procedural defence and it is for the *defendant* to raise it in the defence.[1] It will not be raised by the court on its own initiative, nor should the claimant anticipate it in the particulars of claim.[2]

---

1 PD 16, para.13.1

2 The claimant, or his legal advisors, may well anticipate the 'risk' that a defendant might raise limitation, and might even make an application to the court about it, but no pre-emptive strikes of a "just in case you mention limitation in your defence" kind are ever made in the particulars of claim.

It would be very hard on defendants if they were perpetually at risk of being sued, and so the purpose of the general rule is to put a reasonable but finite limit on the time during which actions can successfully be pursued, and stop unduly stale claims being litigated. Fixed limitation periods have been laid down for different types of cases[3], but a certain amount of flexibility has been built into the system over the years, in particular to help people who may for some considerable time be unaware that they have suffered harm.

The result of an action being time-barred is to extinguish the claimant's remedy.[4] In the case of adverse possession of land and conversion, expiry of the limitation period has the additional effect of extinguishing the claimant's title.[5]

Actions are commenced when the originating process (e.g. the claim form) is issued. *It is important to remember that this is what must happen within the limitation period.*[6] By analogy, third party claims are deemed to be commenced on the date the Third Party/Part 20 claim form was issued.[7] Counterclaims and set-offs are deemed to have been commenced on the same date as the original action – they are, as it were, 'back-dated' to that date.[8]

KNOWING WHETHER AN ACTION IS TIME-BARRED

Determining whether the relevant limitation period has expired in any given situation is basically a *two-stage process*. It involves asking yourself two questions:

(1) How long is the limitation period in this case?

(2) When did it start to run?

Once these questions are answered, in most cases it can easily be determined whether an action has been, or can be, brought in time.

---

3 As set out in the Limitation Act 1980 ('LA 1980'). The periods vary because different types of cases bring with them greater or lesser degrees of urgency, depending on things like how ephemeral the evidence is likely to be, what can be expected of claimants in such cases and/or the nature of the conduct alleged. For example, breach of trust claims brought by beneficiaries against trustees alleging fraud or conversion of trust property have no limitation period at all: LA 1980, s 21(1). This is partly because what is being alleged might well amount to a criminal offence.

4 Strictly speaking the cause of action still exists, but cannot effectively be pursued. If a claimant is unwilling to discontinue a stale claim, the defendant

As to the first question, most time periods are laid down in the Limitation Act 1980, as amended. The important ones are conveniently set out at BCP, table 10.1. Remember that personal injury and fatal accident[9] claims can arise in contract as well as in negligence actions; generally speaking 'personal injuries' describes the nature of the damage caused by a breach, not the cause of action.[10]

As to the second question, time ordinarily runs from the date the cause of action 'accrues', although statute has provided alternatives in some cases. The *nature* of the cause of action will normally dictate when it accrues and time starts to run.

Limitation periods

Thus, looking at both questions together, as they relate to the general run of cases:

(i)   *Non-personal injuries claim founded on simple contract*

The limitation period is six years. Time runs from date of *breach*.

(ii)   *Non-personal injuries claim founded on common law tort (not including defamation)*

The limitation period is six years. Where the tort is actionable *per se* (i.e. without having to prove damage, as with trespass), time runs from the date the tort is *committed*. Most tort actions, however, are only actionable on *proof of damage*[11] (as is the case with negligence, nuisance etc) and in those cases time runs from the date of *damage*, unless the Latent Damage Act l986 provides an alternative.

(iii)   *Claims under the Latent Damage Act 1986*

Where damage (other than for personal injuries) is latent, not patent, a claim in the tort of negligence[12] may be brought under this Act. The *limitation period* is *shorter*, i.e.

---

will usually be able to apply to have the claim struck out as an abuse of process.

5   LA 1980, ss 3 and 4

6   It is enough for these purposes if the claimant has done all he or she needs to do, e.g. by delivering the relevant documents to the relevant court office in time. This is because LA 1980 refers to proceedings being 'brought' in time. See ***St Helens Metropolitan Borough Council v Barnes*** [2007] 1 WLR 879.

7   LA 1980, s35(1)(a). As to Third Parties generally, see Ch. 3

8   LA 1980, s35(1)(b). And see also amendment outside the limitation period at Ch. 11 below.

9   A fatal accident is an extreme personal injury, so these two appear in the rules as something of a twin-set. Therefore (unless I indicate otherwise) when

3 years, but it starts to run *later, i.e. from the date the claimant knew*, in effect, that damage worth suing over was caused by an identifiable defendant.[13] This is analogous to the special rules relating to personal injuries discussed next – you might think of it as applying to sick buildings[14] instead of sick people.

(iv) Personal injuries and fatal accident cases

Here several *special rules apply*. First, the limitation period is *shorter*, i.e. *three years*. Time runs from the date the cause of action accrues (e.g. date of damage, if a negligence action) *or*, to deal with those cases where the claimant does not realise he has been injured until much later, from the *'date of knowledge'*. Analogous provisions apply to fatal accident cases (fatal accidents being the ultimate personal injury).[15] Further, even if time has expired, the court has a *further discretionary power* to allow such cases to continue notwithstanding.

Date of knowledge

This is specifically defined in the Limitation Act 1980.[16] It is important to remember that the requirements are *conjunctive*. There are three (sometimes four) components. In a nutshell, the date of knowledge is the first date when the claimant knew *all* of the following:

(i) that the injury is significant (i.e. worth suing over),

and

(ii) that the injury was caused by the alleged act or omission,

and

(iii) the identity of the defendant.[17]

In essence, if you were to date stamp each individual part of this knowledge

---

I refer to the latter I include the former.

10 See wording of LA 1980, s 11. At one time it was thought that physical or mental injuries caused by intentional trespass to the person (as opposed to unintentional trespass or negligence) were not personal injuries as defined by LA 1980, but this (at best, tortuous) distinction was declared false in *A v Hoare* [2008] 1 AC 844.

11 Sometimes easier to describe than to identify. See e.g. *Khan v R M Falvey and Co* [2002] EWCA Civ 400, [2002] PNLR 28.

12 Contract based actions are not covered under this legislation.

13 See LA 1980, s 14A. There is also a so-called 'long stop' preventing such cases being brought later than 15 years from the negligent act: LA 1980, s 14B.

14 Bear in mind, however, that

puzzle, the date the last piece fell into place (or the latest date recorded) is the date of knowledge.

Note too that date of knowledge is all about the date certain *facts* became known. Knowledge of law, or the legal implications of those facts, is irrelevant.[18] In addition, claimants will be expected to act reasonably (given their situation) in acquiring knowledge for these purposes, for example by making such inquiries and seeking such expert advice as the circumstances warrant.[19]

The date of knowledge provisions were first introduced in the 1960's to assist miners who had suffered damage to their lungs while down the pits, but were unaware of any injury until their disease (pneumoconiosis) manifested itself many years, often decades later. However, there were still some litigants who failed to bring a claim in time even once they had the requisite knowledge – some had taken poor advice from the employers who had caused the harm! As a result, further provision was passed, now s 33 Limitation Act 1980, giving the court a *discretion,* where it thinks it equitable, to let a personal injuries action proceed notwithstanding that it is out of time. In exercising the discretion the court does not extend the limitation period, but, rather, overlooks it. For this reason it is inelegantly known as 'disapplying' the limitation period.

Sec 33 Discretion

Sec 33(3) says that the court should have regard to '*all of the circumstances*' of the case when deciding whether to exercise its discretion, and 'in particular' those factors contained in a relatively long list at s 33(3)(a)-(f). These are largely a matter of common sense and include things like the length and reason for the claimant's delay in bringing the action, the effect of the delay on the cogency of the evidence,[20] the behaviour of the defendant after the cause of action arose, how promptly the claimant

---

although latent damage resulting in financial, rather than personal injury, is most often raised in relation to defective buildings, the legislation is not restricted to this. It can apply, for example, to tort-based claims against solicitors for negligent advice.

15 LA 1980, s 12 and 14

16 LA 1980, s 14.
See detailed discussion in WB or BCP

17 If the act or omission of someone other than the defendant is relevant, as is common in vicarious liability cases, then the identity of that person also needs to

be known.

18 LA 1980, s 14(1)

19 See LA 1980, s 14(3) and *Adams v Bracknell Forest Borough Council* [2005] 1 AC 76.

20 Ss 33(3)(a) and (b). The relevant delay for these purposes is that between the end of the limitation

acted once time (as extended by the date of knowledge provision) began to run and so on. It is worth having a look at this list yourself – but remember *it is not* exhaustive. The specific matters mentioned there are 'exemplary, not definitive'. The discretion is unfettered.[21]

What the court must do is balance the prejudice to the claimant in not being able to continue with the personal injuries action, on the one hand, against the prejudice to the defendant in having to meet a stale claim. The overriding question is one of equity: would it be fair, in the circumstances, to let the case continue? It is for the claimant to convince the court that it is equitable to disapply the limitation period, and the burden is a heavy one. The exercise of this discretion is really in the nature of an 'indulgence'.

Remember that every case is different and which factors or circumstances will determine the outcome will vary from application to application, although whether there can be a fair trial is an important part of the equation.[22] Other factors not specified in the s 33(3) list which might also be relevant include how long the defendant has known about the claimant's claim (the earlier the notification the better for the claimant) and whether the claimant has an alternative claim in professional negligence against his or her legal advisors. Note however that the latter, while obviously pertinent, is not necessarily decisive. There are several drawbacks to suing your own solicitors (not least of which being that you might like them!), so it should not be viewed as an easy option. Indeed, if there can still be a fair trial against the original defendants, there is a lot to be said for allowing the case to proceed against them, as the ones who caused the damage in the first place!

At one time it was held that if an action had been commenced within the limitation period, but the claim had not progressed to trial because of a

---

period and commencing the action. See e.g. *Long v Tolchard* [2001] PIQR P2, CA. Delay during the limitation period would be material to other of the factors.

21 *Nash v Eli Lilly & Co* [1993] 4 ALL ER 383, at 402 (CA). And see discussion in WB, Vol 2, para.8-92ff.

22 See e.g. *Donovan v Gwentoys Ltd* [1990] 1 WLR 472. And see *B v Nugent Care Society* (Practice Note) [2009] EWCA Civ 827, [2010]

WLR 516, CA where the court observed that there may be occasions when it may need to hear oral evidence in order to exercise its discretion properly, as for example, where there were allegations of child abuse and psychological damage.

'self-inflicted' wound resulting, for example, in its being struck out,[23] s 33 could not be used to start a second, identical claim.[24] These were the so-called 'second action cases'. However, this (rather artificial) restriction was removed by *Horton v Sadler*, [25] and such cases will be determined like any other, although why the first action was 'lost' may well be relevant to the court's decision.

Further instances of common limitation periods

(v)   Contribution claims

The limitation period is two years, but time only begins to run from the *date of judgment or settlement* of the main action. Most contribution claims are made by way of an additional claim (for example, third party claim) under Part 20 and are dealt with at the same time as the main action.[26] If this has not happened, then a defendant has a further two years after liability is established (or admitted) to bring his contribution claim.

(vi)   Recovery of land cases

The limitation period here is twelve years. There are detailed provisions set out in Schedule 1 of LA 1980, but (very) broadly, time runs from the date of dispossession or, if later, from the date when the claimant's interest in the land vested.

(vii) Judicial review

This time period is more analogous to lodging appeals.[27] Such claims must be made very promptly and in any case within three *months* after the grounds for making the application arose.[28] The time for making the application can be extended by the court if there are good reasons.

---

23 See Ch. 13
24 *Walkley v Precision Forgings* [1979] 1 WLR 606
25 [2007] 1 AC 307

26 Third party proceedings are discussed in Ch. 3

27 Judicial Review is not an appeal mechanism as such, but rather a challenge to and review of public law functions. It is a very complex area. See Ch. 19
28 CPR, r 54.5(1)

This is a very basic summary of some of the more common limitation periods (the detail in Schedule 1 of the Limitation Act 1980 goes on for four pages!); it is the sort of entry level of knowledge and understanding that an unseen assessment will test. If and when a limitation problem arises in practice (or in a take-home exam), then clearly you will need to check the detail in the relevant statute and/or case law to identify and advise on the issue.

Factors which prevent time starting

Be aware, too, of the various circumstances which can stop the limitation period from *starting* to run when it otherwise would. The most common is where the claimant was a 'child' when the cause of action otherwise arose, in which case time does not start to run until the child becomes 18 years old.[29] As we saw in Chapter 3, a person who has not yet attained the age of majority is said to be acting under a legal 'disability'. So too is a 'protected' person who lacks the mental capacity[30] to conduct proceedings. Like the litigant who has not yet turned 18 years of age, if *at the time the cause of action would otherwise have arisen*, the clamant is of unsound mind (possibly because of the injury suffered), then time will not begin to run until the mental incapacity has ended. Be aware, however, that once time has started to run, *later* mental incapacity *cannot* stop it.[31] It's a bit like a horserace – a legal disability can keep the starting gates from opening; but once they have and the horses have got out, there is no stopping them until the race is over.

Misconduct on the part of the defendant can have a similar effect. If, for example, the action is founded on an act of *fraud* by the defendant, or if the defendant has *deliberately* concealed a fact relevant to the right of action, time will not start to run until the claimant has, or could reasonably have been expected

---

29 LA 1980, s 28
30 Within the meaning of the Mental Capacity Act 2005. See LA 1980, ss 28 and 38(2).

31 It would be very awkward for a defendant if it could, since he would have to keep checking up on the claimant's mental health to know if limitation was running or not. It is easier with the claimant's age, since once you become 18 there is no going back. This is not necessarily true of mental health.

to have discovered the fraud or concealment.[32] Similarly, where the claimant's action is for relief from the consequences of a mistake,[33] time will not start to run until the mistake is, or, with 'reasonable diligence', could have been discovered. A good example of this is *Peco Arts Inc v Hazlett Gallery Ltd.*[34] In that case, the claimant had, on advice of a specialist, bought a drawing from the defendants. It was an express term that the drawing was an original, signed by the artist. Six years later, the drawing was re-valued, and no doubts were cast on its authenticity. Five years after that, it was found to be a reproduction (obviously a very good one). The claimant sued for return of the purchase price as the money had been paid under a mutual mistake of fact. It was held that 'reasonable diligence' is a matter of fact in any given case, and here it meant acting like a prudent buyer of valuable art, which is what the claimant had done. He was thus able to recover.

Further, note that limitation time limits do not, as such, apply in respect of claims for *equitable* relief.[35] These will, of course, be defeated by 'delay' and 'acquiescence'[36] in deciding which the court has a wide discretion – as is in the nature of equity!

Finally, a note of caution: the relationship between the pre-action protocols and problems of limitation must be watched closely. As regards personal injuries actions, to an extent the s 33 discretion is an arguable fallback if proceedings are brought out of time. Having said that, it is a matter of simple common sense that a limitation period should *never* be allowed to expire. Indeed, the notes of guidance to the PI protocol indicate that if a claimant is in the middle of the protocol and the relevant limitation period is about to expire, *'protective proceedings' should be issued*, giving the other parties as much notice of the intention and need to issue proceedings as is practicable.[37] The parties could then invite the court to

---

32 LA 1980, s 32(1)(a) and (b). Re the latter, see examples in *Cave v Robinson Jarvis and Rolf* [2002] UKHL 18, [2003] 1 AC 384. Unlike the situation with the mentally incapable claimant, a deliberate concealment by the defendant after time has started to run can operate to 're-set' the clock, as it were: *Sheldon v R.H. Outhwaite (Underwriting Agencies) Ltd* [1996] AC 102 – in such cases the defendant has control over his own behaviour!

33 In the legal sense.

34 [1983] 1 WLR 1315

35 LA 1980, s 36(1). Sometimes ordinary time limits can assist the court by analogy.

36 Specifically preserved by LA 1980, s 36(2).

extend time for service of statements of case, or allow a stay in proceedings, while the recommended steps in the protocol are followed or completed. This must be of general application.

revision tips

- Make yourself a table of the mainstream limitations periods: when time starts and how long it lasts. Be clear about the different permutations so that you can *recognise a limitation scenario when you see it* in an exam. Watch out especially for personal injuries actions involving children – there may be quite a few variables to consider.

- Remember that the discretion under s 33(3) LA 1980 to disapply the limitation period in personal injuries actions is *unfettered,* and not limited to the factors in the statute. The case law tells us this. What are sometimes referred to as non-statutory considerations (although the statute does say "all the circumstances"!) include the possibility of a fair trial, early notification and possible alternative claims open to the claimant. But every application must be judged on its *own merit*. There is nothing 'off-the-peg' about the s 33 discretion.

It is worth reading ...

Judgment of Waller LJ in *McDonnell v Walker* [2009] EWCA 1257, on the exercise of the court's s 33 discretion. There is a useful comparison between cases where a defendant would suffer no forensic prejudice if the discretion is exercised in a claimants favour (as in *Cain v Francis* [2008] EWCA Civ 1451) and those where it would. It is always instructive to see the principles applied to a real situation!

37   Para.2.11

CHAPTER 11

Amendment of statement of case

In the course of litigation, a party may wish to amend the wording of a statement of case[1] after it has been filed or served. This is a common occurrence, which often happens after disclosure of documents or other evidential information comes to light. Amendments can range from the correction of minor 'slips' to more significant adjustments to the presentation of a case. A claimant who wants to add a claim based on a new cause of action or to join a new defendant, for example, will have to amend the claim form as well as the particulars of claim. A defendant may want to amend the defence or add a counterclaim.

As a general proposition, the overriding objective of dealing with cases justly means that if made in good time, amendments of this kind are often uncontroversial and allowed almost as of right (if not by agreement). It is important that the real issues in any given case are litigated and it would be very harsh if a mistake or omission in a statement of case could not be put right, so long as the other parties are not prejudiced by the correction. However, problems can arise if a party seeks to amend very late in the day and it poses *real* difficulties if a relevant limitation period has expired.

---

1 'Statement of Case' is a generic description for the typical documents setting out a party's case in any litigation, i.e. the claim form, particulars of claim, defence, reply, additional claim forms and any further information given in relation to any of these: CPR, r 2.3.

1. AMENDMENT *BEFORE* EXPIRY OF A RELEVANT LIMITATION PERIOD

The following points provide a summary of the position.

(a) Amendment before service

A party is allowed to amend a statement of case at any time *before* it has been *served* on any other party.[2] *No permission of the court is required*, but a court could later disallow the amendment.[3] Such amendments are obviously made quite early on,[4] given that the exchange of statements of case is one of the first things that happens in any litigation. It makes sense to say that if the other party has not even seen it yet, it is no big deal to make changes to the document before they do.

(b) Amendment after service

However, if the statement of case has *already been served*, as often happens, it can only be amended with the *written consent* of the parties or the *permission of the court*,[5] *unless* the amendment involves a *change of party*, in which case the court's *permission is always required*.[6] This special requirement about amendments involving a change in party is sensible when you think about it – the court is happy for the named parties to sort out the nature of the allegations between themselves, but if *new* or different parties are to become involved, the court would like to know about it. Otherwise it might go a long time thinking the case is Bob v Alice, when in fact it has become Bob and Carol v Ted and Alice (I am showing my age here). Like any host, the court wants to know who is invited to the party! More to the point, it wants to have a say. The main consideration in any decisions to add, substitute, or indeed remove a party is whether the amendment is 'desirable'

---

2   CPR, r 17.1(1)

3   CPR r 17.2. An application to disallow such an amendment should be made within 14 days of service of the amended document.

4   Either between issue and service of the claim form (which can be as long as four months) or between filing (with the court) and service (on other parties) of other statements of case, which is usually a very short period of time. We are not, of course, talking about the several drafts of, say, the particulars of claim which it might take Counsel to get the document ready for the solicitors to file and serve – that is called being (quite properly) a perfectionist. The amendment rules are all about changing documents which have come to the attention either of the court or the other parties.

to ensure that all relevant issues in dispute can be resolved.[7] This ultimately is for the court to decide. As you might expect, however, nobody can be forced to be a claimant.[8]

(c) General principles

In determining an application for permission to amend generally, the courts should, in accordance with the overriding objective, decide where the justice of each case lies. Certainly significant amendments very late in the day can be more problematic[9] than those made relatively early on, although with effective case management this situation should not now often arise. But so long as the amendment is required to determine all of the relevant issues, and is not tactical or foolish, then the justice of the case will almost always, if not inevitably, lie with the person seeking to amend – unless the other party or parties can show that they will be prejudiced *over and above* the fact that time and expense will be incurred in redrafting their own statements of case in response to the amendment, which can usually be dealt with by way of an order for costs against the amending party. As Brett MR put it in *Clarapede v Commercial Union Association*,[10] a case which has stood the test of time;[11] "however negligent or careless may have been the first omission, and however late the proposed amendment, the amendment should be allowed if it can be made without injustice to the other side. There is no injustice if the other side can be compensated by costs." Even so, amendments sought once the trial is underway may invite a greater degree of scepticism than those sought earlier, since by that time it may be apparent that a claim or defence is without merit or that the amendment will serve no useful purpose or that it represents such a departure from the pleaded case that it comes across simply as an act of desperation.[12]

---

5   CPR, r 17.1(2)

6   CPR, r 19.4

7   See generally CPR, r 19.2

8   CPR, r 19.4(4)

9   See e.g. *Kettleman v Hansel Properties Ltd* [1987] AC 189. In that case the defendants were about to lose on the merits of the case at trial and sought to amend at the very last minute to plead a limitation defence, which no doubt could have been pleaded much earlier on. The House of Lords agreed with the Court of Appeal in saying that the amendment should not, in the circumstances of that case, have been allowed.

10 (1883) 32 WR 262

11 See e.g. comments of Neuberger J (as he then was) in *Charlesworth v Relay Roads Ltd* [2002] 1 WLR 230.

12 As in *Ketterman* itself, ibid.

(d) The costs of amending

The *usual order for costs* is that the party *making the amendment* must pay the *'costs of and arising from' the amendment*.[13] Having said that, if a party unreasonably failed to consent to an amendment and in effect forced an unnecessary application to the court, it might be ordered that the amending party pay the costs occasioned by the amendment (since these arise either way), but leaving the recalcitrant party to pay the costs of the avoidable application to the court.[14]

(e) Seeking permission

Permission to amend is sought by application notice. Evidence is not always required, but the proposed amended statement of case must be filed with the application.[15] The rules do not strictly require it, but traditionally *both* the original and amended text (in red) is shown – otherwise it is difficult for the court to know what was being proposed! Multiple further amendments will result in a very colourful display, since with each change a different colour is used.[16]

So usually amendments are not controversial because, most of the time, payment of costs can compensate for the time and trouble they cause. There is one especially important situation, however, where no costs order can compensate for the injustice caused by a proposed amendment, and that is where a relevant limitation period has expired. If an amendment would deprive a party of the defence that an action is statute-barred (which cannot be compensated by any costs order), it will *not* ordinarily be allowed.

---

13 PDs 17 and 19

14 See BCP, para.31.5

15 PD 17, para.1.2(2)

16 There are alternative ways of doing this in the electronic age. See e.g. PD 17, para.2.2(2)

17 LA 1980, s 35(1). This is sometimes referred to as 'relate-back'

18 Note that it says 'may', not 'must'. There is still a discretion to say 'no' if justice requires it.

19 Not all proposed amendments do this necessarily. Some may just simply resolve an obvious discrepancy between the claim form and particulars of claim. See e.g. *Evans v CIG Mon Cymru* [2008] P.I.Q.R., p 17, where the claimant considered suing her employers both for an 'accident at work' and 'abuse at work'. She decided not to pursue the latter bullying allegation. The

2. AMENDMENT *AFTER* EXPIRY OF RELEVANT LIMITATION PERIOD

An amendment to add or substitute a new party or cause of action is deemed to be a separate claim which is commenced on the *same date as the original claim.*[17] This is a purely practical provision, designed to achieve predictability and uniformity. You can see, however, that if the original action was brought *within* the relevant limitation period, but the amendment is made *after* it has expired, the effect of this rule would be to deprive the new defendant (or the original defendant defending the new cause of action) of a limitation defence. No amount of money by way of costs can make up for that. In this situation, therefore, the *general rule* is that a party may *not* amend *once a relevant limitation period has expired.* The idea is that once limitation has expired, a party should not be able to achieve something by way of amendment, which could not be achieved by actually bringing a separate action.

As always, there are *exceptions*, which essentially fall into *three* types of amendment, discussed below.

A. AMENDMENTS HAVING THE EFFECT OF ADDING A NEW CLAIM

As an exception to the general rule, the court *may*[18] allow an amendment, even after the expiry of the limitation period:

(a) To add or substitute a claim/cause of action[19] if it arises out of the *same or substantially the same facts as are already in issue* on any claim previously made in the original action.[20] An obvious example might be a claim in breach of statutory duty being added, after limitation had expired, to an existing claim in negligence, relating to the same accident and facts as already pleaded in the particulars of claim. The court should

particulars of claim sought remedies for an 'accident at work' but because of a typing error, the claim form referred to remedies for 'abuse at work.' After limitation had expired, the defendants attempted to get the particulars struck out because they were irrelevant to the claim form. The claimant applied to amend the claim form so as to substitute 'accident at work' for 'abuse at work' in the claim form. The Court of Appeal (no doubt sensing that there really were bullies at work here) held that the amendment should be allowed and the particulars not struck out. It said that whether a proposed amendment has the effect of raising a new claim had to be determined by looking at the entire claim as pleaded up to that point, not the claim form alone. What was involved

look at the 'essential facts' as already drafted and compare them with those of the proposed pleading.[21] But whether it decides that such amendments involve the 'same or substantially the same' facts as those already in issue will always, to some extent, be a matter of impression, degree, mood and motivation. Every case is different.[22]

(b) To add or substitute a new *personal injuries* claim when the limitation period has been *disapplied under LA 1980, s 33.*[23] Obviously it would be a bit strange if the court could allow a personal injuries action to continue alone, but not in addition to some other existing action.

(c) To allow a party to an existing action to raise a *counterclaim or set-off* for the *first* time.[24] Counterclaims are deemed to have been commenced on the same date as the original claim,[25] so it makes sense that the court may allow an amendment to plead a counterclaim which, were it not for this deeming provision, would be out of time. But it must be an 'original' counterclaim (we are *not* talking about amending an existing counterclaim). So long as the party proposing the amendment has not previously counterclaimed,[26] then this exception will apply. But, again, the court can exercise its discretion to refuse to make the amendment, which it will do if it believes the proposed counterclaim is being used for tactical or other reasons not in keeping with the overriding objective.[27]

B. AMENDMENTS HAVING THE EFFECT OF ADDING A NEW PARTY

As an *exception* to the general rule, an amendment to add or substitute a new party, once the relevant limitation period has expired, may[28] be allowed where:

(a) The court has exercised its *discretion under s. 33 to disapply* the relevant limitation

---

in that case was not the raising of a new claim, but a clerical error.

20   LA 1980, s 35(5)(a) and see also CPR, r 17.4(2). The rule is worded more narrowly than the statutory provision (it does not use the more expansive phrase 'fact already in

issue' but instead refers to amending a claim which has 'already' been made.). But the courts have said that the more expansive words should be read into the rule, otherwise it would be too limiting on a claimant's right to a fair trial. Thus, for example,

if a defendant makes claims or allegations in the defence, they become facts 'in issue' and so give scope for an amendment by the claimant under this provision: *Goode v Martin* [2001] EWCA Civ 899, [2002] WLR 1828.

21   *P and O Nedlloyd BV v*

period in *personal injuries* actions.[29] This discretion can result in the addition of a new party, as much as a new claim (or both simultaneously).

(b) The amendment merely alters the (legal) *'capacity* in which a party *claims*, so long as that new capacity is one which that party had when the proceedings started or has since acquired.'[30] A typical example would be where a person who has brought the claim as an individual, wants to amend to carry on as a trustee (or vice versa). In a sense the party does not change, so much as their legal status. If such an amendment were to have the effect of adding or substituting a party (in addition to changing the capacity of an existing party), then one or other of the exceptions set out in this section would have to apply.[31]

(c) the amendment is 'necessary'.[32] An amendment to add or substitute a party, once the relevant limitation period has expired, will *only be necessary* where:

(i) the original party has died, or been declared bankrupt, and his interest or liability has passed to the new party.[33]

(ii) the amendment is *legally* necessary to maintain the action.[34] This is a highly technical exception which is assumed to cover a very narrow range of circumstances which used to be explicitly set out in the old rules, but which were not replicated in the CPR.[35] It covers things like needing to join the Attorney-General because the proceedings should have been brought as a relator action in his name. For *assessment* purposes, you don't need to know more about this exception than the fact that it exists. If it arises in practice, or a take home exam, you will just have to look it up.

Arab Metals Co [2006] EWCA Civ 1300, [2007] Ch. 182

22 Compare, e.g. *Law v Society of Lloyd's* [2003] EWCA Civ 1887 (amendment refused) with *Senior v Parsons and Ward* (2001) LTL 26/1/2001 (amendment allowed) and

the other examples at BCP, para.31.23.

23 See generally Ch. 10
24 LA 1980, s 35(3)
25 LA 1980, s 35(1)/(2)
26 And is on the opposite side of the record to the defendant to the proposed counterclaim.
27 See e.g. *Law Society v*

Wemyss [2008] EWHC 2515 (Ch)

28 Again, this is 'may', not 'must'.
29 LA 1980. S 35(3) and CPR, r 19.5(4)
30 CPR, r 17.4(4)
31 *Roberts v Gill* [2009] 1 WLR 531
32 CPR, r 19.5(2)(b)

(iii) there has been a *mistake in naming a party* to the original action.[36]

This is a rather vexed, and vexing, area of procedure, not least because aspects of the relevant legislation[37] and the pre-CPR rule[38] have been sprinkled about in two different places in the new rules: Part 17 which deals with 'Amendment' and Part 19 which deals with 'Parties'. As the subject matter at hand is the addition or substitution of parties by amendment, it is perhaps not surprising that this 'division of labour' might have happened, but the relationship between the provisions in CPR, r 17.4(3),[39] and those in CPR, r 19.5(3)[40] has caused no end of judicial headache.

Mistaken name

The main problem is that both sets of rules contain different aspects of the one previous rule, which was stated to allow an amendment to 'correct the name' of a party, even if in a sense this resulted in the 'substitution' of a new party, if the court is satisfied that the mistake was a 'genuine mistake' and was not 'misleading or such as to cause reasonable doubt as to the identity of the person intending to sue or, as the case may be, intended to be sued'.[41] For some reason, the notion of 'correcting' a mistake but only if it was 'genuine' and caused 'no reasonable doubt' about the 'identity' of the party to be substituted made it only into CPR, r 17.4(3), but the idea of the actual 'substitution' of party for one who was 'named in the claim form in mistake' is really all that appears in CPR, r 19.5(3). You might think the neatest solution would be to say that if the substitution is necessary under the latter rule because of a mistake in name, this would then send you back to CPR, r 17.4(3), which sets out the additional requirement of its needing to be a genuine mistake and so on.[42] But you would (at least so far) be wrong.

---

33 CPR, r 19.5(3)(c)
34 CPR, r 19.5(3)(b)
35 See e.g. discussion at BCP, para.14.89 or WB, Vol 1, at 19.5.4
36 CPR, r 19.5(3)
37 LA 1980, s 35
38 This was RSC O 20, r 5.
39 The title to CPR, r 17.4 is 'Amendments to

statements of case after the end of a relevant limitation period'; r 17.4(3) allows an amendment to 'correct' a mistake as to the name of a party.
40 The title to CPR, r 19.5 is 'Special provisions about adding or substituting parties after the end of a

relevant limitation period.'
41 RSC Ord 20, r 5
42 These two sections do cross-refer to each other, although the reference back to CPR, r 17.4 from CPR, r 19.5 is admittedly less compelling than that going in the other direction.

There was also a lot of case law under the old rule, in particular about just what kind of 'mistake' was correctable once limitation has expired and how misleading or not a correction of such a mistake might be. It was fairly clear that where, for example, the right person had been sued but called by the wrong name, this was correctable; but if a person had been sued in mistake for another, this was not. In what was then the leading case,[43] Loyd LJ commented that the notion of the 'identity' of the person intending to sue or intended to be sued was a concept which is "not at all easy to grasp, and can be difficult to apply to the circumstances of a particular case ..." He added that "in one sense a (claimant) always intends to sue the person who is liable for the wrong he has suffered. But the test cannot be as wide as that. Otherwise, there would never be any doubt as to the person intended to be sued, and leave to amend would always be given. So there must be a narrower test." He went on to suggest that where the party is named "*by reference to a description which was more or less specific to the particular case*",[44] then this was the sort of mistake which was correctable without causing reasonable doubt about who was the intended party. So, for example, if in suing a defendant, the claimant gets the right description (e.g. employer, landlord etc) but the wrong name, Lloyd LJ thought that there "is unlikely to be any doubt as to the identity of the person intended to be sued. But if he gets the wrong description, it will be otherwise."[45]

So, along come the new rules. CPR, r 19.5(3) does not specify the need for the mistake to be genuine and not misleading to the person whose name is to be substituted.[46] But CPR r 17.4(3), the old rule, and all the existing case law, does. So where does that leave us?

Trial and appeal judges have been grappling with this problem for some years now, with varying degrees of success. This has occasionally resulted in different, sometimes conflicting solutions, which are then either endorsed or overruled. Some

---

43 *The Sardinia Sulcis* [1991] 1 Lloyd's Rep 201

44 This became known as the '**Sardinia Sulcis** test' and see useful list of examples in WB, para.19.5.8.

45 op.cit., p.207

46 Neither does LA 1980, s 35, but that was so before the CPR.

have approached it by saying the two rules are entirely separate, and only r 19.5 is relevant to a 'substitution' of one name for another as a result of a mistake.[47] At one point, the Court of Appeal said[48] (and I am paraphrasing) "Forget what the old rule said and the related case law, let's just start afresh with the new rules." This approach (which did not really help with some aspects of the problem) was rejected in what is now the leading case of *Adelson and another v Associated Newspapers Ltd.*[49]

The *Adelson* case held that pre-CPR case law *was* relevant to applications to amend out of time to add or substitute a new party. It also approved of the notion that CPR, r 19.5 deals with mistakes in naming parties which requires a new party to be *substituted,* leaving CPR, r 17.4 to deal with cases where there has been a mistake in setting out the name of a party, which needs *correcting.*[50] It also sets out the following principles about applications under CPR, r 19.5(3):

- The court must be satisfied that the person who made the mistake, directly or through an agent, was the person responsible for issuing the claim form;
- The applicant must show that had the mistake not been made, the new party would have been named in the claim form;
- The mistake has to be as to the name, *not the identity* of the party, thus endorsing the *Sardinia Sulcis* test. This can still be a very tricky point to decide – the line between the two can be quite grey. Often there will be some corporate connection between the named party and the one to be substituted.[51] How lenient or harsh a court will be in deciding this aspect of a case can also depend on other factors in a case, which can sometimes be rather quirky.[52] Some, including *Adelson* itself, were applications by claimants to change their own names (when you

---

47   Leaving r 17.4(3) for things like correcting spelling mistakes. See e.g. *Lockheed Martin Corporation v Willis Group Ltd* [2010] EWCA Civ 927 (the appeal was determined on another point, so the comments are obiter).

48   *Morgan Est (Scotland)*

Ltd v Hanson Concrete Products Ltd [2005] 1 WLR 2557. The next appeal court to deal with the point felt bound by this case and so began to postulate (quite understandably) a new 'test' (*"Can you change the name of the party without changing the claim?"*),

which was in fact not a millions miles away from the *Sardicia Sulcis* test. But the latter was about to be rehabilitated in any event.

49   [2007] EWCA Civ 701, [2008] 1 WLR 585

50   As decided in *Gregson v Channel Four Television Corporation* (2000) CP Rep

might think they would know who they were from the outset!), and in those cases the court is more apt to think there has been a change of mind about who should sue, rather than a mistake in naming that party. In other cases, whatever the nature of the mistake, it was made by lawyers, against whom an action for professional negligence could be brought. This also tends to make judges more, shall we say, judgmental. One can usually imagine the sort of mistake in naming a party which the court would clearly allow to be corrected, even if by way of substituting a new party, as well as the sort of mistake which the court would clearly not allow – it's the situations in the middle which can be a lot more difficult to call.

- No injustice should be caused if the application is granted. This is how the court can factor in questions about the genuineness of the mistake and whether the substituted party has been misled, without actually referring to CPR, r 17.4(3).[53] If there are concerns, especially if the party to be substituted would be completely taken by surprise by the amendment, then the court can exercise its discretion (remember the rule says 'may', not 'must') to refuse to make the amendment.

Finally, note carefully that because of the wording of CPR, r 19.5(3), *only substitutions* (and *not additions*) are allowed under this head of amendment.[54]

C.   AMENDMENTS HAVING THE EFFECT OF ADDING A NEW DEFENCE[55]

Here the *emphasis is different* because limitation periods basically concern claimants, not defendants. Thus, amending a defence after the action's limitation period has expired is not usually a problem.

---

60. It may still, at times, be difficult to distinguish between these two.

51   As in *Adelson* itself.

52   In the *Lockheed Martin Corporation* case, op.cit., there was no cause of action against the defendant whom the claimant wanted, by amendment, to proceed against!

53   So problem solved? Watch this space – I would not be surprised if the Supreme Court had a go at it ... or maybe the CPR rules committee might beat them to it.

54   *Broadhurst v Broadhurst* [2007] EWCA 1828.

Somehow, Lord Phillips in the *Adelson* case managed to turn 3 claimants into 1, but disallowed the amendment on other grounds.

55   This is sometimes called amendments affecting accrued rights (i.e. the right of defendants to plead a limitation defence).

So here, the general rule is that the court *will* allow a *defendant to amend the defence, even after the limitation period* has expired, *unless* the claimant can show that he or she would be *prejudiced by it in a way which cannot be compensated in costs*. This would be the case, for example, where a defendant suddenly blames another person whom the claimant cannot now sue because the action against that person is statute-barred. In *Cluley v RL Dix Heating*,[56] for example, the claimant sued the defendants for breach of contract. The original defence admitted the contract but denied breach. After the limitation period for the contract action had expired, the defendants sought to amend their defence to deny the contract, and alleged that the claimant should have sued other parties. The amendment was not allowed, because it was now no longer possible for the claimant to sue any other parties, because limitation had expired, and the defendants must have known much earlier whether they had a contract with the claimants or not.

In this sort of situation, the position can be summarised in this way:

A defendant will be allowed to amend his pleadings to raise a new defence allegation, even after the relevant limitation period has expired, unless:

- the effect of the amendment is to blame another party whom the claimant cannot now sue,

and

- it is the defendant's fault in not seeking to amend earlier.[57]

However, if on a closer look, it turns out that the claimant knew all along of the facts giving rise to the defence amendment, that amendment may be allowed.[58]

---

56 (2003) LTL 31/10/2003

57 *Weait v Jayanbee Joinery Ltd* [1963] 1 QB 239

58 As in *Turner v Ford Motor Co* [1965] 2 ALL ER 583. There is a useful, short exposition of these two cases at BCP, at para.31.24.

revision tips

Differentiate between:

- Amendments sought *before* versus *after* the limitation period has expired

and

- *The different types of amendments sought after expiry* of the limitation period.

It is worth reading ...

Neubeuger J's (as he then was) judgment in *Charlesworth v Relay Roads Ltd* (No 2) [2000] 1 WLR 230. In this case judgment had been given but not officially drawn up. Limitation had not expired, but talk about a last minute application to amend!!

CHAPTER 12

Renewal of claim form

In Chapter 10 we looked at the prescribed time periods for bringing proceedings, after which, with certain exceptions, a defendant will have an unanswerable limitation defence. To avoid a case being time-barred, therefore, a claimant should start the action before the relevant limitation period has expired. An action is commenced when the claim form is *issued*. Once this happens, the next step is to *serve* it on the defendant while the claim form is still valid for service.[1]

The claim form is valid for service for *four months* if it is to be served within the jurisdiction – time runs from the date the claim form is issued. Where it is to be served *outside* the jurisdiction, which can be more time-consuming than serving inside the jurisdiction, the period of validity is extended to *six months*.[2] The defendant does not need to receive the claim form during the period of validity, but the claimant must have *completed the steps* required by the rules to effect the chosen method of service.[3] The claimant has until midnight on the last day of the period of validity to do this.[4]

A claim form must be served while it is valid. If a claimant has a reason for not being able to do this, an extension may be granted either with the consent of the party to be served[5] or by the court. Extending the period of validity is sometimes referred to as 'renewal' (like a library book), and as we shall see, the rules are very strict (like some librarians). If the limitation period in the action has not

---

1 CPR, r 7.5
2 CPR, r 7.5(2)
3 See generally Ch. 4 on service.
4 CPR, r 7.5(1). Assume, for example, an action founded on contract (with a 6 year limitation period) with service to take place within the jurisdiction. If the claimant used both (limitation and validity) time periods to the full, in theory the defendant need not be served until 6 years plus 4 months from the breach. But it is never a good idea to leave these things to the last minute – the courts hate this.
5 Only written consent will be effective in these circumstances: CPR, r 2.11 and *Thomas v Home Office* [2007] 1 WLR 230.

yet expired, there is no great reason to panic since an alternative to renewal would be to issue fresh proceedings.[6] *It is where the relevant limitation period has expired that serious problems arise.*

When the court serves the claim form, renewal problems should not often occur. But where claimants choose to serve the claim form themselves, problems can arise. The key to understanding renewal is to see the *relationship* between the limitation period in the action and the period during which the claim form is valid for service – but *not to confuse the two.*

1. RENEWAL APPLICATIONS DURING THE PERIOD OF VALIDITY

Renewal is typically sought when a claimant is having difficulties serving a defendant. The general rule is that an application for an extension of the claim form's validity for service should be made *before* the claim form expires.[7] In such cases, sometimes referred to as 'prospective applications', the court has a *general discretion* to renew. The court will exercise the discretion in accordance with the overriding objective; allowing the renewal if it can do so justly, but mindful of the importance of ensuring that cases progress expeditiously. In particular, the court will look closely at the *attempts* made to serve (both when and how) and the *reason* for the need to renew – the better the reason, the more likely they are to allow the renewal: *Hashtroodi v Hancock.*[8] The balance of hardship may well be relevant, as could the implications of the claimant's merely issuing fresh proceedings if the application to renew is refused.[9] The main thrust of the court's approach to renewal has always been that a claimant should issue *and* serve proceedings promptly. This is neither expensive (in the scheme of things), nor difficult. If any hiatus in proceedings is desired, it can

---

6   There would be a price to pay, because you would have to pay to start fresh proceedings, but all would not be lost.

7   Or as specified by court order: CPR, r 7.6(2)

8   [2004] 1 WLR 3206

9   See e.g. *Hoddinott, Hoddinott and R.G. Hoddinott Ltd v Persimmon Homes (Wessex) Ltd* [2007] EWCA Civ 1203 where this was one factor among many.

occur *after* service of the claim form, not before.

So what amounts to a good enough reason? Not much, is the short answer. Historically, under the old rules, reasons which were *not* thought to be good reasons included: negotiations in progress, strength of claimant's case, an honest mistake, difficulty in obtaining evidence, and delays by the claimant in applying for public funding (although delays in the granting of funding might amount to a good reason).

Reasons which *were* considered to be good reasons under the old rules included a defendant evading service, a defendant explicitly asking not to be served, or saving a defendant costs. Note the theme here: either the defendant is behaving badly or making service difficult, or the claimant is doing the defendant a favour. The cases under the CPR have continued in this vein.[10]

Remember that decisions in individual cases are merely a *guide* to the outcome of any given renewal application which has been made prospectively, although the reasoning can be enlightening. Every case is different and courts have a complete discretion. Having said that, the cases confirm a generally *restrictive* approach even in these cases. The overriding objective is, of course, overriding in such situations.

2. RENEWAL APPLICATIONS MADE AFTER EXPIRY OF THE CLAIM FORM

This is a much more difficult scenario. Where the application to renew is made *after* the claim form has *expired* (sometimes called a 'retrospective' application), the court's *discretion is very much constrained* by the fact that it must be shown that (a) the claimant has taken 'all reasonable' steps, but failed (or the court was unable) to serve the claim

---

10 Compare, for example, *Hoddinott* case (delay in receiving the expert's report on quantum was not a good reason; the claimant should have served the claim form and sought an extension of the time for serving the particulars of claim instead) with *Imperial* *Cancer Research Fund v Ove Arup & Partners Ltd* [2009] EWHC 1453 (TCC), June 23, 2009, (the claimant's need to evacuate the premises, investigate a water leak and obtain a expert's report on the liability of the defendant, and possibly others, was a good reason, especially since the defendants had been slow to disclose plans and documents when asked.). The WB has a good summary at para.7.6.2.

form in time *and* (b) the application was made promptly.[11] Although not contained in the rule, reasons why the application was made after the claim form expired would not go amiss, either. This is an *exceedingly narrow* set of criteria, really focusing *only* on failed attempts to serve.

Furthermore, there is virtually no escape from the confines of CPR, r 7.6(3). In a line of cases,[12] the Court of Appeal decided that CPR, r 7.6 constitutes a *complete code*, so that recourse may not be had to other powers[13] under the CPR, nor even it seems the overriding objective, to mitigate the severity of the rule – except in *very exceptional* circumstances. These possibilities are:

(i) To apply retrospectively for an order for alternative service;[14]

(ii) To get an order dispensing with service under CPR, r 6.16. This will only be granted in exceptional circumstances, and only it seems if an attempt has been made by the claimant to serve;[15]

(iii) To remedy, under CPR, r 3.10, what is in effect a 'de minimus' or technical error in service.[16]

Each of these is a possible circumvention, but the circumstances need to be truly exceptional. The long and the short of it is: the rule is strict, and is strictly enforced. Too many exceptions would dilute the message: serve the claim form in time!

An application for renewal is made to the Master or District Judge under Part 23, using an application notice supported by written evidence. The application is made without giving notice to the other side.[17] If renewal is granted, the first the defendant may know about it, therefore, is when the (extended) claim form is served. A defendant who wishes to dispute the extension should first acknowledge

---

11 Albeit that the period of validity has already passed. See CPR, r 7.6(3). It is the steps taken to serve the claim form during its validity which matter: *Drury v BBC & Carnegie* [2007] EWCA Civ 497

12 E.g. *Kaur v CTP Coil Ltd* (2000) LTL 10/7/2000;

Vinos v Marks & Spencer plc [2001] 3 ALL ER 784; *Godwin v Swindon Borough Council* [2002] 1 WLR 997.

13 For example the general power to grant extensions of time, to grant relief from sanctions or remedy procedures in error, all

found in Part 3. See generally, discussion of case management at Ch. 13.

14 Under CPR, r 6.15(2). The ability to apply retrospectively for this order is a relatively recent development, brought about by the 2008

service in the normal way, stating an intention to defend, and *then* apply on notice to have the order extending the validity of the claim form discharged. The same would apply to a defendant who has simply been served with an invalid claim form, although in this case the claimant will likely cross-apply for an appropriate court order.[18] In either case, it is important for defendants to act promptly in these circumstances, since delay could be taken as acceptance of valid service.

The rules on renewal essentially reflect the fact that, at the very least, the court must be satisfied that there was a compelling reason for a claimant not doing something as cheap and easy as 'popping' the claim form in the post (or letting the court serve it!). The ultimate no-no, of course, is to apply for renewal after *both* the limitation period and the claim form have expired, when the action will effectively be lost. Not only is r 7.6(3) very strict in its own terms, but the courts have always been extremely reluctant to deprive a defendant of a limitation defence, especially when the claimant issued proceedings at the very last minute. *Do not forget*, however, that so long as the limitation period in the action has *not* expired, it always remains the case that (unless the court has barred a claimant from re-litigating, and at admittedly at some cost) a *fresh* action can be commenced.

continues/...

---

changes.

15 *Anderton v Clwyd County Council (No 2)* [2002] 1 WLR 3174.

16 See e.g. *Steele v Mooney* [2005] 1 WLR 2819; *Phillips v Symes (No 3)* [2008] 1 WLR 180.

17 See generally Ch. 4

18 Unless it is simply easier and no more expensive (assuming limitation has not expired as well) to issue another claim form and start again.

revision tips

- Be clear about the interrelationship, but also the difference between the limitation period in an action and the period during which the claim form issued in the case is valid for service. Do not confuse the two.

- Be clear about how very strict the rule is if the application to renew is made after expiry of the claim form. Even the overriding objective does not help here!

- If the claim form has become invalid for service, but the limitation period in the action has not yet expired, starting again is a possibility which should always be considered. It might even be the cheaper option!

It is worth reading ...

The judgments of Dyson LJ (who was then the Court of Appeal's resident expert on renewal, until he went up to the Supreme Court) in:

- *Hoddinott v Persimmon Homes (Wessex) Ltd* [2007] EWCA Civ 1203, [2008] 1 WLR 806. This is partly a case about when and how a defendant disputes the court's jurisdiction, but also discusses the approach which the court should take when an application to renew the claim form is made while the claim form is still valid.

and

- *Drury v BBC & Carnegie* [2007] EWCA Civ 96. An interesting defamation case. Eady J, whose decision was appealed against, is one of the foremost experts in the world on this complex subject. But even he was wrong-footed by the constraints of the court when faced with an application to renew after the claim form had expired!

CHAPTER 13

Case management and sanctions

Once a defendant has filed a defence and the allocation questionnaires have been returned (or dispensed with), the Master or District Judge, as interim judge, will essentially need to consider three things:

1. whether the claim or defence (or part of it) should be *curtailed at this stage*, for example by means of striking out[1] or summary judgment.[2] If appropriate, the court will fix an early appointment to hear argument from both sides;

2. *allocation* to the appropriate track. Several factors will be relevant, including complexity, evidential needs and predicted length of trial, but normally the value of the claim will dictate which track it goes on;[3]

3. giving *directions*. Directions upon allocation are generally given using standard forms, adapted to the individual needs of the case at hand, although parties can ask the court to make agreed directions. Typically these include disclosure of documents,[4] exchange of witness statements, and expert evidence.[5]

---

1 Read on.
2 See discussion in Ch. 5

3 See generally discussion in Ch. 8
4 See generally Ch. 9

5 See generally Ch. 17

Once allocated, a case then proceeds on its given track through its interim stages. Active management of this progress by the courts is a crucial part of the ethos and effect of the CPR – without it, the overriding objective cannot be achieved. It had long been recognised that the old system resulted in delay and expense which was often disproportionate to the issues or amount at stake in a case. Lord Woolf's answer was to put the court firmly in the driving seat.

CPR, r 1.4(1) thus places a *duty* on the court to further the overriding objective by *actively managing cases,* which includes encouraging a co-operative approach to litigation, identifying the real issues at an early stage and disposing summarily of others, controlling the pace and progress of cases, considering whether the ends justify the means and so on.[6]

The *ammunition* given to the court for this purpose is found in CPR, Part 3, which gives the court an exceedingly wide range of powers. These include making orders on its own initiative (without being asked, and with or without a hearing)[7]; making orders with built-in punishments (so-called 'unless orders'[8]); imposing (and giving relief from) sanctions for non-compliance with court directions and orders; extending or refusing to extend time; controlling the nature and extent of evidence to be adduced at trial and so on. In a nutshell, the court can do nearly anything it likes. Part carrot, but a lot of stick! Let's look at some of these powers and sanctions in turn:

A. STRIKING OUT

This is an attack on a party's statement of case or conduct of that case. Strictly speaking, causes of action are not struck out as such, but the term is used rather loosely. Of course if, say, a claimant's particulars of claim are struck out in their entirety, it follows that the action will be stayed or dismissed.[9] If a whole defence

---

6 CPR, r 1.4(2). It is worth reading and digesting this rule in its entirety.

7 Any party who is unhappy with such an order can apply to have it varied or set aside. See generally CPR, r 3.3.

8 As in, "Unless you do what I say, you will be in trouble." A typical 'unless' order might sound like this: *"Unless by (date/time) the defendant do file and serve a list of documents giving standard disclosure, the Defence will be struck out and judgment entered for the claimant, damages to be decided by the court."* It thus contains both the order and the punishment (and any consequence).

9 As to 'stays', see below

is struck out, the inevitable result will be judgment for the claimant. If only part of a statement of case is struck out,[10] then the rest of a viable claim or defence can continue. Striking out is the *most severe sanction* the court can impose.

The court may strike out all or part of a statement of case if it appears:

(i)   that it discloses *no reasonable grounds* for bringing or defending the claim;

(ii) that it is an *abuse* of the court's process or is otherwise likely to obstruct the just disposal of the proceedings;

(iii) that there has been a *failure to comply* with a rule, practice direction or court order.[11]

Ground (i) and (ii) cover statements of case which do not amount to a legally recognisable claim or defence[12] or which are unreasonably vague, incoherent, vexatious, scandalous, obviously ill-founded or otherwise amount to an abuse of process.[13] It is important to note that, where relevant, the court can and should exercise this power at the stage of issuing a claim or filing a defence, thus saving a party the expense of applying to strike out. A court official, for example, who receives a claim form that fails to meet the standards required, will issue it, but may then consult the judge who in turn may, on his or her own initiative, make an appropriate order in the circumstances. Possibilities include staying proceedings pending the filing of a 'proper' statement of case, requesting the filing of relevant further information, or, in the worst cases, striking out the offending statement of case (and entering such judgment as the other party may be entitled to).[14] The court may order a hearing to canvass the options.

Ground (c) covers cases where the problem lies not in the statement of case itself, but in the *way* the claim or defence has been conducted. Sanctions for

---

10 See wording of CPR, r 3.4(1)

11 CPR, r 3.4(2)

12 See examples in PD 3A

13 See e.g. *Pickthall v Hill Dickinson LLP* [2009] EWCA Civ 543 (commencement of proceedings knowing that the cause of action is vested in someone else is an abuse of process. Only the person with the vested right of action can bring the claim).

14 PD 3, paras 2-4

non-compliance are discussed below, but striking out on this basis should be a last, not first resort. Note the following:

(a) Built-in strike out sanctions

Sometimes the strike out sanction is *built into* the rules themselves (for example, where there has been non-payment of fees payable at the track allocation and listing stages, the court will send a notice stating the date by which these must be paid, failing which, according to the rules, the claim will be struck out[15]) or is built into a court order (the 'unless order'). In both such cases, the sanction follows *automatically* upon the stated event, unless a reprieve is given.[16]

(b) Strike out versus summary judgment

Striking out and summary judgment may be viewed as something of a twin-set, in the sense that many cases falling within CPR, r 3.4(2) may also fall within Part 24, which provides for summary disposal of claims or defences which have no reasonable prospect of success.[17] The overlap is not complete (summary judgment is not about non-compliance, and various procedural requirements relevant to Part 24 do not apply to CPR, r 3.4) but both possibilities should be considered in relevant cases.[18]

(c) Deadly weapon

Striking out is the court's *most draconian weapon*, and should be reserved for the most obvious and serious cases. In *Biguzzi v Rank Leisure plc,*[19] the Court of Appeal drew attention to the fact that there are several alternatives to a strike out[20] to be considered in any given situation before deploying the weapon of last resort. But each case must be decided on its merits. In the case of *Raja v van Hoogstraten,*[21] the defendant had arranged for the claimant to be killed in order

---

15 CPR, r 3.7(2)-(4)
16 Under CPR, r 3.9., see below
17 See generally Ch. 5
18 PD 3, para.1.7
19 [1999] 1 WLR 1926
20 As to which, read on
21 [2006] EWHC 1315 (CH)

22 Under the old rules, 'dismissal' of a claim or defence (not a statement of case, as such) was a sanction which took two forms, only one of which survived the advent of the CPR. This involved allegations of deliberate abuse of court procedures. This is now more than adequately covered by CPR, Part 3, which can deal with the contemptuous litigant, as well as the merely lazy and disorganised. The other, known as 'dismissal for want of prosecution' has been rendered virtually

to prevent him giving evidence – it does not get much more serious than that!

B. RANGE OF SANCTIONS FOR NON-COMPLIANCE
WITH DIRECTIONS AND ORDERS

The court has various weapons which it can use to actively manage cases and give effect to the overriding objective. The power to impose sanctions for non-compliance is critically important for maintaining control of the conduct of litigation. Generally speaking, the philosophy behind the CPR will not work if the court's bark is always worse than its bite. The court now has more choice, and a greater range of sanctions at its disposal than previously,[22] which should assist in ensuring that in any given case the 'punishment fits the crime.' Again, note the following:

(a) Timetable directions

Not *all* acts of non-compliance are of the most serious kind. An example of a minor default would be a failure to comply with timetable directions.[23] So long as the key case management events in a case remain unaffected,[24] the parties should seek to resolve such problems between themselves by agreeing a new date for compliance or some other solution. Furthermore, an 'innocent' party faced with an opponent who has not complied with a timetable *direction* may neither let sleeping dogs lie (by sitting back and letting the default get worse by the passage of time) nor immediately rush to the court. Instead, the middle grounds of a *written warning* should be given.[25] This should warn the defaulting party of the intention to make an application to the court if the direction is not complied with by a reasonable (stated) time. If this does not do the trick, an application to the court may be made for an *order* to enforce compliance or for a sanction to be imposed, or both. Sanctions may range from a costs sanction (minor) to the more draconian 'unless' order, but should be proportionate.

---

extinct. This was an allegation by a defendant that a claimant was not pursuing the action with acceptable speed. Given active management of cases by the court, this type of action should now be confined to the status of museum relic.

23 Directions tend to be more impersonal than orders. It is a bit like the difference between *"I want you children to play quietly in there"* (a direction) and *"Tommy! Put down that vase!"* (an order). Breach of the latter is considered (other things being equal) more serious than breach of the former.

24 See Ch. 8

25 PD 28, para.5 (fast track) and PD 29, para.7 (multi-track)

(b) Pre-action default

Another type of default is non-compliance with the pre-action protocols. Minor breaches will not cause much concern and certainly should not be viewed as an excuse itself for non-compliance, but where a failure to comply with the protocol results in unnecessary litigation and/or costs, sanctions can follow. These would focus on punitive costs and/or interest orders as a punishment for not trying hard enough to avoid litigation. It is now a requirement that the parties plead in their statements of case whether or not a relevant pre-action protocol has been complied with,[26] so lack of compliance should come as no surprise at the end of a trial.

(c) Built-in sanctions other than strike out

We saw that the strike out sanction is sometimes built into some of the provisions of the CPR in case of non-compliance. This applies to other sorts of sanctions as well. An example is CPR, r 35.1 which says that if a party fails to disclose expert evidence as required,[27] that party will not be allowed to rely on that expert evidence, unless the court gives permission.[28] This is a common sense, tailor-made sanction which is intended, and usually does, encourage compliance!

(d) Relief from sanctions

When a sanction is built into an order (an 'unless order') or mandated by a rule or practice direction, it will *automatically* take effect unless the defaulting party applies for (and is granted) 'relief from the sanction' under CPR, r 3.9.[29] In deciding whether to grant relief, the court should consider all of the circumstances of the case (including the overriding objective), but in particular the factors listed in the rule, which include whether the default was intentional, whether the defaulter has otherwise been a cooperative and compliant litigant, the cause of the default,

---

26 PD Pre-action conduct, para.9.7

27 See generally below at Ch. 17

28 Some rule-based sanctions are more discretionary, allowing the court to impose the penalty if it chooses.

29 The application must be supported by written evidence.

the prejudice to both parties and so forth. A fair trial is obviously an important factor.[30] In deciding whether to grant relief or not, the court *should look at all the relevant factors systematically, giving each its appropriate weight, and strike a balance applying the overriding objective.*[31] It perhaps goes without saying that as part of this process, the court should ask itself whether the sanction itself had been correctly ordered in the first place.[32]

(e) Worst case senarios

Only in *exceptional* circumstances will the court let a failure to comply with a direction or 'unless order' lead to the postponement of the trial.[33] Where (in the worst case scenario) an action has been struck out following a failure to comply with an 'unless order' (or other contemptuous behaviour), a second claim brought on the same basis (even if not statute-barred) would normally also be struck out (as an abuse of process).[34]

(f) Punishment to fit the crime

The cases on sanctions since the inception of the CPR show that each case must be decided on its own merits and that pre-CPR cases are only useful if they speak to the overriding objective. Cases rooted in the old value system will be irrelevant and unappreciated in court. A noticeable theme of the cases is that the courts should be fair and flexible in exercising their wide and varied powers – ensuring that any penalty is commensurate with the nature of the default. As one case put it, it is necessary to concentrate on the 'intrinsic' justice of each case in light of the overriding objective.[35] Striking out in this context is very much a last resort, especially if there is fault on both sides.[36]

---

30 It is a paramount consideration in any decision to *apply* the strike out sanction: *Hansom v E Rex Makin* [2003] LTL 18/12/2003.

31 *Woodhouse v Consignia plc* [2002] 1 WLR 2558

32 *Tarn Insurance Services Ltd v Kirby* [2009] EWCA Civ 19

33 See e.g. *Woodward v Finch* [1999] CPLR 699.

34 *Johnson v Gore Wood and Co* [2002] 2 AC 1

35 *Purdy v Cambran* [1999]

36 But sometimes patience runs out (usually after years of inactivity and non-compliance) as in *Duggin v Wood* [2001].

C. EXTENSION OF TIME AND CORRECTING IRREGULARITIES

The court has general power to extend or abridge time (or to refuse to extend or abridge time), to allow (or refuse to allow) the parties to overlook procedural errors and/or take steps itself to remedy procedural errors.[37] As we have seen, however, this power may not be used in respect of applications to renew invalid claim forms which have expired.

D. STAYS

This is a bit like the dog command. A 'stay' is an order producing a *temporary halt to proceedings* which can in effect become a permanent state of affairs.[38] While a stay is in effect, no other steps may be taken in the case (except an application to remove the stay).[39] The power arises and is applicable in all sorts of situations. Some examples are:

- A stay of proceedings in a personal injuries case so long as the claimant unreasonably refuses to undergo a medical exam.
- A stay of proceedings while a preliminary point is argued which may have the result that the action will proceed no further.
- If a claimant accepts an offer of settlement,[40] the proceedings will be stayed, effectively ending the case.
- A stay of execution pending an appeal.
- A stay in proceedings for a month to attempt a settlement.
  This is requested in the allocation questionnaire (and so occurs after the defence has been filed).

---

37 Most procedural errors are 'irregularities', which means they do not invalidate the proceedings and are capable of correction by the court. CPR, r 3.10

38 It is not, however, the same thing as discontinuing an action or getting judgment.

39 But it does not stop time running for other purposes.
40 See Ch. 15

E. DISCONTINUANCE

This is something a claimant (or a person in position of a claimant) does if he or she wishes to abandon the whole or part of a claim against the defendant. The claimant merely serves a standardised notice of discontinuance on the defendant (agreeing to pay the defendant's costs). The claimant does not require the permission of the court, so long as no interim remedy has been granted which might need 'unravelling'.[41]

If permission is required, the claimant will usually be given it, subject to appropriate orders as to costs and any corrective orders which might be needed (for example, to repay an interim payment). The court is usually only too delighted to be relieved of cases, although very occasionally it may feel that a case has progressed so far that the claimant ought to lose openly and publicly.[42]

---

revision tip

Read all of CPR 3 and PD 3A carefully.
The rules themselves are clearly set out. You need little else to remind you of the court's powers!

It is worth reading …

Lightman J's judgment in *Raja v van Hoogstraten* [2006] EWHC 1315 (CH) – interesting on all sorts of levels. It is not all that often that such murder and mayhem goes on in the Chancery division!

---

41 Or where there might be another claimant left in the lurch. See CPR, r 38.2(2)

42 *Fox v Star Newspaper* [1900] AC 19, HL. Similarly, and for the same sorts of reasons, a defendant can apply to set aside a notice of discontinuance: CPR, r 38.4

PART FOUR

typical defendant's initiatives

CHAPTER 14

Security for costs

In the past, claimants made much of the running in litigation; the claimant, after all, is the party who sets the ball rolling and, generally speaking, it was historically the claimant who set the pace of the proceedings. Under the CPR, of course, all that changed – it is the court which now controls and sets the agenda.

Even so, defendants (if all they are doing is defending) will still of necessity spend much of the time reacting either to something the claimant has done (not least of all bringing the action) or by the court's management of the case. Defendants may respond with deadly effect, of course, but nevertheless they are often prodded into action by something or someone else. It is also worth remembering that a claimant with a weak case does not have to bring proceedings (and would be well advised not to do so.). Unless and until a claimant sees reason, however, a defendant with a strong defence[1] really has little choice but to defend.

That being the case, and despite the fact that there are obviously many requests or applications which either party to litigation can make if necessary,[2]

---

1   Not so strong as to succeed in striking out the claim, perhaps, but still good enough to win at the end of the day.

2   For example, a request for further information, an order for disclosure of a particular document, an order to strike out, and so on.

there are three very important procedural initiatives *typically taken by defendants.* One of these is bringing in third parties. We looked at this in the context of parties and additional claims in Chapter 3. The other two are applications for security for costs, discussed in this chapter and offers of settlement, discussed in the next.

Occasionally a claimant brings an action against the defendant simply for its nuisance value. The case may have a limited prospect of success,[3] but it has every ability to cost the defendant time, inconvenience, and expense. More mundanely, and much more commonly, a defendant may feel confident that there is a good chance of defeating a claim brought against him, but at the same time be concerned that the claimant, as loser, will be unable to meet any order for costs made against him.[4] In this context an impecunious claimant can be as much of a problem as an impecunious defendant.

Some, *but by no means all,* defendants are able to get protection in this kind of situation, in the form of an order for security for costs. If granted, security can be ordered in any number of ways. One is by the claimant paying a specific amount of money into court. The order for security must specify how and when security must be given, until which time the action may go no further.[5] The money is held as a fund out of which the successful defendant's costs can be paid.[6]

Thus, the court has a *discretion* to order a person *in the position of claimant*[7] to give security for his opponent's *costs* where the defendant can establish that the claimant is one of those sorts of claimants against whom it is *possible* to get such an order.

There are essentially *two hurdles* to be surmounted. The defendant must *first* establish that the claimant is one of those kinds of claimants against whom an order for security is *possible.* This is a *very narrow class of* what might be thought of as qualifying *claimants.* [8] In a nutshell, the possibilities[9] are where:

---

3   If it is completely and obviously without merit, of course, the claim could be struck out or the defendant might get summary judgment.

4   As to costs, see generally Ch. 18.

5   The preferred form of order will give the defendant liberty to apply to the court (e.g. to have the claim struck out) if the claimant does not give security as ordered. This is typical in the Commercial Court. The alternative is an 'unless order'. See generally Ch. 13 and WB, para.25.12.8.

6   If the defendant loses, of course, the money will go back to the claimant.

7   Note that this would also include, for example, a counterclaiming defendant, who for the purposes of the counterclaim is a claimant. See CPR, r 25, 12(1) which refers to the order

(i)   The claimant is ordinarily resident outside the
      (domestic or European[10]) jurisdiction;

(ii) The claimant is an impecunious[11] limited company;

(iii) The claimant has changed his address so as to evade service;

(iv) The claimant failed to give a correct address in the claim form;

(v)   The claimant is an impecunious, nominal[12] claimant;

(vi) The claimant has taken steps in relation to his assets which would
      make it difficult to enforce an order for costs against him.[13]

If a defendant *cannot surmount this first hurdle*, that is the end of the story – there would
be *no scope* for an order for security for costs. Note, too, that impecuniosity is *not, by
itself,* a qualifying claimant characteristic. It is *part* of the equation for conditions
(ii) and (v), above, and may be relevant if the court is in a position to exercise its
discretion, but impecuniosity alone is not enough to get the defendant over this first
hurdle.

Even if the first hurdle is surmounted, however, it does not necessarily follow
that the defendant will get security. There is a second. Such orders are *discretionary*
and to make the order the court must be satisfied that having regard to 'all the
circumstances' it is 'just' to do so. This is all the rule says. Older cases[14] attempted
to list the sorts of factors which the court might look at in order to do this. For
example: are there any special difficulties in enforcing a costs order? Is it obvious
(without conducting a mini-trial) that the merits favour one side or the other? How
clear is it that the defendant will win and not get his costs? Could the defendant
recover costs from someone other than the claimant? What impact would the
order have on the claimant? Would it stifle a genuine claim? Has the claimant's
impecuniosity been caused by the defendant's conduct at all? These are really just

being made in favour of 'a
defendant in any claim'.
Claimants who try to avoid
being claimants for these
purposes can also be
subject to an order: CPR, r
25.14. For the purposes of
this discussion I will just use
the descriptions 'claimant'
and 'defendant', as this is

8   the usual scenario.
    This is my expression,
    not the CPR's.

9   See wording of
    CPR, r 25, 13

10 As discussed in Ch.
    4 (Service outside the
    jurisdiction).

11 'Impecunious' is used as
    shorthand. The wording in

the rule is phrased in terms
of there 'being reason
to believe' the claimant
'will be unable to pay the
defendant's costs if so
ordered'.

12 'Nominal' essentially means
    that the claimant is just a
    frontman. Claimants suing
    in a representative capacity

common sense considerations focused on the purpose behind the application – the risk that the defendant, if successful, will not recover his costs.

In the post-CPR case of *Nasser v United Bank of Kuwait*[15] the court said that its discretion was to be exercised by applying the overriding objective (no surprises there) so as to afford a 'proportionate protection' against the 'difficulty identified' by the condition relied upon in making the application for security for costs. So, for example, if the claimant is resident outside the jurisdiction, how easy or difficult it would be to enforce a costs order will be especially relevant. If the claimant is an impecunious limited company, the court might be more focused on how to protect the defendant without stifling a genuine claim. Is the defendant being a bully? Did the defendant contribute to the company's financial difficulties?

Delay in making the application might also be relevant. Every case, and every application, will be determined on the basis of its individual facts.

An application for security for costs is a with notice application made to the Master or District Judge, as the case may be. The application notice must be supported by written evidence, setting out the basis for the application and facts relevant to the exercise of the court's discretion.

If the court is minded to make an order for security, the next question is: for how much? The first point to make is that the amount of security to be ordered is *entirely within court's discretion.* Having said that, the amount chosen should 'be neither illusory nor oppressive.'[16] A conventional approach has been to fix the amount of security at about $^2/_3$rds of the estimated costs up to the stage of proceedings for which security is ordered (so past as well as future costs can be included in the figure). It is common to order security in convenient stages, rather than one huge amount right up to end of trial (the case might settle, after all), but there is no hard and fast rule.[17] Orders should be case-specific.

---

are specifically excluded from the description.

13 It is not necessary to establish any particular motivation here, simply that whatever has happened to the assets have made them less accessible to a debtor.

14 See, especially, *Lindsay Parkinson and Co Ltd v Triplan Ltd* [1973] QB 609

15 [2002] 1 WLR 1868

16 *Hart Investments Ltd v Larchpark Ltd* [2008] 1 BCLC 589

17 The claimant may apply to discharge or vary an order for security. This would be appropriate if the order was wrongly granted in the first place or there has been a significant change in circumstances since the order was made. See e.g. *Gordano Building Contractors v Burgess* [1988] 1 WLR 890.

Do not lose sight of the fact that this is an order about security for *costs*. It is nothing to do with damages. Winning defendants do not, of course, get damages; they *avoid* paying them. But (other things being equal) they would normally be entitled to their costs from the losing claimant.[18]

Joint claimants can complicate matters, especially if one, say, is resident outside the jurisdiction, but the other is not. Assuming no other ground is relevant, it is clear that an order cannot be made against the claimant who lives in this country, since that person is not what we are calling a qualifying claimant. But would the court make an order against the other claimant who does come within CPR, r 25.12?

The courts get edgy about claimants who reside beyond the reach of the English (and European) courts, concerned that it is too easy for them to scurry away without meeting their litigation obligations, including payment of costs if they have lost or abandoned the case. This may be why they are head of the list of qualifying claimants! But does the fact that there is another claimant within the jurisdiction make it more or less likely that the order will be made against the one who is not? As you might expect the answer is that it depends on the circumstances, and in particular how confident the court is that the defendant will be able recover his costs from the resident claimant. Thus, it may be possible to get an order against the foreign claimant if the two claimants are not relying on the same cause of action or each claimant will be solely responsible for his own share of the defendant's costs (or it is impossible to predict the liability on costs). Conversely, it may not be appropriate to grant the order against the foreign claimant where both claimants are relying on identical causes of action and will be jointly responsible for costs, and there are sufficient funds to enforce against – if, in effect, the defendant could recover all of his costs from the claimant who is inside the jurisdiction.[19] In essence, the court has to balance the protection afforded the

---

18   See generally discussion in Ch. 18

19   See discussion in *Slazengers Ltd v Seaspeed Ferries International Ltd* [1987] 1 WLR 1197.

defendant by the claimant within the jurisdiction against concerns about allowing foreign claimants to bring actions here without giving security.

revision tips

- Remember that it is *defendants to any claim* who apply for orders for security for costs. Watch out especially for counterclaims, when roles are reversed! When dealing with any problem question in an assessment, make a quick note of who is doing what to whom.

- Focus on claimants who are non-resident or impecunious companies – these are the most common types of qualifying claimant against whom such orders are sought – both in practice and in assessments.

- Remember the two hurdles!

It is worth reading ...

The judgment of the Court of Appeal in *Spy Academy Limited v Sakar International Inc* [2009] EWCA Civ 985. Not the thriller its name implies, but still a good read. And a fine example of some of the issues that arise in the exercise of the court's discretion whether or not to make an order for security. And there is an order for specific disclosure in the story too, so it's two for the price of one!

CHAPTER 15

Part 36 and offers of settlement

A formal offer of settlement is something defendants are more apt to do than claimants, but claimants can and increasingly do make such offers as well. CPR, Part 36 now deals with the whole range of situations where a formal offer to settle a case might be made: by a claimant or by a defendant; before or after a claim has been commenced; where the relief sought is money and where it is not. These are known globally as 'Part 36 offers.'

As we have seen, much of the CPR is focused on getting parties to avoid unnecessarily resorting to, or prolonging litigation. They are, for example, asked to consider alternatives solutions, to focus on the real issues in dispute, to be open and cooperative in the conduct of litigation. Part 36 offers perform a vital part of this process by encouraging parties to settle their dispute at the earliest possible stage, rather than fighting it out to the bitter end. A party who receives a realistic offer of settlement will be motivated to accept it, because otherwise the risk is that the person making the offer ('offeror') will be awarded the costs incurred of continuing the litigation, if the person to whom the offer was made ('offeree') fails to achieve a better outcome at trial. This can be a very heavy price indeed.

Advising on the terms of an offer of settlement, and whether to accept or reject such offers, requires considerable professional skill and experience. At this point what is important is to understand how the Part 36 scheme works in principle, which is what this chapter aims to help you do. The system was rationalised in April 2007, when the current provisions came into operation.

It is useful to distinguish between offers made by defendants and offers made by claimants.

1. PART 36 OFFERS BY DEFENDANTS

The principle behind the Part 36 procedure is that a claimant should accept an 'acceptable' offer by the defendant to settle the case rather than proceed to trial regardless, thereby increasing the costs the defendant would have to pay when the claimant only wins at the end of the day what was earlier on offer. If a claimant fails to accept an 'acceptable' offer, the sanction is that he pays the costs of unnecessarily continuing.

For many years, in money claims,[1] defendants actually parted with their money when putting formal offers on the table. These were known as 'payments into court' and were abolished in 2007.[2] Now *only the offer* goes on the table, whatever the nature of the claim. Defendants thus make formal Part 36 offers to settle, in the proper form,[3] which must normally remain on the table for at least 21 days,[4] for the claimant to accept or not.[5]

In a nutshell this is how Part 36 works: if the claimant accepts the offer during this initial period, then all proceedings are stayed. The defendant will be required to pay the claimant's costs up to that period. If the claimant does not accept the offer, the case continues and the trial judge will *not be told* about the offer.[6] If at the end of the trial, the outcome for the claimant is more advantageous

---

1   Non-money claims were never susceptible to payments of money into court, so these always involved a formal written offer.

2   Transitional rules exist to deal with pre-April 2007 cases where payments into court had already been made. Special cases still requiring a payment into court are now covered by CPR, Part 37 (not 36)

3   CPR, r 36.2 and PD 36A, para.1

4   Assuming there are more than 21 days until trial: CPR, r 36.3(c)

5   These offers are not so much rejected, as not accepted.

6   There are exceptions in certain specialised cases, but this is an important general rule.

than what was on offer,[7] then costs would be apt to 'follow the event' in the normal way,[8] meaning that the losing defendant pays the winning claimant's costs. If, however, the outcome for the claimant is *no better or is worse* than what was on offer, the costs incurred *after* the offer was made (+ the initial 21 days) will be awarded against the otherwise successful claimant. From that point, the claimant will have to pay the defendant's costs – and, of course, bear his own.

Strategically, the amount of a defendant's Part 36 offer should tempt the claimant into compromising the case, without offering too much!

Here are a couple of points to note generally:

(i)   A defendant can make a Part 36 offer at *any stage* of proceedings (even during the pre-action phase and even during trial) and can *increase* the amount at any time.

(ii) A defendant's Part 36 offer is treated as including interest.

(iii) The claimant should be able to determine to what the offer relates and can seek clarification where necessary.[9] It is important to be clear about whether the offer is in full and final settlement of all claims, or just some of the claims, and whether it takes into account any counterclaims or interim payments which have been made. The offer must make clear the costs consequences of acceptance.

(iv) Usually, a defendant wants to offer the whole amount appropriate before the heaviest costs are incurred so as to take advantage of the costs protection. The earlier the realistic offer is made, the fuller the protection for the defendant. Having said that, it would be silly to make an offer without a fair degree of evidential information.

(v)   Normally offers are made and accepted under Part 36 without the

---

7   Where the claim is for money, this can usually be determined by comparing the amount on offer with the amount awarded (comparing like with like so far as interest on the sum is concerned), although other factors may come into play: See e.g. *Carver*

v BAA plc [2008] EWCA Civ 412. Comparing offer with outcome can be a lot more tricky with non-money claims.

8   All other things being equal, see *Carver*, ibid.

9   CPR, r 36.8(1)

intervention of the court. For example, it is the *exception, not the rule* for the claimant to need permission to accept a Part 36 offer. Examples include where the claimant is a child or otherwise acting under a legal disability[10] and where the trial has already started.[11]

BCP's Procedural Checklist 29 is a useful resumé of the procedural detail. What follows is an overview, looking at four different possible scenarios. Let's assume the defendant makes a Part 36 offer in a *money* claim, well before the trial date and complies with all necessary formalities:

(a) The first 21 days

There is initially a period of 21 days from the making of the offer (called the 'relevant period'), during which the claimant may accept the offer *and be assured of getting costs*. The claimant must notify the defendant in writing[12] that the offer is being accepted. It will follow that the claimant is entitled to 100% of his standard basis costs[13] up to date of serving the notice of acceptance – these would include, typically, the cost of getting counsel's opinion on whether to accept or not. The defendant *cannot* withdraw the offer (or change its terms to be less advantageous) during this period, unless the court gives permission.[14] Nor does the court have power to order payment of only a proportion of the claimant's costs.[15]

(b) After the 21 days (but before trial)

After the initial 21 days has expired, assuming the offer has not been withdrawn, the claimant may still accept it, subject to the parties' agreeing liability for costs. The claimant will not necessarily get costs incurred after the end of the initial 21 day period; quite the reverse in fact. The usual outcome would be that the claimant gets

---

10 So the court can ensure that the interest of the vulnerable claimant are being served: CPR, r 21.10

11 CPR, r 36.9(3)(d). Because some great revelation may have occurred at the trial which puts the offer in a new light.

12 There is no particular

format – a letter will do: CPR, r 36.9(1). The notice must also be filed with the court: PD 26, para.3.1. There is no equivalent procedure for rejecting an offer. Even a counter-offer does not necessarily amount to a rejection of a Part 36 offer, which can

remain on the table and capable of acceptance. See *Gibbon v Manchester City Council* [2010] EWCA Civ 726

13 See discussion of costs below at Ch. 18

14 CPR, r 36.3(5). An application for such permission would be made

his costs up to that point, but the defendant would normally be entitled to costs from the end of the initial 21 day period until the date of acceptance. Where the parties cannot agree, the court will make an order as to costs (including the costs of having to ask the court to make the order as to costs!)

Where a defendant's Part 36 offer has not been accepted by the end of the initial 21 day period, the defendant can withdraw it and/or make a new offer. No permission of the court is required.[16] Note that a withdrawn offer cannot give rise to an 'official' costs sanction under Part 36, but it can still be 'put into the mix' and taken into account in the court's wide discretion (as can any informal offer) in deciding final costs orders.[17]

(c) At trial

If a claimant wants to accept a Part 36 offer once the trial of the action has started, this brings into play two conflicting propositions. The first is that the claimant requires the court's *permission* to accept the offer *once the trial* has started. Maybe the claimant's case is not going so well, and it would be unjust to let him take advantage of an offer which he has spurned for so long. But the rules also require that in the normal course of events the *trial* judge must *not know* about any Part 36 offers which have been made. So how does a claimant ask for permission from the court without the court finding out that the offer has been made?

Ask another judge, is the short answer. Of course, if (as is commonly the case) the defendant does not object to the claimant accepting the Part 36 offer even at this late stage, then it is unlikely to cause a problem because the only remaining issue will be the question of costs. The defendant might object, however, if the trial has revealed unanticipated weaknesses in the claimant's case. This happened in the old case of *Gaskins v British Aluminium Co.*[18] After failing in his application to the

---

in accordance with Part 23 (PD 36, para.2.2(1)).

15   There is a deeming provision to this effect. See WB discussion at 36.10.1 and *Lahey v Pirelli Tyres Ltd* [2007] 1 WLR 998.

16   CPR, r 36.3. The claimant should be given written notice of the new offer. The new offer (whether better or worse than the previous one) will take effect once the claimant has been notified: CPR, r 36.2(2)(a).

17   See generally, discussion of costs in Ch. 18

18   [1976] 1 All ER 208

trial judge for permission to accept the payment-in (as it was then), the claimant then made a second application to the judge for a re-trial because he now knew about the fact of the payment-in. The Court of Appeal was not enamoured with this argument, especially as the only reason the trial judge found out about the payment into court was because the claimant had told him. They also pointed out that it would be strange if a claimant whose case is going badly at trial could get a new trial simply by seeking permission to accept the amount on offer, and if this is refused, necessarily getting an order for a re-trial. It was up to the judge to decide whether, all things considered, carrying on with the trial in such circumstances created an injustice.

This essentially remains the case, especially for an inadvertent disclosure of the fact of a Part 36 offer.[19] Even after an inappropriate disclosure at trial, the judge should think long and hard before ordering a new trial, and in particular about the expense and proportionality of such a course.[20] But where a claimant seeks permission to accept the defendant's offer after the trial has begun, the rules now suggest a simple solution – unless the parties are happy for the trial judge to deal with the matter, the claimant should simply apply to another judge.[21]

In the majority of cases, acceptance even at this late stage will be granted, although the court's discretion is unfettered and if the circumstances (and in particular a *change* in circumstances) warrant it, as in the *Gaskins* case, then permission will be denied.[22] If acceptance is allowed, either by consent or with the court's permission, the usual rule is that the claimant recovers costs up to the end of the initial 21 day period, and the defendant recovers costs thereafter – a claimant who has left it this long to accept the offer will end up paying a lot of money in costs!

---

19 *Garratt v Saxby* [2004] EWCA Civ 341
20 If the disclosure was intentional or clearly the fault of one party, and a new trial ordered, no doubt that party (or possibly his legal advisors) would be asked to pay (a considerable amount) for the wasted costs. Junior Counsel beware!
21 The same would apply to an application to withdraw the offer: PD 36, para.2.2 and 3.2
22 For a current case on this, see *Capital Bank plc v Stickland* [2004] EWCA Civ 1677
23 Assuming there was no other reason to deviate from the general rule that the winner gets his costs. See e.g. *Allison v Brighton & Hove City Council* [2005]

(d)   The claimant never accepts the offer

One used to talk about the need for the claimant to better or 'beat' the offer (or payment-in, as it used to be) in order to avoid the cost penalties of failing to do so. If the claimant recovered more in damages (even one penny more) than the amount on offer, it was more or less guaranteed that he would be entitled to all of his costs.[23] But if the claimant fell short of this mark, the penalty would kick in – the claimant would gets his costs up to the end of the initial 21 day period, but *thereafter* he would have to *pay* the defendant's costs (*and of course bear his own*), unless such an order were unjust. It is easy to see how serious this consequence can be – it can take a large bite out of a damage award.[24] And there can be some very hard cases, given the difference one penny can make.

The costs consequence remains essentially the same today, and the courts can still depart from the normal costs penalty if justice demands it.[25] But the vocabulary (for money claims) has changed somewhat. Instead of referring to a failure to 'better' the defendant's offer, the current expression is (the somewhat more amorphous) failure to obtain a judgment more 'advantageous' than that offer.[26] This has given the courts some scope for dealing more holistically, as it were, with the hard cases. There is really no problem if the offer was £5,000 and the claimant is awarded £10,000 at trial. No one would doubt that the claimant had won outright.

But what about a case like *Carver v BAA plc*?[27] In that case, the amount claimed by Ms Carver against her employers for an injury caused at work eventually climbed (unlike the faulty lift, which was the cause of her injury) to about £20,000. Liability was admitted; the issue in dispute was quantum. The defendants made interim payments and at least two Part 36 offers. Judgment was eventually given for just under £5,000, which amounted in effect[28] to only £51 more than the

---

EWCA Civ 548 (where the claimant exaggerated the claim and so got only 25% of costs in the pre-offer period). And see Ch. 18

24 Or consume it altogether!

25 By CPR, r 36.14(4), in deciding this question, the court will take all the circumstances into account, including the nature of the Part 36 offer, when it was made, what the parties knew at the time the offer was made, and any other relevant conduct of the parties.

26 CPR, r 36.14(1)

27 op.cit (footnote 7)

28 When comparing like with like and adjusting for interest.

defendant's Part 36 offer to settle. In the meantime, some £80,000 in costs had been incurred! The offer had been beaten in the 'pennies and pound sense', but was it 'more advantageous'? The Court of Appeal decided that the expression 'more advantageous' was 'more open-textured' than its predecessor and enabled the judge to consider: [29]

> A more wide-ranging review of all the facts and circumstances of the case in deciding whether the judgment, which is the fruit of the litigation, was worth the fight ... Litigation is time consuming and it comes at a cost, emotional as well as financial. Those are, therefore, appropriate factors to take into account in deciding whether the battle was worth it. Money is not the sole governing criterion.

The trial judge had decided that it had not been worth the extra financial and emotional cost of going to trial for an extra £50 and so the outcome was not more advantageous for Ms Carver. He thus decided that the appropriate order was that the claimant get her costs up to the end of the initial 21 day period, but thereafter no order as to cost was made, which meant that both parties had to pay for their own costs from that date.[30] The Court of Appeal upheld the order.

It can be difficult, of course, to put a price on emotional factors, and later judgments have expressed concern[31] about the subjective nature of the exercise as set out in *Carver*. In *Gibbon v Manchester City Council*[32] a note of caution was sounded about the court imposing its own views about the emotional consequences of litigation onto the parties or using *Carver* as a justification for a wide-ranging investigation in cases when, in financial terms, it is absolutely clear that the claimant has achieved a better outcome. Where, on the figures, this is obviously

---

29 op.cit., per Ward LJ, at p.123

30 This is a middle ground between one paying the other's costs as well as their own. The trial judge thought it was 'unjust' to go quite that far. See wording of CPR, r 36.14(2) and Ch. 18.

31 Especially Jackson J (as he then was) in *Multiplex Constructions (UK) Ltd v Cleveland Bridge UK Ltd* [2008] EWHC 2280 (TCC) and Jackson LJ (as he later became) in his *Review of Civil Litigation Costs* (see Ch. 18).

32 op.cit.(footnote 12)

so, then this will normally be the governing consideration.

Finally, remember that defendants can also make Part 36 offers in *non*-money claims. The process is just the same as for money claims,[33] but when one is not dealing with hard cash, it can be more challenging to determine, in any given case, whether a judgment at the end of a trial is more advantageous than an offer which was made, but never accepted. In such cases, the court simply has to look at the case in the round, a fact which Ward LJ noted in the *Carver* case. As he put it:[34]

> it is quite clear that in non-money claims, where there is no yardstick of pounds and pence by which to make the comparison, all of the circumstances of the case have to be taken into account. Why, therefore, should the rule be different where a money claim is involved.

One difference, of course, is that in a money claim, there is the financial result to put in the mix – in a non-money claim, there is not.

2. PART 36 OFFERS BY CLAIMANTS

Claimants can, and often do, make Part 36 offers themselves. In other words they can offer to settle the action on stated terms in exchange for not pursuing the case to trial. Indeed, a defendant's Part 36 offer which is not accepted may well be met with a claimant's own Part 36 offer (a formal counter-offer in effect).[35]

A claimant's Part 36 offer will be made and accepted just as any other Part 36 offer. The main difference is the costs consequence of a defendant not accepting an 'acceptable' offer by the claimant (and it is important to remember that the roles

---

33   Under the previous version of the Part 36 rules, there used to be a distinction between payments-in for money cases and offers for non-money cases. The latter did employ the notion of determining whether the outcome was more advantageous than the offer (or not), which then became applicable once payments-in were abolished and parties only ever made offers.

34   *Carver*, op.cit. p.123

35   But, curiously you might think, such a counter offer does not operate as a rejection of the first offer: CPR, r 36.9(2). And see *Gibbon case*, op.cit.

are reversed from the situation where the defendant makes the offer). If an offer is made and never accepted, and the outcome at trial is more advantageous to the claimant than his offer, various cost or interest 'penalties' may ensue – in effect because the defendant forced the claimant to litigate to the bitter end to get justice. Unless it thinks it unfair, the court will choose from a range of possibilities: a punitive rate of interest to be applied to the damage award and/or costs to be paid at the indemnity (rather than standard) rate for the period after the initial 21 days expired and/or interest on those costs.[36]

Fairness and proportionality should dictate what, if any, penalty is levied. In particular, a defendant who comes close to winning may have been perfectly justified in not accepting a claimant's offer.[37] But every case is different. In one, a chemist sued a former colleague at Boots[38] for libel after she had accused him of rape. He was never charged, but following an investigation his employers moved him to another branch. The claimant said the allegation was completely false and had caused severe damage to his reputation. He made a formal Part 36 offer to settle for £25,000 in damages. The defendant did not accept the offer and at trial the claimant was awarded £400,000(!). According to the newspaper report, costs were ordered to be paid at the indemnity rate.[39] Finally, bear in mind, that (as with defendant's offers) there may be reasons to depart from the normal costs order if the circumstances warrant it.

---

36 CPR, r 36.14 and generally Ch. 18
37 See e.g. *Daniels v Commissioner of Police for the Metropolis* [2005] EWCA Civ 312
38 The retail chemists
39 *Garfoot v Walker,* Independent, 8 February 2000

revision tips

- Have a look at Form N242A used for making Part 36 offers to settle

- Revisit Part 36 when revising costs orders

- Be confident about the implications of making and responding (or not) to Part 36 offers. This is fertile examination territory.

It is worth reading ...

The judgment of Ward LJ in *Carver v BAA plc* [2009] 1 WLR 113, which is a clear and enjoyable review of the evolution and purpose of Part 36 in the context of an interesting case where the claimant's 'victory' had come at a terrible cost. Few would doubt that the costs order in that case was a sensible one, but the element of uncertainty introduced by the decision caused consternation. In the conjoined appeals of *Gibbon v Manchester City Council; LG Blower Specialist Bricklayer Ltd v Reeves and another* [2010] EWCA Civ 726 the Court of Appeal considered this aspect of *Carver* (especially in the context of the second case, which suffered from an abundance of Part 36 offers!). The judgment of Moore-Bick LJ in that case is, again, very readable and easy to follow. He puts *Carver* in its place without doing any harm to common sense.

PART FIVE
trial matters

CHAPTER 16

Preparations for trial

Civil cases do not often go all the way to trial. Some are put down early by the court; most are compromised by the parties. Trials vary in their complexity, but one thing they all have in common is that they are very expensive. The cost of many trials will far exceed the expense of all the interim proceedings in the case put together!

If, however, the parties cannot agree a settlement, the dispute will have to be determined by the court. In such cases, there may be a number of pre-trial matters or preparations to bear in mind. These can include:

A. NOTICES

'Notices to admit' and 'notices to prove' further the overriding objective by helping to narrow the issues in a case in a cost-effective way. This shorthand is not very descriptive. To make it clearer, I will supply the missing element(s) (in brackets).

(a) Notice to admit (facts)

One party can serve on another a notice to admit such facts or part of his case as is set out in the notice. These tend to focus on what are *essentially uncontroversial matters*.

No application to the court is required. A party just serves the notice on his opponent (no later than 21 days before trial), setting out the facts to be admitted.[1]

---

1   CPR, r 3.18

To the extent that the facts are admitted, they cease to be an issue at trial.[2] To the extent they are not admitted, there is no sanction built into this specific provision, but the cost rules are wide enough to produce the result, as existed under the previous rules, that the party refusing to admit the facts in the notice may have to pay the costs of proving those facts at trial, regardless of the outcome of the case.

The cost rules require the court to have regard to the *conduct* of the parties when making an order for costs, including whether it was 'reasonable for a party to … contest a particular issue'.[3] Much will depend, therefore, on how silly or sensible it was not to admit the fact or facts in question. The procedure must not be used oppressively, or indeed unreasonably. In other words, parties should not ask their opponents to admit what is clearly a real issue in dispute. No costs consequences would follow when an opponent predictably refuses to make such an admission.

Suppose, for example, a claim in negligence following a car accident, the outcome of which will depend on how well those in control of the cars were driving at the time. To ask the defendant to admit his negligence would be ridiculous – that is the main issue in dispute. But if the defendant had failed to admit the fact of the accident itself, then (assuming it clearly happened as alleged), then serving on him a notice to admit this fact would be appropriate. If he does not admit it, the claimant will still have to prove it, but the defendant will be ordered to pay the costs of doing so, unless he can come up with a good reason for putting the claimant to proof of the fact.

(b) Notices to prove (the authenticity of documents)

The gist of this is that it is assumed, and one is *deemed* to admit, that documents *inspected on disclosure* by the other side have not been tampered with or otherwise fabricated. This is because, generally speaking, it is not the authenticity of a document which

---

2   The admissions can only be used against the party in the proceedings in which the notice was served and only by the party serving the notice: CPR, r 3.18(3)

3   CPR, r 44.5(3). And see generally Ch. 18

is at issue in any given case, but rather the document's evidential or legal effect. If, however, authenticity *is disputed*, a 'notice to prove' its authenticity must be sent to the disclosing party. This puts the disclosing party on notice that authenticity of those documents is in issue.[4]

B.   REFERENCES TO THE EUROPEAN COURT AND HUMAN RIGHTS QUESTIONS

These are two *different* considerations, and they must not be confused!

(a)   References to the European Court

Sometimes cases tried before our national courts raise issues about the application or interpretation of the laws of the European Community, by which (as members) we are bound. The intention is that these should be applied consistently throughout the European Union. If the domestic court in question cannot answer the question without doing so, a reference to the European Court of Justice in Luxembourg ('ECJ') may be necessary. The court would usually do this before the trial starts (as a preliminary issue) – in any event, if a reference is made, the domestic trial will be stayed until a ruling by the ECJ is given. Only a County Court or High Court judge can make an order of reference.

If the issue has already got to the highest court in the land[5] (usually the Supreme Court), then that court *must* make the reference unless the point has already been decided (and there is no need to re-refer, as it were) or it is obvious how the community law is to be applied. Lower courts *may* make a reference if it 'is necessary to enable it to give judgment'.[6] This discretion is quite wide.

A good example is the pub landlady in Portsmouth, Karen Murphy,[7] who has been taken to court by the English Premier League for screening football matches

---

4   CPR, r 32.19

5   The court from whom there is no further judicial remedy: Art 234(3) of the EC Treaty

6   Art 234(1) and (2).

7   See e.g. "Pub Landlady 1-0 up over cheaper TV football," Guardian, 4 February 2011.

via a Greek satellite instead of paying Sky, which holds the rights to broadcast in the UK. Sky's fees are considerably higher than those charged Ms. Murphy by the right's holder in Greece. The case began in the criminal (magistrate's) court, but the High Court became seized of the matter on appeal on a point of law. Because the case turns on laws governing 'freedom of movement of services' within Europe, the judge made a reference to the ECJ. The first step in the process is the opinion of the Advocate General (who effectively advises the Court), who has said that selling on the basis of 'territorial exclusivity' is an attack on the internal market in Europe. The case against Ms. Murphy will not be able to continue until the High Court finds out whether the full Court agrees (as they are apt to do). Until the ECJ gives its judgment on the question referred to it, the action against her will remain on hold.

For more detail on ECJ references, see generally CPR, Part 68 and accompanying Practice Direction.[8]

Human Rights Issues[9]

The effect of the Human Rights Act 1998 ('HRA 1998') is to make rights under the European Convention for the Protection of Human Rights and Freedoms ('Convention on Human Rights') 'directly enforceable' against 'public authorities', thus obviating the need for individuals to apply to the European Court of Human Rights.[10] 'Public authorities' include, but are by no means limited to, the courts, which under s 3 must minimise interference with the Convention, and interpret legislation so as to be compatible with it. Where a court is satisfied that a provision in primary legislation is not compatible with a Convention right, it may make a 'declaration of incompatibility.'

Lay clients are apt to find breaches of their human rights around every

---

8   Plus practitioner commentary in WB or BCP (Ch. 75)

9   BCP devotes an entire chapter to this subject (Ch. 88)

10   This is a very different jurisdiction to the European Court of Justice!

corner. But parties must be cautious to raise points only when appropriate.[11] The rights which are most likely to figure in civil litigation are Art 6 (right to fair trial), Art 8 (right to respect for private life), and Art 10 (freedom of expression).

Procedurally, note the following:

- Details of any human rights point raised must be set out in the statement of case (or appeal notice).[12]
- Claims for declarations of incompatibility may not be heard by a judge below the status of High Court Judge.[13]
- If there is a real prospect of a declaration of incompatibility being made, this is obviously a factor in deciding whether to transfer a case from the County Court to the High Court.[14]
- Declarations of incompatibility strike at Acts of Parliament, so the government has an interest which is protected by allowing the relevant minister to 'intervene'.[15] Appropriate notice must be given.[16]

It is very important *not to confuse* the rules designed to ensure that sufficient safeguards are in place when arguing a human rights point in the domestic courts, with the procedure required on those occasions when it is necessary to refer a point of EU law for adjudication by the ECJ. The latter is more akin to appealing a particular point to a higher authority; the former merely ensures that all interested parties are before the English court, where the human rights point will be argued before a judge of sufficient standing.

continues .../

---

11 See e.g. *Williams v Cowell* [2000] 1 WLR 187
12 PD 16, para.15.1
13 PD 2B, para.7A(2)
14 CPR, r 30.3(2)(g)

15 Another means by which parties are sometimes added to proceedings. CPR, r 19.4A(2)

16 CPR, r 19.4A(1)

C.   TRIAL ARRANGEMENTS

When a case is listed for, or is approaching trial, the court may have to make decisions (in consultation with the parties) about any number of things, such as whether there are any preliminary issues to be dealt with (for example, if a disputed point of law is particularly relevant to the outcome or there is a reference to the ECJ); whether there is any reason why the trial should not be conducted in public, as is the general rule;[17] and how the trial itself should 'play out.' This latter is called the trial 'timetable' and involves considerations of how long should be spent conducting various aspects of the trial, including speeches, reception of expert evidence and the extent needed for cross-examination. Decisions may need to be made about the reception of certain evidence.[18] The parties can express views on these in the pre-trial checklist; in multi-track cases, such decisions will usually be made on a pre-trial review. Have a quick look at BCP's checklist 28.

D.   TRIAL BUNDLES

Trial 'bundles' should be filed by the claimant, who is responsible for their preparation.[19] The parties should agree the contents, so far as this is possible. Rival bundles are never lodged. Unless there is some ruling or order to the contrary, all the documents in the bundle are admissible as evidence of their contents.[20] Have a look at PD 39A, para.3 which sets out the requirements for trial bundles, including what should be included in them and their presentation. The idea is that all participants have easy access to the relevant documents in the case.

E.   SKELETON ARGUMENTS

We have seen that these are used for the more complex interim applications. They are also required for High Court trials[21] and are often a good idea for those in the

---

17   CPR, r 39.2

18   For example, evidence by deposition. See generally Ch. 17

19   CPR, r 39.5(2)

20   Where possible, originals of all relevant documents should be in the bundle: PD 39, para.3.3

21   *Practice Direction (Civil Litigation: Case Management)* [1995] 1 WLR 262

County Courts. Skeleton arguments allow the judge to do effective pre-reading and focus the mind of the advocate who prepares it. They are not, however, a substitute for effective questioning and oral advocacy.

revision tips

- Be careful not to confuse references to the European Court of Justice with the raising of human rights arguments in domestic trials.
- Have a look at what is on a pre-trial checklist. This is Form N. 170 and can be found on the WB online service via Westlaw.

It is worth reading ...

The judgments in *Williams v Cowell* [2000] 1 WLR 187, an interesting case about a bi-lingual Welshman who refused to speak English in court (even though it was his second language). He claimed that being forced to do so violated his human rights. There is a heartfelt plea from the judges (one of whose surnames is Judge!) about not turning trials into 'human rights seminars.'

CHAPTER 17

Evidential matters in civil cases

By and large whether a case succeeds or fails at trial will depend on the facts of the case. What view the court takes on these will in turn depend on the quality of the evidence before it. It is therefore very important to have a firm grasp of the rules and principles about the admissibility and reception of evidence in civil cases, not only for any examination you will be required to pass (that goes without saying) but also as a foundation for embarking on practice with confidence.

Of necessity this is a quick review of a vast subject. For more depth and detail, consult the text of your choice.[1] If the truth be told, criminal evidence is the more entertaining branch of the subject, and most books will concentrate on it. BCP, however, usefully has an entire chapter devoted to civil evidence,[2] written by Adrian Keane, lead author of the *Modern Law of Evidence*.[3] And for a really enjoyable and enlightening introduction for the intelligent beginner, I recommend Christopher Allen's *Practical Guide to Evidence*.[4]

There are two important principles to bear in mind when considering the evidential issues in this chapter.

(i) Whether an item of evidence is admissible will depend in the first instance on the law of evidence. Evidence must be *relevant*, but it

---

1   And do make a choice if you can, if learning the subject for the first time. Textbooks differ in their approach, and you may find that one works better for you than another. It is like cars – take a test drive before committing yourself to a major purchase!

2   Ch. 47
3   Keane, A. et al, (2010) 8th Edn. Oxford University Press.

4   Allen, C. (2008) 4th Edn. Routledge-Cavendish.

will only be admissible if, in addition, it is *not excluded* by any of the exclusionary rules of evidence[5]. These are considered below.

(ii) The CPR gives the court an *overarching discretion to exclude* otherwise admissible evidence, if this is in keeping with the overriding objective. The rules specifically provide that the court may control the evidence in a case by giving directions as to *what evidence it wants to hear, on what issues and in what form.*[6]

This chapter covers a lot of territory. For the sake of convenience, I have divided it into three sections: pre-trial evidential considerations; admissibility and reception of special categories of evidence; and witnesses and the course of testimony.

1.   PRE-TRIAL EVIDENTIAL CONSIDERATIONS

A.   BURDEN AND STANDARD OF PROOF IN CIVIL CASES

Burden of Proof

The burden of proof is the obligation imposed on a party to prove a fact in issue. A party who fails to discharge this burden will lose on the issue in question. This is often referred to as the 'legal burden' and should be *distinguished* from the so-called 'evidential burden', which is not a burden of proof at all.

In civil cases, the pleadings will tell us what facts are in issue – they will consist of all of the matters (not admitted by the defendant) which a claimant must prove in order to succeed in his case, plus any matters raised by the defendant (not admitted by the claimant) which must be proved in order to succeed in the defence and/or any counterclaim. The facts in issue are thus partly determined by the *substantive law* (for

---

5   The various rules of evidence tend to focus on what cannot be admitted at trial, not what can.

6   CPR, r 32.1

7   If you put the statements of case side by side, and contrast and compare, it should be clear what the issues in dispute are.

The particulars of claim should state concisely the facts relied upon in formulating the cause of action and the remedy sought, including any interest (CPR, r 16.4). The defence must respond comprehensively and make clear what is

admitted, what is denied (setting out the defence version of events) and which allegations the claimant is otherwise required to prove. (CPR, r 16.5). If necessary, a claimant may 'reply' to the defence, but this will only be necessary if an

example, the constituent elements of a breach of contract claim), and partly by the *statements of case*.[7]

It is important to understand that only *one* party bears a burden of *proof* on any given fact in issue.

In civil cases the incidence of the legal burden is determined by reference to various, sometimes competing, principles.[8] The first general principle is: "He who asserts must prove". So if, for example, the claimant sues in negligence, it will be for him to assert in the particulars of claim, and thus prove (except as admitted by the defendant) the nature of the duty of care owed to him by the defendant; breach of that duty by the defendant; and the recoverable damage suffered as a result. And, if, for example, the defendant alleges contributory negligence, the burden is on him to prove this. In 99% of cases, the principle "He who asserts must prove"[9] tells us in a civil case where the burden of proof lies.

But sometimes, especially when dealing with contractual clauses which limit or exclude liability, it can be difficult to know who is asserting what. There may also be a particular outcome which the court, in the circumstances, thinks is fair. In such cases, other principles come into play, including: "It is more difficult to prove a negative than a positive" and "Place the burden on the party who can more easily discharge it."

In the case of *Constantine (Joseph) SS Line Ltd v Imperial Smelting Corp. Ltd* [10] the court was unable to make a finding as to the cause of an explosion on a ship, at which point the allocation of the burden of proof on this issue (was it caused by negligence or not?) became decisive, as is the way with these cases.[11] The House of Lords, concerned to arrive at a just result, held that the charterers bore the burden of proving the ship owner's negligence because it was difficult, if not impossible, for the ship owner to prove a negative – that they were not negligent.

---

issue has been raised which was not dealt with in the particulars of claim. Replies are not intended to reiterate allegations.(CPR, r 16.7).

8　There are some exceptional cases where special rules apply, as where a specific burden of proof is imposed

by certain clauses in a standard form contract.

9　Or should have asserted in the case of a poorly drafted statement of case: see *BHB Billiton Petroleum Ltd v Dalmone SpA* [2003] EWCA Civ 170 which said that the pleadings are a guide to what is

being asserted, but not necessarily definitive.

10　[1945] AC 154

11　Although courts should resolve cases in this way only as a last resort and not as an excuse for indecision: *Stephens v Cannon* [2005] EWCA Civ 222.

As Viscount Simon LC put it:[12]

Does the application of the doctrine require that the owners should affirmatively prove that those on board were keeping a good lookout, were obscuring lights, were steering as directed and so forth?

Ease of proof is the principle which unites the *Constantine* case with that of *Levison v Patent Steam Carpet Cleaning Co.*,[13] but the result was different. The difference is sometimes explained by the fact that the latter is a bailment case, but in reality this was a device to achieve justice in the case. The claimants had sent an expensive Chinese carpet to the defendants for cleaning. The defendants failed to return it and concluded that it had been stolen. They relied on a clause in their contract with the claimants limiting their liability for loss, the effect of which was to make them liable for £44 rather than the £900 the carpet was worth. Lord Denning MR hated exclusion clauses on the best of days, and they were only operative if the party relying on them had not been in 'fundamental breach' of contract. The question then arose: was it for the Levisons to prove the defendant's breach or for the defendants to disprove it? The Court of Appeal held that it was for the defendants to prove that they had not been guilty of a fundamental breach, because they could more easily discharge the burden. The Levisons did not know what went on at the cleaner's premises; the defendants were the ones who knew what had happened to the carpet once they took possession of it and so were better placed to show that they had handled the carpet properly (or not, as it turned out).

The approach to this issue, then, is largely pragmatic and one of fairness in different circumstances. Thus, on those rare occasions (and they *are* rare) when "He who asserts must prove" does not provide the answer to the question (or seems to answer it in the wrong way, perhaps), the court will be apt to find it by asking which

---

12   op.cit. at pp.161-2
13   [1978] 1 QB 69

party would find it easier to discharge the burden of proof on the issue in question, even if that involves proving a negative.

Standard of proof

The standard of proof in civil cases is the 'balance of probabilities'.[14] This is so even where the allegation is so serious as to amount to the commission of a criminal offence (for example, fraud or assault). The courts have wrestled over the years with how to deal with such allegations in a civil context, but it now seems clear (if it was not before) that *the standard stays the same*, however serious the allegation. Previous attempts, including that of Lord Nichols in *Re H and others*[15] to distinguish between the standard of proof (which is immutable) and the strength of evidence which might be required to meet that standard were frowned upon (perhaps a bit unfairly) in *Re B (Children) FC*,[16] another child abuse case where nobody's evidence could be believed on some key issues of fact. The court was at pains to say, in slightly exasperated tones,[17] that:

> Once and for all, there is only one civil standard and that is proof that a fact in issue more probably occurred than not ... Inherent probabilities are simply something to be taken into account, where relevant, in deciding where the truth lies ... [and] neither the seriousness of the allegation nor the seriousness of the consequences should make any difference to the standard of proof to be applied in determining the facts.

'Evidential burden'

The evidential burden is *not* a burden of *proof*. It is an obligation to put forward enough evidence on a particular issue to allow the question to go before the fact finder for a decision; the burden is discharged when there is sufficient evidence to

---

14 This translates into proving that it is 'more probable' or 'more likely' than not that something happened.

15 [1996] AC 563 (a gruesome child abuse case).

16 [2008] 2 FLR 141 (UKHL 35), [2009] 1 AC 11

17 Lord Hoffmann quoted here, at ibid. [13]. In an earlier case he had given a useful example by saying that as a matter of common sense it would take more compelling evidence to satisfy the court that "the creature walking in Regent's park was, more likely than not, to be a lioness, than to be satisfied to the same standard that it was an Alsatian." *Secretary of State for the Home Department v Rehman* [2001] 1 AC 153, at [55].

justify, as a possibility, a favourable finding. The evidential burden is a low threshold – certainly discharging it does not by any stretch mean the legal burden of proof will be discharged. A party bearing a legal burden of proof on an issue, who cannot even discharge the evidential burden on that issue, will lose, without the other side having to say anything.[18]

By and large the party with the legal burden on an issue also bears the evidential burden, so they tend to go together as a twin-set. The are several exceptions in criminal cases where a defendant has an obligation, when raising certain defences,[19] to put forward sufficient evidence to make the issue a live one; but the burden of proof remains squarely on the Prosecution to disprove that defence beyond reasonable doubt. The only situation in a *civil case* where the legal burden of proof and an evidential burden might be 'split' between parties in a similar way is by virtue of the operation of a rebuttable presumption 'of the evidential variety',[20] where adducing some evidence to the contrary is all it takes to rebut the presumption operating in favour of the person with the legal burden of proof. This is discussed in the next section.

Presumptions

So-called 'presumptions' can have an effect on the burden and standard of proof. They operate, to a greater or lesser degree, by allowing fact finders to draw certain conclusions ('the presumed fact') for other facts ('the primary facts'). One tends to refer to three 'types' of presumption, although only one is a 'real' presumption.

(i) 'Presumption of fact'

This is not a presumption so much as an inference to be drawn, as a matter of common sense, from certain facts. Such presumptions are really just examples of commonly

---

18 Except "I win!" Submissions of no case to answer are much more prevalent in criminal cases than in civil, where such actions would likely be struck out or summarily determined well before trial.

19 For example, self-defence, duress.

20 See below

recurring circumstantial evidence. The way these operate is that if the primary fact is proved, the presumed fact *may* be presumed. There is *no compulsion*.

Examples from the criminal law include notions like the 'doctrine of recent possession', which is an inference to be drawn from the fact that a person is in possession of recently stolen goods. An example more germane to civil cases is the so-called 'continuance of life' which allows a fact-finder to conclude that if a person was alive on a certain date then, unless there is evidence to suggest otherwise, that person was still alive on a later date. This depends, of course, on how long the period is and how well the person was in the first place.

This presumption can also work in individual cases. Remember the case of the missing canoeist who 'came back from the grave'?[21] He was presumed dead on the basis of the alleged circumstances of his disappearance (parts of a broken canoe, clothes found washed up on the beach and so forth) and the fact that he had apparently not reappeared, made this a logical inference.[22] The coroner had been under no compulsion to agree, however, because less than seven years had passed.[23]

(ii) *Irrebuttable (or conclusive) presumption of law*
This is not a presumption so much as a rule of substantive law. It works like this: if the primary fact is proved, the presumed fact *must* be presumed. It is compulsory. This kind of presumption is incapable of being rebutted.

One good example of this in civil cases is the deeming provision regarding service of the claim form[24], which effectively creates an irrebuttable presumption of due service. Another is s 13 Civil Evidence Act 1968, which says that in the context of defamation proceedings, a person convicted of an offence shall be *conclusively* taken to have committed that offence. This is a rule to avoid re-running criminal cases in the context of the civil claim.[25]

---

21 See e.g. Telegraph online for 4 December 2007, which includes a video of him looking very much alive!

22 As it happened he hid in the house next door while his wife waited to claim the life insurance money, then they both fled to Panama.

23 At which point the 'presumption of death' could have been relied upon. See below.

24 See generally Ch. 4

25 Civil Evidence Act 1968, s 13(1)

(iii) Rebuttable presumptions of law

These are true presumptions, of which there are many examples.[26] Their purpose is two-fold: (a) to *save time* and effort when in 99 cases out of 100 the presumed fact follows from the primary fact (for example, the 'presumption of legitimacy') or (b) to *resolve a dilemma* (for example, the 'presumption of death'). As to the latter, these are only applicable when there really is a dilemma. If the court will make the inference you want from the facts at hand, you do not need to resort to a dilemma-resolving presumption!

Rebuttable presumptions operate as follows. If the primary fact is proved, the presumed fact *must* be presumed, *unless* there is evidence to the contrary.

A rebuttable presumption casts a burden on the party against whom it operates. How onerous this burden is (that is to say, how much evidence is needed to rebut the presumption) varies from presumption to presumption. In some cases, the presumption can be displaced if *some* evidence to the contrary is produced (a so-called 'evidential presumption'); in others, it can only be displaced on the balance of probabilities (a so-called 'persuasive presumption'). As a broad generality, the greater the social interest in the state of affairs to which the presumption is directed, the harder it is to rebut it. For example the presumptions of legitimacy and marriage are harder to rebut than the presumption of proper working order, since the law is reluctant to brand people harlots and bastards!

As one example, the presumption of death works like this: if there is no acceptable evidence that a person was alive at some time during a continuous period of seven years or more, that person will be presumed to have died at some time during that period if it can be proved that:

- people exist who would be likely to have heard from him/her during that period;

---

26 See generally discussion at
BCP, para.47.11 to 47.20

- they have not heard of him/her during that period;

and

- all appropriate enquiries have been made[27]

Note that the presumption is merely that death occurred at the latest by the end of the seven years. It says *nothing about the date of death*. It would seem that, in civil cases anyway, this is an 'evidential presumption',[28] which would be consistent with the law being reluctant to declare dead, people who may be alive! But there is no clear authority, perhaps because any substantial evidence that the person was alive would stop the presumption from operating in the first place.

Presumptions of this kind may conflict. If they are of equal strength (for example both 'evidential presumptions'), they are thought to cancel each other out, so that the case is determined on the basis of the ordinary rules regarding the burden of proof, although again the court will have regard to policy considerations.

B. PRIVILEGE AND RELATED CONCEPTS

Many of the exclusionary rules of evidence have developed out of a desire to ensure a fair trial. The justification for the principles relating to privilege and public interest immunity, however, have nothing to do with this motivation, important though it is, but with another competing objective which is given priority, namely that there are occasions when the benefit in withholding evidence from inspection by the court or an opponent should prevail over the public interest in openness and putting all of one's 'cards on the table.' For this reason, it impinges on the rules about disclosure of evidence.

It is important to distinguish (a) between the various forms of privilege and (b) between privilege and public interest immunity claims. There are essentially three

---

27 *Chard v Chard* [1956] P 259
28 See *Prudential Assurance Co v Edmunds* (1877) 2 APP Cas 487

types of privilege: privilege against self-incrimination; legal professional privilege (which itself takes two forms); and 'without prejudice' communications (often referred to as a privilege, but perhaps more accurately described as a 'protection'). We have considered the first of these when discussing search orders, so the discussion below will focus on the others.[29]

Public interest immunity is not a privilege as such – it imposes a *duty*, not a right to withhold disclosure and gives the court power to exclude evidence on the grounds that its disclosure would damage the public interest. It can and should be distinguished from legal professional privilege.

The litigation context in which these issues usually arise in the first instance is on disclosure of documents and other evidence. The basic principles are as follows:

Legal professional privilege

There are two 'heads' of legal professional privilege. It is important to distinguish between them:

Head 1: 'Legal advice privilege'

Confidential communications between professional legal advisor and client (or any person representing that client) made in connection with the giving or receiving of legal advice to that client are protected by legal professional privilege. *This is so whether or not litigation is contemplated.*[30] Here the communication is a two-way street and can be thought of in the form of a straight line, with the client at one end and the legal advisor at the other.

Legal advice is not confined simply to telling a client about the law; conversely, not all advice (and certainly not every communication) is privileged.[31] In complex cases, issues can arise about who is a client (if not an individual) and what is legal (as

---

29 For special rules about the protection (or not as the case may be) of journalist's sources, see Contempt of Court Act 1981, s 10.

30 Compare this with Head 2.

31 See the interesting list in BCP, para.48.47

opposed, say, to financial[32]) advice. But the essential idea is straightforward enough. The reason for this privilege, of course, is that it is in the public interest that people should be able to get legal advice in complete confidence. Other parties are therefore not entitled to know of the content of such communications.

Head 2: 'Litigation privilege'

This brings a third person into the equation. *Confidential communications* between a professional legal advisor and/or his client *and a third party*[33] are privileged where the *dominant* purpose in creating the document (or making the communication) is to use it or its contents to obtain legal advice or help in the conduct of *litigation* which at that time was at least reasonably in prospect.[34] The typical example is an expert's report. So long as the right person (i.e. the person commissioning the document) has the right motivation (litigation), then it is immaterial whether the litigation actually takes place. Here the lines of communication form a triangle, involving three parties instead of two.

The rationale here is that parties should be free to *conduct* litigation confidentially. A party thus need not produce such documents for inspection at the disclosure stage. This can be useful when, for example, litigants receive an unfavourable report from their own expert. As we shall see, such evidence as one proposes to *rely* on is routinely disclosed pre-trial[35] in the interests of openness.[36] But a party who does not want to rely on such a privileged document, can bin it.[37]

Without Prejudice protection

In a sense this can be viewed as something of a 'mirror image' of litigation privilege, because it also involves the solicitor or client and another person – specifically the other party to the litigation. *Without prejudice communications (oral or written) made in a*

---

32 See e.g. *Three Rivers District Council v Bank of England* (No 6) [2004] UKHL 48, [2005] 1 AC 610

33 Not in the Part 20 sense, of course.

34 *Waugh v British Railway Board* [1080] AC 521

35 But usually post-disclosure of documents

36 In effect, a party must waive his privilege in such documents if he wants to rely on it at trial.

37 Although it might well provoke a re-evaluation of the case!

genuine attempt to seek a settlement of a dispute, are protected from disclosure *to the court* at trial (the other side, of course, knows all about it). The purpose of this rule is to encourage open and effective negotiation by removing the fear that any admissions apparently made during the negotiations will be used at trial against the party who made them, the attempts to settle having (rather obviously) failed. There is thus a focus on protection from the revelation of *concessions or admissions,* although most attempts to by-pass the rule by cutting and pasting around the admissions in otherwise protected correspondence have failed.[38]

The court will look at the substance, rather than the form of the communication, so that the over-enthusiastic use the words 'without prejudice' (usually written in bold letters by amateurs) does not necessarily afford protection to the document (and vice versa – a document may be protected even if those words are not used). It is the *purpose* behind the document which matters. Note that, in effect, the protection extends to negotiations which *fail.* If or to the extent that they *succeed and the case settles,* the protection has served its purpose, and so the without prejudice communications leading up to that settlement would now be admissible to prove, where relevant, the *terms of the compromise agreement.*[39] Otherwise, the longstanding principle of 'once privileged, always privileged'[40] would seem to apply; the protection is only to be lost in exceptional circumstances.

Public Interest Immunity ('PII')

This is a very different concept to those discussed above. Certain documents *must* be withheld from disclosure and/or inspection if it is found that revealing their existence or contents (or both) would be injurious to the public interest. Public interest immunity is thus a *duty, not a privilege* and claims fall into two types: class claims (a claim that all documents of a certain class need to be protected) and individual claims (a claim

---

38 See e.g. *Re New Gadget Shop Ltd* [2005] EWHC 1606 (CH)

39 As in 'the claimant promises to discontinue the action in consideration of the defendant agreeing to pay £X and pay the claimant's costs.'

40 *Calcraft v Guest* [1898] 1QB 759

that a specific document needs protection because of its contents). The former are regarded more suspiciously than once was the case.

Typically, a relevant minister provides a certificate stating the grounds for objecting to disclosure and/or inspection. The certificate is not conclusive and it is for the *court* in each instance to determine where the public interest lies.[41] To this end the court must *balance* the public interest in concealment against the public interest in the fair and open administration of justice.

It is for the party seeking inspection to show why the public interest lies in openness. This can be made difficult by CPR, r 31.19(1), which says a PII claim may be made *without notice*, and any order made on such application must *not*, unless the court orders otherwise, be served on any other person. Thus it strikes both at disclosure *and* inspection, unlike legal professional privilege which prevents inspection but not disclosure as such.[42] With a PII claim, the other side may have no idea what is going on, which can have obvious human rights implications.[43]

2. ADMISSIBILITY AND RECEPTION OF SPECIAL CATEGORIES OF EVIDENCE

A. OPINION EVIDENCE

As a *general rule*, opinion evidence is not admissible at trial. Witnesses must normally confine themselves to telling the court about the facts, and not express opinions about those facts. To do so would either be considered an irrelevance (unless the state of mind of the holder of the opinion is pertinent) or an intrusion on the role of the judge[44] deciding the case, whose opinion is really the only one that matters.

There are, however, some *important exceptions* to this general rule. One relates

---

41 *Conway v Rimmer* [1968] AC 910

42 Since its existence appears, however obliquely described, on the disclosure list. See generally Ch. 9

43 See discussion at BCP, para.48.69

44 Most civil cases are decided by a single judge, but there are or still may be juries in some cases, most notably libel actions: see CCA 1984, s 66/SCA 1981, s 69

to the opinions of other tribunals; the others, to the opinions of certain kinds of witnesses.

Previous judgments

Judgments of a court are a form of opinion evidence, since a finding of guilt or a finding of negligence, for example, is really nothing more than the opinion of the tribunal trying the case. Before statutory intervention, there was a rule that verdicts in previous criminal or civil cases were not admissible in subsequent cases as evidence of the facts on which they were based. This is known as the rule in *Hollington v Hewthorn*.[45] The logic of that decision is that the opinion of a previous court on facts which were not rehearsed in front of the present tribunal are irrelevant (in accordance with the general exclusionary rule). It is the opinion of the present tribunal that counts.

This decision had its obvious drawbacks and so was reversed for civil cases by the Civil Evidence Act 1968, s 11. This creates a rebuttable presumption that a convicted person (whether convicted on a guilty plea or not) *committed the offence(s)* in question, 'unless the contrary is proved'. A very typical example of the use of s 11 would be in a personal injuries action arising out of a car accident. If the defendant driver had, in respect of the same accident, been convicted of dangerous driving, this would be cogent evidence of his negligence, since the criminal standard of proof is higher than the civil standard.

For precisely this reason, it is very difficult, but not impossible, to discharge the burden of rebutting this presumption. According to Lord Diplock in *Hunter v Chief Constable of West Midlands Police*,[46] although the standard to be met in proving the contrary was the 'balance of probabilities', in the face of a conviction after a full hearing this is "likely to be an uphill task".[47]

---

45 *Hollington v Hewthorn and Co Ltd* [1943] KB 587

46 [1982] AC 529

47 ibid, at 544

The conviction must be pleaded in the particulars of claim. Details of the date and type of conviction, and a statement of its effect, including the issue in the case to which it relates, must be included.[48]

Non-expert witnesses: perception evidence

An ordinary witness will be allowed to express an opinion as a way of conveying facts which were personally perceived, where breaking down what was observed into its constituent factual parts would be difficult, if not impossible. It is useful to think of this as *'perception' evidence*. Examples include: "He was drunk", "The car was very old", "The weather was stormy." Where the 'opinion' best conveys the facts perceived, it will be admissible.[49] This is a common sense exception, which is about ordinary witnesses describing ordinary things. It is very different from the next exception.

Expert witnesses

Admissibility

Often issues raised in cases require a level of understanding which ordinary people (including judges) do not possess, unless they have special training. For example, if the claim were against a surgeon for carrying out an operation negligently, it would be difficult for the judge to know what a specialist, carrying out such an operation, would (or should) have done in the circumstances, which will be important in deciding liability. The judge is a judge, not a doctor. This is where the important role of the expert witness comes into play.

As an exception to the general rule, therefore, *relevant expert opinion* evidence is admissible where needed to decide a case. It is important to appreciate the necessary requirements for admissibility. The first is that the court *needs*[50] the assistance of the

---

48 CPR, PD 16, para.10.1

49 Civil Evidence Act 1972

50 See e.g. *Liddell v Middleton* [1996] PIQR p36 CA on when accident reconstruction experts would and would not be necessary.

expert to do its job properly, because the matter at issue is beyond normal human behaviour and experience. The second is that help comes from a *suitably qualified expert* competent in a *relevant and recognised area of expertise*. How experts gain their expertise is not usually important, so long as the expertise has been acquired, although these days most experts will be 'professionally' qualified. But it is important to remember that an expert may only give expert opinion evidence on matters within his expertise. So in our example, a doctor is a good start, but not good enough. The appropriate expert would be a surgeon (usually a consultant) with recognised expertise in the specific type of operation carried out on the claimant – in effect, the sort of person the claimant may, with hindsight, have wished operated on him.

Remember that expert witnesses are expressing opinions on certain facts in the case at hand (such as, in our example, what actually happened during the operation in question). It is important to appreciate that those underlying facts must themselves be proved by admissible evidence. These are called the 'primary facts' and this is known as 'laying the proper groundwork.' Having said that, the research or reports or other materials ('secondary facts') which an expert uses or relies upon in forming and expressing to his opinion need not themselves be admissible, but will be made available for the court and the other parties to examine.

Cases often turn on the nature and quality of the expert evidence. Expert evidence tends to trump non-expert evidence (if the issues calls for expertise).[51] If each side has an expert, whose evidence conflicts, it is fairly obvious that a judge will have to choose whose is to be preferred. But bear in mind that it is ultimately the judge, not the experts, who decide the case, and expert evidence (even where the expert has been jointly instructed, so there is only one speaking to the issue) can be rejected if there are sensible grounds for doing so. This will be rare, but it happens.[52]

---

51   This does not always follow. See e.g. *Fuller v Strum* [2002] 1 WLR 1097, where the evidence of attesting witnesses to a (contested) Will was preferred over a handwriting expert.

52   See e.g. *Armstrong v First York Ltd* [2005] 1 WLR 2751

Reception

One of the most significant procedural changes wrought by the CPR occurred in the area of expert evidence. In the old days, parties brought along their own experts (who may have had varying degrees of interest in the overall justice of the case) to slug it out in court against each other – the court exercised little control over the process. The situation is completely different today. Not only does the court control the pace of litigation, but it also manages the amount of, and manner in which any evidence is received – this is *particularly so as regards expert evidence.*

This dramatic reversal of the former freedom of litigants to conduct their cases as they wished was brought about by the very strong feeling that the 'bonfire of the vanities' arising from the widespread, adversarial use of experts had become a lengthy and costly exercise in bias.[53] So, for most straightforward, lower value claims, out goes the 'tame' expert witness for both sides; in comes the single expert, either jointly selected and instructed or court-appointed.[54]

Expert evidence is not usually allowed in small claims track cases, so the discussion below concentrates on fast track and multi-track cases. As we have seen,[55] directions concerning expert evidence will usual be made when allocating a case, or at a case management conference.[56]

The first point to make is that 'no party may call an expert or put in evidence an expert's report without the *permission* of the court'.[57] If there is no order, there is no expert. Secondly, the court is under a duty to restrict evidence to 'that which is *reasonably required* to resolve the proceedings'.[58] The burden will lie on the party seeking to rely on expert evidence to justify doing so and the principle of *proportionality* will be an important consideration. The court will have to balance the desire to save costs against the requirement to do justice.[59]

In larger, more complex claims, *competing experts* on each side will often

---

53 Experts have always owed a duty to the court in expressing their views, but one-sided instructions undermined their independence.

54 This concept was borrowed from family law cases dealing with care of children.

55 See generally Ch. 13

56 Experts should be served with a copy of any direction or order which affects them: PD 35, para.6A

57 CPR, r 35.4

58 CPR, r 35.1

59 This is an in-built tension in the overriding objective

be necessary and so are still permitted. This is most likely to happen in *multi-track* cases.[60] But in smaller claims, the value of two opposing experts will not ordinarily justify the expense, particularly where they are merely being used to lend 'authority' to facts which can be proved in other, more straightforward ways – for example by admitting certain readily understandable statistics. In many cases where the question, "What is good practice?" is capable of being answered by one knowledgeable person in the relevant field, the court will not need or want to sample from a buffet of experts' opinions – the fixed price menu will do. Joint instruction of a mutually acceptable expert – the so-called single joint expert[61] – is the norm in *fast track* cases.[62]

The single jointly instructed expert
Pre-trial

This is what is usually ordered in a fast track case.[63] The parties may already have agreed to this, which the court can sanction, or the court can make a direction on its own initiative, even if the parties do not want it!

Such an order requires that the parties participate both in the selection and the instruction of the expert.[64] If possible the parties should try and agree a single set of instructions for the expert, but if this is not possible, they should disclose to each other the (different) instructions they have given the expert.[65] The expert's report itself,[66] of course, is also disclosed to both parties. If necessary, written questions can be put to the expert by one or other party, but only by mutual agreement (or court order) if the query goes beyond simply *clarifying* what is in the report. Any answers given to such questions are treated as part of the expert's evidence.[67] In a sense, this sort of witness belongs to both parties, and to neither party, because the expert's principle allegiance is to the court.[68]

---

60 If the court is considering a single joint expert in a multi-track case, a case management conference must be called, unless the parties agree.

61 See discussion of nomenclature in Ch. 2

62 In fast track cases, the court essentially asks itself, "Is expert evidence really necessary?" and if so, "Is there any reason why such evidence should not come from a single joint expert?"

63 It is possible, if not common, for the court to order that the expert evidence be limited to that already gathered by the claimant in investigating the strength of his case. It does save time and money, but can carry the risk of bias.

64 See discussion in Ch. 2 about selection process. And see PD 35, para.8.1 for detailed guidance about instructing experts.

At trial

The way in which expert evidence is *received* at trial is also controlled by the court. In fast track cases, the presumption is that expert evidence will be given in the form of a *report* – and not orally. The expert will *not* attend in person to give evidence unless the court orders.[69] Remember that fast track cases only last one day and the trial costs are fixed. To be allowed to have the expert there at the trial, the court would have to be satisfied that oral evidence from the expert has probative value which would outweigh the attendance costs.

In any event, the report prepared by the single joint expert would 'represent' the evidence in the case on the issues to which it relates, and the report should not normally be amplified or tested in cross-examination[70] at trial, although as always the discretion remains with the court.

In complex cases, or where the expert evidence is very technical or controversial, the court will more likely allow the parties to have their own expert, as is the norm on the multi-track. In such cases, the rules about how instructions should be given, and the form reports should take, still apply. As does, with even greater purpose, the requirement that the expert's primary duty is to the court, and not to the party instructing him. In addition, the court may direct a discussion between the experts, if this would help to identify areas of agreement and narrow the issues in dispute. At least some of this evidence will normally be given orally at trial.[71]

Disclosure of expert evidence pre-trial

An expert's report, as we saw earlier, is the quintessential example of a privileged document, which protects it from inspection by an opponent at the disclosure *of documents* stage. However, a party who seeks to *rely* on such evidence at trial *must*

---

65 CPR, r 35.8(2)
66 See CPR, r 35.10 and PD 35, para.2.2 as to the form of expert's reports.
67 CPR, r 35.6(3)
68 CPR, r 35.3

69 CPR, r 35.5

70 Remember that the single joint expert is the one expert – it is not a competition.
71 When it can be cross-examined on in the usual way.

disclosure it to the other side *before the trial.* In effect, the privilege must be waived if a party wants to *make use of* the evidence at trial. This rule ensures that the parties can know the nature and strength of the case against them, and so make informed decisions about compromising the action. It is very important, and sanctions for non-compliance are severe. A party who fails to disclose an expert's report, may not use the report at trial or call the expert to give evidence orally unless the court gives permission.[72]

Where the parties instruct a mutually agreed expert, then disclosure in effect occurs all along the way. Where directions allow the parties to instruct their own expert, then they will be directed to exchange the expert evidence they propose to call. Usually such disclosure is ordered to be mutual (or simultaneous, so one has not seen the other's beforehand), but in some cases it may be appropriate to allow sequential disclosure. It is important to remember that it is only evidence which a party proposes to *rely* on at trial which needs to be disclosed; if it is not part of the case, it need not be disclosed, and this can include draft reports.[73]

Sometimes an expert's report is disclosed, but not relied upon at trial. In such circumstances, any party to whom the report was disclosed may *put the report in evidence himself,* although not for the purpose of impugning it.[74]

B.   WITNESSES OF FACT

Just as with expert's reports, the rules[75] also provide for the *early exchange* of the evidence of the *witnesses of fact to be adduced* at trial. This is done by exchanging witness statements. We saw that these are used as the means of putting evidence before the court when making interim applications.[76] They are also the format[77] in which the evidence to be given by a witness at trial is disclosed to the other side.

---

72   CPR, r 35.13
73   *Jackson v Marley Davenport Ltd* [2004] 1 WLR 2926

74   There is a general rule that parties may not impugn their own witnesses. The main exception to this is the so-called 'hostile witness', as to which see below.
75   The main rules are found at CPR, r 32.4 and 32.10
76   See generally Ch. 4

77   With permission, the court may exceptionally allow disclosure by exchange of a witness summary.

Again, the point is to promote openness in the conduct of litigation. Note the procedural similarities with expert evidence:

- Directions for the exchange of witness statements are usually made upon allocation to the fast- or multi-track, or at a case management conference. They may be made at other occasions, as necessary. Witness statements are not usually exchanged in small claims track cases.
- Normally *mutual* exchange is required, which takes place after disclosure of documents.
- Privilege in the witness statements is *waived on disclosure.*
- If the evidence is *not exchanged* as directed, the witness may *not be called* to give oral evidence, unless the court gives permission. Whether the court gives permission will depend on the circumstances of the case and the nature of the default. Whatever decision the court makes should be proportionate.
- Statements that need to be exchanged are those of the witnesses a party *intends to call at trial.* There is no need to disclose a statement from someone who will not be called as a witness at trial.

In addition (fairly obviously) witness statement should only include matters capable of being adduced at trial. They should not include inadmissible evidence.

---

78 CPR, r 32.5 and see below
79 Or by affirming

Use of witness statements at trial

By the party calling the evidence:

A witness statement is not evidence in itself, unless it is admitted as a hearsay statement.[78] Rather it is a means of disclosing what the evidence will be. It is a longstanding principle that normally evidence is given at trial orally and on oath.[79]

Having said that, the rules invoke a useful time-saving device: where a witness is called to give evidence, his witness statement shall *stand* as his *evidence-in-chief*,[80] *unless the court orders otherwise.*[81] However the evidence-in-chief is given, it will start off in the same way (the witness will be called, take the oath, identify himself etc) and end up in the same way, when the witness is tendered for cross-examination. To the extent that the statement stands as the witness's evidence-in-chief, the gap between those two will be very short.[82]

Where witnesses do give evidence-in-chief orally, they may 'amplify' their statement and/or give evidence on new matters which have arisen since the statement is made, *only* if the court gives permission.[83] There needs to be a good reason, in keeping with the overriding objective, not to confine witnesses to their statements, since the other side may be taken by surprise by new material, which is precisely what the rules about disclosure are intended to avoid.

By the other side:

Where the witness is called to give evidence:

The other party or parties may *cross-examine* the witness on *any* aspect of the disclosed witness statement, regardless of how much of the evidence in the statement might have been referred to in any oral examination-in-chief.[84]

---

80 In effect, the court treats the witness as having given the evidence in the witness statement.

81 Which the court might do if the evidence is very complex or if there are doubts about the credibility of the witness or the court otherwise wants to hear the evidence directly from the witness.

82 Such witnesses would need to verify that the statement is theirs and true to the best of their knowledge.

83 CPR, r 32.5(3)

84 If the witness statement stands as the evidence-in-chief, then it has effectively been covered in its entirety in any event.

Where the evidence is not adduced at trial in any form[85]

In this situation, any other party may themselves put the *disclosed* statement in as hearsay evidence.[86] The rules now expressly provide that a witness statement can only be used for the purposes of the proceedings in which it was disclosed, unless the witness consents in writing or the court gives permission or the witness statement has been put in evidence at a hearing in public.[87]

C. HEARSAY EVIDENCE IN CIVIL CASES

Admissibility

The rule excluding hearsay evidence is a venerable, if not always venerated, rule of evidence. An assertion made otherwise than by a person while giving oral evidence in the proceedings, which is tendered to establish the truth of what was asserted, is hearsay. Very broadly, the rule excludes second-hand evidence, of the "Mary told me she wore a red dress to the party" variety, which cannot be easily tested under cross-examination. If the issue is whether Mary did wear a red dress to the party, let's hear from her what she had on at the time.

To understand whether an out-of-court statement is or is not hearsay, one must focus on the *purpose* to which the evidence is being put. In relation to any item of evidence one must ask: "What job of proof is this statement being asked to do?" Is the tribunal of fact being asked to believe that what was said in the statement is true[88]? Or is it relevant for some other purpose – for example, to show that the statement was made, or the tone of voice in which it was made.[89] If the former, the assertion is hearsay; if the latter, it is not.

There are now many exceptions to the rule against hearsay. The common law rule was abolished in civil cases many years ago,[90] principally because juries are rare in civil trials. It is still important, however, to know whether or not an item of

---

85 Including as a hearsay statement – see below

86 CPR, r 35.5(5). It is not very common that evidence which is not going to be adduced at trial will be disclosed to the other side, but it can happen. And occasionally the party to whom it has been disclosed can make use of it.

87 CPR, r 32.12

88 Often referred to as 'truth of contents.'

89 The person who heard the statement can give direct evidence of these facts.

90 By the Civil Evidence Act 1995 ('CEA 1995')

evidence is hearsay in a civil case because of the need to give notice to the other side of the intention to adduce such evidence. If the evidence is not hearsay, the special rules do not apply.

Reception

Thus, in civil proceedings, all hearsay – of whatever degree[91] – is admissible, except where the live witness, as it were, would not have been competent to testify.[92] But there are requirements to tell the other side of the intention to adduce hearsay evidence.

The only issue for the judge, when considering hearsay evidence, is what *weight* to ascribe to it. This depends in part on common sense considerations, including how easy it would have been to call the witness to give direct oral evidence, how closely in time the statement is to the event it describes, whether it involves multiple hearsay, whether there is any ulterior motive in keeping the witness away.[93] It can also depend on the extent to which the party relying on the hearsay evidence has complied with the notice rules.[94]

Hearsay comes in different shapes and sizes. Where the hearsay evidence takes the form of the witness statement of a person *not* being called to give oral evidence, then the party intending to adduce that evidence must, when exchanging the statement, 'inform' the other parties of that intention and explain why the witness is not being called.[95] No formal notice as such is required. It is important to appreciate that in this situation, parties on the other side may request that the 'live' witness attend to be *cross-examined* on the statement – if indeed he or she is alive (a dead witness is a particularly compelling reason for wanting to adduce a hearsay statement). The purpose of the general admissibility of hearsay evidence is not, after all, to keep witnesses who can give evidence away from a party's opponents.

---

91 CEA 1995, s 1(2)(b)
92 E.g. because of unsound mind.
93 CEA 1995, s 4(2)
94 Relating to adducing such evidence at trial. They do not apply to interim hearings: CPR, r 33.3
95 CPR, r 33.2(2)

If the hearsay is merely contained *within* the evidence of a witness who *is* being called to give evidence, then beyond the exchange of the witness statements nothing further need be done. The other side, by reading the witness statement, can instantly see the nature and source of the hearsay contained within it.

But if the hearsay takes some other form (e.g. an invoice from a shop or a diary entry), then the party wanting to adduce the evidence complies with the rules by serving a proper 'notice' to the other side, clearly identifying the hearsay evidence, stating the intention to adduce the hearsay statement and again giving reasons for not calling the maker of the statement (e.g. the person who wrote up the invoice or made the diary entry).[96] Such a notice must be served no later than the time for exchanging witness statements.[97]

Remember that a failure to comply with the notice rules does not render the hearsay evidence inadmissible as such, but it can affect the *weight* attributed to it and/or result in an adverse costs order.[98] But always bear in mind that ultimately it is for the court to decide what evidence it wants to hear, on what issues and in what form.[99] *The bottom line is that the court has the power to exclude admissible evidence.*

Finally, note that the more crucial the evidence, the less you will want to rely on hearsay evidence – it carries less weight than evidence which can be tested by, and stands up to, cross-examination. In other words, just because you can do something, does not necessarily mean you want to. Other alternatives, such as evidence by deposition, may need to be considered.[100]

D. CHARACTER EVIDENCE IN CIVIL CASES

The law has always been more lenient about the reception of bad character evidence in civil cases without juries – that is to say most civil cases. The assumption is that judges alone are able to make the necessary distinctions between evidence which is

---

96 CPR, r 33.2(3)
97 CPR, r 33.2(4)
98 CEA 1995, s 2(4)
99 CPR, r 32.1

100 An alternative to admitting a hearsay statement if the evidence is important, but the witness may be unavailable for trial, is to apply for an order that the witness evidence be taken on oath before trial under CPR, r 34.8-34.12. This is a costly alternative to a hearsay statement, but if the evidence is vital, this option allows the evidence in effect to be cross-examined and tested in a formal setting.

relevant to culpability and evidence which is relevant to credibility – an important distinction in principle, but one which in any case can be difficult to maintain.

Character evidence can be relevant in one of three ways:

(i) It can be a fact in issue (as in defamation cases);

(ii) It can be relevant to a fact in issue if it demonstrates that it is more likely that the party is or is not capable of doing what is alleged. This is known as evidence of 'disposition' or 'propensity';

(iii) It can be relevant to the credibility (or 'credit') of a witness. If the witness is an habitual liar, perhaps their version of events is not to be believed.

It is useful to distinguish between good and bad character evidence.

Bad character going to credibility

Witnesses giving testimony in a civil case, including parties to proceedings, are open to attack on their credibility as witnesses by means of evidence of bad character, subject to the restrictions set out in *Hobbs v CT Tinling and Co Ltd*[101] and the court's general discretion to control cross-examination.[102] According to the *Hobbs* case, such questions are only proper if the nature of the imputation would *seriously affect the opinion of the court as to the credibility of the witness on a matter to which he had testified.*[103] If the evidence of bad character is very remote in time or character, it will struggle to meet this test. Indeed an attempt to 'delve into a man's past ... to drag up such dirt as can be found'[104] might smack of desperation.

---

101 [1929] 2 KB 1
102 CPR, r 32.1(3)
103 op.cit., (per Sankey LJ)

104 See e.g. *R v Sweet-Escott* (1971) 55 CR App R 316 (per Lawton J, at p 320). Criminal cases, of which this is one, are now governed by statute, but nevertheless they retain the same principle.

Bad character going to propensity

As regards evidence of *disposition or propensity* (to do something 'bad'), the test for admissibility in civil cases is one *of relevance*. If the evidence is of potential *probative* value in relation to the fact in issue, it will be admitted unless its prejudicial effect would be *disproportionate*.

The leading case is *O'Brien v Chief Constable of South Wales*,[105] involving an allegation of malicious prosecution following a miscarriage of justice review. The House of Lords held that the test in civil cases is different, and less strict, than in criminal cases. Lord Philips said that the test was that of relevance in that the evidence is admissible if it is 'potentially probative' of an issue in the claim. He went on to say that the policy considerations giving rise to the position in criminal cases (and in particular the Criminal Justice Act 2003) should be kept in mind by a civil court when giving effect to the overriding objective. Where the risk of prejudice was 'disproportionate' to its relevance, the judge should manage the case accordingly by excluding the evidence, but the civil courts are *not* bound to apply the criminal test to a civil suit.

Any arguments on whether evidence of bad character should be admitted, therefore, will turn on its probative value (which need not be huge) measured against its prejudicial effect, which should not be disproportionate to the persuasive value of the evidence. Criminal lawyers will recognise this balancing act – it is not very different[106] from the general discretion to exclude prosecution evidence in criminal cases. Bear in mind, however, that the implications of losing most civil actions are not generally so severe as to make it particularly easy to convince a judge that it would be disproportionate to allow in relevant evidence of this kind. But again, every case is different and actions raising the most serious allegations will be those where this balancing act is most difficult to execute.

---

105 [2005] 2 AC 532

106 In criminal cases the court is concerned to see if the probative value 'outweighs' the prejudicial effect. 'Disproportionality' is a somewhat wider notion.

Good character evidence

Some of the older cases suggest that evidence of good character is never admissible in civil cases, presumably because even very virtuous people can be careless once in a while. It must be doubted whether this could be so in a case involving very serious misconduct or allegations of a criminal nature. Perhaps a more modern approach is to say that admissibility depends on relevance and the probative value of the evidence, bearing in mind than none of us are perfect all of the time.[107]

3.   WITNESSES AND THE COURSE OF TESTIMONY

A.   COMPETENCE AND COMPELLABILITY

As you prepare for trial, it is important to know whether the witnesses you want to call are legally capable of giving evidence – and if so, whether they can be made to give evidence if they are unwilling to do so voluntarily. 'Competence' refers to the first of these; 'compellability', to the second.

The *general rule* is that *all* persons are *both competent and compellable*. Exceptions in criminal cases involve spouses and civil partners of the accused and defendants themselves. There are *no such exceptions in civil cases*. An important exception relating to children (and persons of unsound mind) applies in *both* criminal and civil cases. The tests differ, although they borrow from each other.

Children

Test for competence

The manner in which a child's[108] evidence is given is tied up with competence.

The first question is whether the child is competent to give *sworn* evidence.

---

107 See e.g. *Hatton v Cooper* [2001] RTA 544, a case arising out of a collision where there was little evidence of what had actually happened. The Court of Appeal held that the trial judge improperly relied on evidence from the claimant's employer to the effect that the claimant was an excellent driver. But in so doing, the court referred not to a blanket ban as such, but its lack of probative value in the case ("completely worthless" was how Jonathan Parker LJ put it.)

108 A person is a child in the legal sense if under the age of 18.

The test is one which used to govern both the civil and criminal law, and is known as the test in the case of *R v Hayes:*[109] does the child *understand the 'solemnity of the occasion'* and the *special duty to tell the truth,* over and above the ordinary social duty to do so? This is sometimes referred to as being '*Hayes* appreciative'. The idea behind the *Hayes* test was to move away from the need for belief in the divine sanction against lying, and so secularise the test for the giving of sworn evidence.

If the child does not satisfy the *Hayes* test, the court can look to s 96 of the Children Act 1989, which applies to a child who is called as a witness, but who does not, in the court's opinion, understand the nature of the oath (in the *Hayes* sense). Such a child's evidence can be heard *unsworn,* if, in the court's opinion, the child understands that it is his duty to tell the truth and he has sufficient understanding to justify his evidence being heard.[110] This in essence is not only about intelligibility, but also about being able to distinguish between the truth and a lie. It seems to be a somewhat stricter test than in criminal cases.[111]

If the child does not pass the requirement for the giving of unsworn evidence either, then that child is not competent to give evidence.

Procedure for assessing competence

It will be for the court to form an opinion on these matters before hearing the child's evidence (obviously). The judge will do this (possibly on an earlier occasion if the issue is controversial) simply by asking the child some questions, in part to determine intelligibility and in part to ensure the child understands the importance of telling the truth, especially in the context of a trial. Except in family law cases,[112] all such inquiries will be made in open court. Whether a child warrants such an examination is a matter for the judge – there is no fixed age for these things, but as a rule of thumb, inquiry would be made of a child under 14, although much would

---

109 [1977] 1 WLR 234
110 Children Act 1996, s 96(2)

111 In criminal cases, children who are 14+ years of age and *Hayes* appreciative can give sworn evidence (and there is a rebuttable presumption that a child of 14+ is *Hayes* appreciative). Children under 14 can give evidence unsworn if they can understand and give intelligible (not to say intelligent) answers to questions: Youth Justice and Criminal Evidence Act 1999, ss 53-57.

112 These are not covered by the CPR and will usually be heard in private.

depend on the child in question. The 'watershed' which divides children who are normally thought to be able to give sworn evidence from those who are too young to do so tends to fall between about eight – ten years. Following *Hayes,* questions will be secular in nature. It will be for the person tendering the child as a witness to prove the child is competent.

A child who is judged competent to give evidence (whether sworn or unsworn) will also be *compellable* to give that evidence. If this seems a little harsh, remember that arrangements can be put in place to assist the child in giving his or her evidence.

Special arrangements

Special arrangements can be made for any vulnerable or frightened witnesses, including children. The general rule that evidence is to be given orally and in open court is qualified by the court's ability to control the way in which evidence is received. For example, CPR, r 32.3 provides that a witness may provide evidence through a 'video link' or 'by other means'. In *Polanski v Conde Nast Publications Ltd*[113] it was said that videoconferencing orders are readily available to all litigants in civil proceedings. 'Special measures' as they are called in criminal cases, include screens, videotaping examination-in-chief and cross-examination by video link and so on. There does not seem to be any reason these cannot equally be employed as appropriate[114] in civil cases. Consideration and decisions about such measures can be made at a pre-trial review, if not earlier.

Note too that interpreters, signers and so on can be used to help witnesses with special needs give their evidence.

---

113 [2005] 1 WLR 637

114 If the witness statement stands as the evidence-in-chief, then it is really only the cross-examination which you need to worry about.

Persons with mental incapacity

In civil cases, persons with mental incapacty must be able to satisfy the *Hayes test* and give sworn evidence. It is important to remember that not all mental incapacity leads to an inability to give evidence on oath. If this is not possible, however, note that there is *no provision* enabling such a person's evidence to be heard unsworn.

Just as with children, the court will assess the competence of the witness before the evidence is heard. It may be necessary to hear expert evidence about the mental condition in question, and in particular how it would impact (or not, as the case may be) on the ability to give sworn evidence.

Again, if the witness is found to be competent, that witness is also compellable to give evidence. Special measures may be put in place as appropriate.

B. EXAMINATION-IN-CHIEF

There are some important evidential and procedural rules relating to the course of presenting one's own evidence and examining witnesses-in-chief. It is as well to remember that, although a judge may ask questions of a person giving evidence from time to time, it is essentially the advocate's job, not the judge's, to question witnesses. Moreover, the credibility of the witnesses's evidence is an important aspect of getting one's case across. There are, however, limits on what an advocate may do to bolster the quality of the evidence being presented. Because of the prevalence of letting a witness's statement stand as the evidence-in-chief, these rules are less important in civil cases then they once were. Indeed examination-in-chief is something of a dying art in such cases, but you need to be aware of these rules for those occasions when you need to re-examine a witness following cross-examination or indeed when called upon to examine a witness in chief in the old-fashioned way. It does happen from time to time. These rules also appear in assessments!

The rule against asking leading questions in examination-in-chief

Leading questions are those which include or suggest the answer in the question, thus leading the witness from the one to the other. An obvious example might be: "And was the weather warm and sunny?" The purpose of the rule is obvious and really just a matter of common sense: the evidence is meant to come from the witness, not the advocate. The rule, however, is not applied strictly where the subject matter of the question is not in dispute.

The so-called 'hostile witness'

An advocate conducting an examination-in-chief should know what the evidence of that witness is! Sometimes, witnesses get muddled or say the wrong things or suddenly remember something differently. There is nothing an advocate can do about a witness who is 'unfavourable' in this sense, except soldier on as well as possible.[115] However, if a witness actively does not wish to tell the court, truthfully, what he knows, then that witness may, with the court's permission, be declared 'hostile'. This allows the advocate in effect to cross-examine the witness to the extent of putting to him his witness statement which is inconsistent with what he is (or is not) now telling the court. It is not a happy situation to have such a witness on your hands (the witness is supposed to be on your side!) and mercifully it does not happen very often. But having the witness declared 'hostile' and making the best of it, is better than just sitting down with a baffled look on your face.

The rule against previous consistent statements

A 'previous consistent statement' is a statement made by a witness on an occasion before the trial which is *consistent* with that witness's testimony at trial. The general rule, in both civil and criminal cases, is that such statements (also called

---

115 An allied principle is that an advocate may not impugn his own witness.

self-serving statements) are not admissible in evidence by the witness who made them to bolster his or her *credibility in court*. The rationale for the rule is that the evidence does not improve with repetition, and there is a risk that a witness may be tempted to manufacture evidence and so artificially increase the credibility of his story by merely repeating it several times before the trial takes place. Do not confuse this rule with the hearsay rules – they interact with one another, but they are different.

As ever, there are exceptions to this rule. The two which are applicable to civil as well as criminal cases are (i) rebuttal of allegations of recent fabrication and (ii) memory refreshing documents.

(i) Rebuttal of allegation of recent fabrication

This is a common sense exception. If, under cross-examination, a witness's version of events is challenged as being a 'recent' invention, it would be very unjust if the general rule prevented that witness rebutting that allegation by pointing to earlier statements which are consistent with his evidence-in-chief. If, however, the allegation is that the story has been untrue from the outset, then the general rule would prevail.

(ii) Refreshing memory

This rule is based on the assumption that evidence-in-chief is given orally. To the extent that it is, it is useful to distinguish between refreshing the memory before giving evidence ('out of the box') and while giving evidence ('in the box').

continues ... /

In the box:

This is all about *facilitating* the giving of oral evidence by reference, while giving oral evidence, to a memory refreshing document – for example, a log book or diary entry. To establish that such a document may be used, the advocate must establish that it was made *'contemporaneously'*.[116] The document must be produced for inspection by the court and opposing parties. Such documents can be used not only to refresh or 'jog' a memory (in which case a true copy will do if the original no longer exists), but also where the witness no longer has any independent recollection of the events in question, but can give evidence of the accuracy of the document (in which case the original must be produced). In either case, it is important to remember that it is the testimony of the witness, *not the document*, which constitutes the evidence in the case.[117]

Out of the box:

It is a matter of common sense (and practice) for witnesses to refresh their memories from notes made by them, and in particular their own witness statements, *before* going into court to give their evidence. This is done routinely and is uncontroversial; the giving of evidence is a test of veracity, not a feat of memory. Opposing counsel would be entitled to see any document used in this way. Usually, this would be the witness statement, which should have been exchanged and will be in the trial bundles. If the witness statement is not to stand as the evidence-in-chief, the witness will not have access to it while the evidence is given (if, as is more usual, the witness statement does stand as the evidence-in-chief, then the witness will simply have access to his statement, verify it as being his and true to the best of his knowledge, and then be tendered for cross-examination).

---

116 This needn't be literally contemporaneously, but it should have been made as soon after the events as possible and in any case while they were still 'fresh in the mind'. *R v Richardson* [1971] 2 QB 484

117 But see below about the possible effects of cross-examination.

It is open to the judge, as a matter of discretion and in the interests of justice, to permit a witness who has *started* giving oral evidence-in-chief, to take a break and refresh his or her memory (out of the box) from a statement made by that witness closer to the time of the events in question – again, usually the witness statement. This is allowed if:

- the witness says he cannot now recall all of the details of the event because of lapse of time;
- the witness made a statement much nearer the time of the event, which records his recollection at that time;
- the witness did not read this statement before giving evidence;

and

- the witness wishes to read the evidence before continuing.

If the judge gives permission, the witness can either withdraw or read the statement 'in the box' (during a sort of 'time out'), but in either case the document must again be removed from the witness before continuing to give oral evidence-in-chief.[118]

Evidential status of memory refreshing documents

A document used to refresh the memory *does not, as such, become evidence* in the case. It merely *facilitates* the witness in giving his or her oral evidence. The cross-examining advocate is entitled to inspect any memory refreshing document, without making it evidence in the case. Equally, he or she is entitled to cross examine on the contents of the document without making it evidence, provided the questioning does not go beyond the parts used by the witness to refresh his/her memory. However, where the advocate's cross examination goes *beyond* the parts

---

118 *R v Da Silva* [1990] 1 WLR
31. The witness can only
do this once!

of the document used in examination-in-chief, this entitles the party calling the witness to put the *document* in evidence and to let the tribunal of fact see it.[119] This principle is of greater significance in criminal cases, but the fact remains that, where relevant, an advocate will always have to weigh up the possible advantage of cross-examining beyond the memory refreshing parts of such a document against the possible disadvantages of the entire document being put in evidence. Once the document itself becomes evidence in this way, it will of course be admitted for the truth of its contents.[120]

C. CROSS EXAMINATION

There are two particular important rules relating to cross-examination.

(a) The rule against rebuttal on collateral issues

There is a general rule, applicable to both criminal and civil cases, that answers on cross-examination given by a witness on *'collateral'* matters (e.g. questions relating to the credibility of the witness) are incapable of being rebutted. This is sometimes called the rule of 'finality of answer', which is a confusing description because the rule does not mean that the tribunal of fact must accept the truth of the answer, nor does it mean that the questioner should not be given every reasonable opportunity to extract the admission in cross-examination which he seeks. What it does mean is that evidence may not be adduced by the party asking the questions to rebut the answer given by the witness. Hence, it might be better described as the rule *against rebuttal*.

The point of the rule is to prevent advocates getting off the point and cases spinning out of control on peripheral issues.

The difficulty with applying this rule is that it is not always easy to determine

---

119 *Senat v Senat* [1965] P 172

120 Because there is no rule against hearsay in civil cases. See discussion above.

what is relevant to an issue in the case, and what is relevant only to credibility or some other purely collateral issue. The rule only precludes rebuttal on matters relating to the latter. And, of course, there are the inevitable *exceptions* to the rule. They are:

- previous convictions
- allegations of bias
- general reputation for untruthfulness

and

- physical and mental disability affecting reliability.

Thus, if a witness does not accept in cross-examination that, for example, he has previous conviction or suffers from a mental disability affecting reliability (assuming this fact is only relevant to the credibility of the witness), then by way of exception to the general rule, evidence of this fact can be put in evidence to rebut the witness.

(b) Previous inconsistent statements

Clearly, one of the most effective ways of undermining a witness in cross-examination is to put to that witness a statement made by him or her on an earlier occasion which contradicts the evidence given at the trial. These are known as previous *in*consistent statements. Believe it or not, ss 4 and 5 of the Criminal Procedure Act 1865, which sets out the manner in which such statements are to be put to a witness, applies to civil as well as criminal cases.[121] The point is to protect witnesses from being unfairly surprised during cross-examination and to give them a chance to correct their evidence.

---

121 So long as they are relevant
   to a matter in issue.

In a nutshell, the circumstances of the making of the statement are put to the witness, who is given a chance to accept that the statement was made and that it is true, before being contradicted. Under s 5, which relates to documents only, the witness should be shown the statement, asked to read it and then asked if he stands by his evidence on oath. This may be enough for the witness to see the need to change his testimony. If not, the advocate may put the document into evidence to show, at the very least, inconsistency. In civil cases, the document will also go in for truth of contents because there is no rule against hearsay.[122] Again, the advocate will have to weigh up the advantages in doing this against any possible disadvantages (e.g. other aspects of the document which support or confirm the other side's case).

---

122 The same is true in criminal
    cases by virtue of the
    Criminal Justice act 2003.

revision tips

- Appreciate the differences between **legal professional privilege (LPP) and public interest immunity (PII)**: the former confers a right to withhold from inspection; the latter, confers a duty to withhold from disclosure. LPP resides in the client, and can be waived; PII is a matter of public interest and it is for the court to determine where it lies, given that one starts from the proposition that in general the public interest is 'better served by candour than suppression.'

- Remember also to distinguish between legal advice privilege and litigation privilege, both heads of LPP.

- Regarding expert evidence:

  - The **norm** in **small claims track** cases is **no expert evidence**

  - Use of the **single joint expert** on any given issue is the **norm on the fast track**, the evidence to be admitted in **written form**

  - **Separately instructed experts, giving oral evidence, will be more acceptable** and common in **multi-track** cases.

  - The expert's duty is **to the court**, to express true and complete professional opinions.

- Do not confuse the **evidence-in-chief** with the **cross-examination** rules affecting the course of testimony.

It is worth reading ...

The judgment in *Warner v Penningtons* (A Firm) [2010] EWHC 1753 (Admin). This case is not long and it covers at least 5 aspects of litigation in addition to expert evidence, including summary judgment and third parties (of which there are several). A good one for a revision check!

PART SIX
last orders

CHAPTER 18

Paying the piper:
costs and public funding

Costs are a highly significant aspect of civil procedure – they overshadow almost every aspect of the litigation process, from start to finish. At least four different parts of the CPR are devoted to the subject.[1] A related issue is how litigation is financed. Litigants are primarily responsible for paying their own legal fees, which will be incurred on their behalf from the moment they first engage solicitors.[2] If someone is publicly funded, it will be the Legal Services Commission ('LSC') who pays the lawyers, with or without contributions from the litigant himself. One way or another, costs quickly add up.

There is, however, a generalised expectation that a losing litigant will usually be required to pay the costs of the winner. This obviously helps the winner with his legal bills. But the extent to which this is what the court actually orders can depend on other factors, and in particular the conduct of the litigants. The courts have become very adept at case specific costs orders. The interplay between costs and public funding can, moreover, throw up a host of special considerations. The unifying theme is: who pays for the privilege of litigation?

Much of this book, as indeed much of civil litigation, is devoted to what goes on before trial. There are a host of *interim* applications which might be made, at the end of which there will be an order for costs. These are known as interim

---

1 CPR, Parts 44-47

2 A solicitor's bill typically includes the solicitor's remuneration for work spent on the case (at an hourly 'charge-out' rate), together with counsels' and any experts' fees, counsel's brief fees, court fees and any other standard or fixed charges, expenses and disbursements.

costs orders. You need to be aware of the various possibilities, some of the more common of which are conveniently set out in the rules, with an explanation of what each one means.[3] Most are self-explanatory, although there are some interim costs orders which sometimes confuse beginners. One is understanding the difference between 'costs in the case' and 'claimant's (or defendant's) cost in the case'. 'Costs in the case' means that whoever wins the substantive case at trial will recover (from the loser) the costs of the interim application. 'Claimant's (or defendant's) costs in the case' is a little more favourable to the named party: it means that if the named party wins at trial, he will recover from the loser the costs of the interim application, but if he loses, he will *not* be asked to pay the other side's costs of that application.

Where the court decides the parties should each bear their own costs, then the order can either be 'each party to pay its own cost' or 'no order as to costs.' In most cases, the result is effectively the same if the court really does make no order as to costs (that is to say, is silent on the matter).[4] This order is appropriate when there are no obvious winners and losers, or everyone is a winner and loser, or it just seems fair in the circumstances.

Although much of what follows also applies to interim costs orders, the focus of this chapter will be *final* costs orders, i.e. costs orders made after final determination of the issues at trial. In particular it will review basic principles, and highlight some of the more complex issues that can arise in making such orders.

Let us start with two propositions: the first is that the costs payable by one party to another are in the *discretion* of the court.[5] It is important to remember this. Nevertheless, there are various principles, guidelines and indeed rules and statutes which affect, inform, and sometimes restrict the exercise of this discretion, the most pervasive of which is that *normally the loser pays the winner's costs.*

3 PD 44, para.8.5. BCP, para.66.29 also has a useful list of the common costs orders, interim as well as final, and their meanings.

4 There are some exceptions but only in very specialist cases; CPR, r 44.13.1

5 CPR, r 44.3(1)

Remember, too, that it is the advocate's responsibility to seek the appropriate order for costs. This includes knowing what to expect regarding how (or how quickly and accurately) costs will be quantified, in any given case. There are basically three choices. Costs will either be:

(i) *Fixed,* in which case set amounts will be used which are 'fixed' by reference to the value of the case. Fixed costs are used for early disposal of cases (for example summary judgment) and also for trial costs on the *fast* track.

(ii) *Summarily assessed,* that is to say, quantified on the spot and on a somewhat rough-and-ready basis. On a summary assessment winners will typically ask for their costs to be assessed using the figures in their schedule of costs, which will have been filed beforehand. It will be for the other side to argue that certain figures should not be allowed, either at all or in a reduced sum.[6] Summary assessment is used for short, and so somewhat predictable, interim applications and the costs leading up to trial on the fast track. This is *not,* however, an appropriate method of calculation for publicly funded litigants.

(iii) The subject of a *detailed assessment.* This is a complex procedure used for long interim applications, and multi-track cases. This is appropriate for cases of any complexity and where the receiving party is publicly funded.[7]

Subject to this, there are essentially *two issues* to think about regarding *final* orders as to costs: (1) *who pays?* and (2) *how much?*

---

6   Applying the same sorts of principles, discussed below, about what is a reasonable amount, reasonably incurred.

7   PD costs, para.13.9. As to costs payable by a publicly funded party see PD Costs, para.13.10 and discussion below.

1. WHO PAYS?

The *guiding principle*[8] is that, as a general rule, costs should (as it is sometimes quaintly put) 'follow the event'. Officially, this is described as meaning that an 'unsuccessful' party will be ordered to pay the costs of a 'successful' party.[9]

Notwithstanding, in deciding what order to make, *the court must have regard to all of the circumstances,*[10] including the complexity of the case, the amount of money involved, and so on. CPR, r 44.3(4) particularly requires the court to have regard to the *conduct* of the parties: for example, was the appropriate pre-action protocol complied with? Did the claimant exaggerate his claim? Was it reasonable to pursue a particular allegation?[11] The idea was that the CPR should move away from 'all or nothing' costs awards, and towards those which are more case sensitive, and the court was given wide powers to achieve this, even if it means awarding different costs on different aspects to different parties. The possibilities include ordering (either by themselves or in combination):[12]

(i) a proportion of another party's costs
(also called 'percentage orders');

(ii) a stated amount in respect of another party's costs;

(iii) costs from or until a certain date only
(sometimes called 'time specific' orders);

(iv) costs incurred before proceedings have begun;

(v) costs relating to particular steps taken in the proceedings;

(vi) interests on costs from or until a certain date,
including a date before judgment.

---

8 This principle, which is hardwired into the civil costs system, seems to have survived the extensive review of the question of costs by Lord Justice Jackson (Review of Civil Litigation Costs (Ministry of Justice, December 2009). For a summary of the recommendations see BCP, 66.1/WB para.44.3.1

9 CPR, r 44.3(2)
10 CPR, r 44.3(4)
11 CPR, r 44.3(5)
12 See range of possibilities in CPR, r 44.3(6)

Issue based costs alone can get complicated, and not a little messy, which is why using some (or a carefully chosen selection) of these other alternatives, and in particular 'percentage awards' have become increasingly popular. Nowadays, when a party is 'partially successful', the trial judge will be apt to award that party a *percentage* of generalised costs (to reflect the extent to which the party was in fact 'successful'), rather than awarding actual costs on a more piecemeal basis. It can sometimes be simpler and save a lot of hassle.[13]

In any event the courts are very sophisticated these days about fine tuning costs orders to be case specific. In *Straker v Tudor Rose*[14] it was said that the trial judge should first identify the successful party and then consider whether there were reasons for departing from the general rule and, if so, to make clear the factors justifying this. In *Midland Packaging Ltd v HW Chartered Accountants* [2010] EWHC B16 (Mercantile), for example, the claimant had clearly won in money terms, having been awarded substantial damages, and beaten a Part 36 offer made by the defendants. But the judge decided that in other respects the success had only been partial. In particular the claimant had grossly exaggerated the amount of the claim and had been unsuccessful on points which occupied a significant amount of the hearing. The judge concluded that the defendant had in fact been successful on six out of eight issues which the court had to determine and that there had been no real attempt to settle by the claimant, who had overplayed its hand and fought the case to the bitter end. He therefore awarded the defendant 75% of its costs from the date of its Part 36 offer (plus 21 days), to be offset against the costs otherwise due to the claimant.

---

13 See e.g. *English v Emery Reimbold and Strick Ltd* [2002] 1 WLR 2409. But see below discussion about multiple parties.

14 [2007] EWCA Civ 368

2. HOW MUCH?

A. AS BETWEEN THE PARTIES

There are two 'bases of assessment': the *standard* basis and the *indemnity* basis. Both of these only allow such costs as were reasonable in amount and reasonably incurred, but the standard basis (and only the standard basis) has a *further* requirement of *proportionality.* Any doubts on any of these matters are resolved in favour of the pay*er* on the *standard* basis and in favour of the pay*ee* on the *indemnity* basis. The indemnity basis of payment is therefore the *more expensive* for the payer and is only used in exceptional circumstances or to be punitive. As the name implies, *the normal basis of assessment is the standard basis.* Unless specific reference to the indemnity basis is made, the presumption is that costs are assessed on the standard basis.[15]

B. AS BETWEEN SOLICITOR AND OWN CLIENT

Conditional Fee Arrangements (CFAs) and Insurance have now joined the traditional retainer as a means of privately funding all types of civil work.[16] These are also known as 'no win, no fee' agreements and the idea is that if the client loses the case, he will not have to pay anything to the firm acting *for him*; but if he wins the case, his lawyers will be entitled to charge him at the usual rate, plus a pre-arranged uplift by way of a 'success fee'.[17] The extent of the success fee is intended to reflect the risks involved in taking on the action, so that if the case is a sure winner, the success fee should reflect this, although sometimes if types of cases are viewed in the round, the success in one case can be viewed (by the solicitors, anyway) as financing failure in another.[18]

Do not confuse CFAs (which are a legitimate, and increasingly common form of funding) with 'contingency fee' agreements. The latter (which effectively take

---

15 CPR, r 44.4

16 Except family cases. Some people also have legal expenses insurance as part of home and other insurance.

17 This will be set at a percentage, which can be as high as 100% of the costs otherwise chargeable to the client. It is *not* a percentage of the damage award! See generally discussion at BCP, para.6.3ff.

18 Note that these days the courts prefer two-stage to single-stage success fees, to reflect varying degrees of effort and risk. Typically there will be a lower success fees for cases that settle early (say 25%) and higher success fees (say 100%) for cases which go to trial (or settle at the court door).

a percentage of the client's winnings) are *not* a permitted form of funding in this country.[19]

Bear in mind that the 'no win, no pay' description only refers to what a client must pay to his *own* lawyers. It is important to appreciate that a litigant who loses may still have to pay quite a lot in the form of costs to his winning opponent. This can be a very significant pay-out, made all the more painful if the litigant is a claimant who has also won no damages! This eventuality is usually catered for by insurance policies known as 'After the Event' policies.[20]

The courts are not often asked to make any determination in respect of the fees owed by parties to their own legal team, but it can and will if there is a dispute. As regards the traditional retainer, as well as certain aspects of CFAs, when there is such an assessment, the basis is the *indemnity basis modified* by various presumptions regarding client approval and so on – a basis, clearly, which is *more* 'expensive' than the standard basis.

It is easy to see, therefore, that even if the case is won, what a party has to pay his own solicitors (whether the solicitors' bill is disputed or not) is usually *more* than what will be recovered from the unsuccessful opponent in litigation. This used to be particularly true of CFA funded litigation, but the court can now order the loser to pay both the success fee (sometimes at a set rate) and the relevant insurance premium (which protects against paying loser's costs).[21] But there is still likely to be some gap between outlay and what one, as winner, recovers in costs from the loser.[22] This discrepancy, which may vary in its size, is one of the risks of litigation. Even if relatively small it represents 'nuisance value' and is relevant to any decision to litigate or settle. Lay clients are much better informed these days, than they used to be, about how much of a bill they are running up with their solicitors, and so should have a clear idea both

---

19 The jurisdiction of England and Wales.

20 You can find detailed discussion of funding arrangements in BCP Part B.

21 CPR, r 43.2.1(l) and (o). Losing to a CFA funded opponent can be a disaster.

22 Sometimes referred to as 'otherwise unrecoverable costs'. See CPR, r 44.3B for excluded items in CFA cases.

before and throughout the litigation of what the costs-benefit risks are all along the way.[23]

C.   PUBLIC FUNDING AND COSTS

Assistance under the Community Legal Service ('CLS') replaced legal aid in 2000. It sought to tighten up eligibility and excluded certain types of claims from its ambit, most notably *personal injury actions* (save for clinical negligence).[24] The means testing is strict[25] – public funding is really only available to the very poor. There is something of a sliding income scale under which litigants receiving public funding will be required to contribute some money of their own towards the cost of their representation.

In addition there are nine criteria for full representation, which include considerations like alternatives to litigation, whether the small claims track can deal with the claim, whether a CFA is a viable option. An important factor in money cases[26] is the cost-benefit ratio, which is a crude way of assessing value for money. In the general run of such cases, funding will only be granted if:

(i)   The prospects of success are very good (80%+),
and the value of the claim *exceeds* the likely level of costs.

(ii) The prospects of success are good (60% – 80%),
and the value of the claim is *twice* the level of likely costs.

or

(iii) The prospects of success are moderate (50% – 60%),
and the value of the claim is at least *four times*
the level of likely costs.

---

23 Solicitors are under a professional duty to provide this information to clients.

24 It is expected that these claims can be successfully funded by CFAs. If the current government has its way, a lot more claims will be added to the list of excluded cases, including clinical negligence.

25 Based on gross and disposable income and disposable capital.

26 In non-money claims the test is whether the likely benefit outweighs the costs, such that a person paying privately would be prepared to risk the litigation.

So, when it funds a case, how much does the Legal Services Commission ('LSC'), which administers the CLS, pay out to its lawyers?[27] Rates of pay are usually agreed and closely monitored, but mirror assessment on the *standard* basis. Thus the LSC's costs of financing the litigation of a publicly funded party would *theoretically* be the same as the costs that would be recovered from the loser (assuming that party is not also publicly funded), because those are also normally assessed on the standard basis.

However, the LSC may have costs or authorise expenditure that is not recoverable from the losing litigant; these might include various administrative costs, the cost of extending funding and so on. Thus there will be a gap between what the LSC expended in the litigation and what it recovers in costs from the losing litigant (and any contribution from the funded litigant). *This shortfall is not written off by the LSC!* A winning publicly funded claimant will be required to make up the difference out of his damage, or other award. That is to say, the LSC has a *first charge* on any *'property recovered or preserved'* by a publicly funded litigant *to recoup their costs of financing that person's litigation.*[28] This is known as the *'statutory charge'* and it arises whenever the LSC has to pay *more* to finance a funded party's litigation than it recovers from that person's own agreed contribution to his representation, plus any costs paid by the other side.

The statutory charge is of critical importance and is of particular relevance where the publicly funded *winning claimant* does *not* get an order for costs against the loser. It can mean that a huge proportion of any damage award would just go to the LSC, pursuant to the statutory charge, to pay for the litigation costs incurred by them.[29]

Let's look at two typical situations where public funding affects costs orders:

---

27 This work is now contracted out to whole firms and organisations

28 Access to Justice Act 1999 ('AJA 1999'), s 10(7)

29 This often arises in family law cases where the property which was 'recovered or preserved' is the family home. Typically the LSC would take a charge, but not execute it in such a case.

(a) Where the loser is publicly funded

If the loser is publicly funded, s 11 of the Access to Justice Act 1999 ('AJA 1999'), comes into play. This provision limits a publicly funded loser's liability to pay costs to that amount, if any, which it is 'reasonable' for him to pay, having regard to all the circumstances, including the resources of the parties and their conduct. Certain items are excluded from consideration as a resource in this context, including the first £100,000 of the publicly funded person's 'dwelling house'.[30]

Obviously there is a correlation between a litigant's ability to qualify for public funding and his lack of resources, so it is not uncommon to find that due to the operation of this statutory 'costs protection', a publicly funded loser will be ordered to pay little if anything in costs to the winner. A privately paying claimant will thus want to think twice before suing an impecunious defendant who will be publicly funded, since that claimant (unless insured) will likely have to pay for the pleasure of winning, to say nothing of the fact that the defendant may well not be able to pay any damages either!

But at least claimants can choose whether to litigate. This is not true of defendants. What about the privately paying defendant who has no choice but to fight or settle, while the claimant is publicly funded? In this situation, help may be available from AJA 1999, s 18 which allows the court to order that the LSC pay the costs of the successful defendant if *certain strict conditions* are met. In summary (for first instance cases) an order for costs against the LSC can be made if the following criteria are met:

(i)   The party in whose favour the order is made is:
      - *successful* (the matter was 'finally decided in that party's favour'),
      - *unassisted* (not publicly funded),

---

30   Community Legal Services
      (costs) Regulations 2000,
      SI 2000/441, reg 7(1).

- *a defendant* (did not start action at first instance[31]);

(ii) The *loser's own liability to pay has been considered* (under AJA 1999, s 11);

(iii) It is *just and equitable* to make the order;

and

(iv) The defendant would *suffer financial hardship* if an order were not made. This last requirement is meant to exclude insurance companies and 'wealthy folk' who would not really miss the money.[32]

(b) Part 36 offer scenario.

We saw how Part 36 offers work in Chapter 15. Let us assume a publicly funded claimant is suing a defendant, who has made a Part 36 offer. The claim is a money claim and the offer is not accepted so the case goes to trial. If at trial the claimant's damage award is 'more advantageous' than the defendant's Part 36 offer, then costs may well 'follow the event' as usual.[33] If, however, the award is not as advantageous as the Part 36 offer, then the costs situation is effectively reversed after the initial 21-day period for acceptance. But this claimant is publicly funded and AJA, s 11 precludes the court ordering a funded party to pay more than a reasonable amount (if any amount) in costs.

Of course, the claimant has just won some damages and the defendant might well say that the claimant should pay costs out of the money which has been recovered in the action. The LSC, however, may say that they have a first charge against that fund for financing the claimant's litigation pursuant to the statutory charge. *Cook v Swinfen*[34] considered this and decided that the defendant was the one who got priority over what is now the LSC. That is to say, the defendant is entitled to set off some or all of damages he is obliged to pay the claimant in damages against costs he is entitled to recover from the claimant who failed to better his offer of

---

31 Beware the defendant bringing a counterclaim. He becomes a claimant in respect of that action.

32 Per *Denning MR in Hanning v Maitland (No 2)* [1970] 1 QB 580

33 Assuming no other reason to deviate from the general rule.

34 [1967] 1 AER 299

settlement.[35] Now, of course, whatever amount in damages is left for the claimant after the defendant has held back the costs payments to which he is entitled, will be subject to the statutory charge – overall, a devastating result for the claimant.[36]

D. SPECIAL COSTS SITUATIONS

Finally, there are two situations that are not at all unusual, which require a variation on the usual costs theme.

(a) Multiple defendants

When a claimant sues two defendants and is successful against one but not the other, a strict application of the general rule would mean that while the claimant would get costs from the unsuccessful defendant, he would have to pay the costs of the successful defendant. But where it was *reasonable* to proceed (and continue to the end) against both defendants (for example, because the defendants were blaming each other and it was impossible to anticipate who was liable), an adaptation of the general rule may be possible. The court has discretion to order, in effect, that the losing defendant pay the winning defendant's costs. This sort of order comes in two forms:

(i) Bullock Order[37]

Here the claimant is ordered to pay the costs of the winning defendant, but once paid these can be recovered from the losing defendant in addition to the claimant's own costs. The order would sound something like this:

> Judgment for C against (unsuccessful) D1 with costs
>
> The case against (successful) D2 dismissed; C to pay D2's costs
>
> D1 to pay to C the costs so paid by C to D2.

---

35 A variant of this is the so-called 'Lockley Order' which allows interim costs payable by a publicly funded litigant to be set-off against any eventual award of damages. *Lockley v National Blood Transfusion Service* [1992] 1 WLR 492.

36 Furthermore, to the extent that an unassisted defendant does not recover all of his costs from the legally aided claimant, there may be scope for getting an order from the LSC. See the interesting case of, *Kelly v London Transport* [1982] 1 WLR 1055 which considered the meaning of 'successful' in the context of the old system of payments into court.

37 This gets its name from *Bullock v London Transport Omnibus Co* [1907] 1 KB 264, CA.

(ii) Sanderson Order[38]

Here the payment of the successful defendant's costs comes straight from the losing defendant, instead of being routed through the claimant. This sort of order is appropriate if the claimant is insolvent or publicly funded, as there will be greater certainty that the money will actually reach the winning defendant. Thus the order might sound like this:

> Judgment for C against D1 with costs.
>
> The case against D2 dismissed
>
> D1 to pay D2's costs.

The choice of order is completely within the discretion of the courts. It is normal for the courts to want to protect the successful defendant as a first priority, as that party had no choice but to defend the case. Having said that, where everyone will get burned no matter what the court does, it is a proper exercise of the court's discretion to attempt to spread the pain as fairly as possible.[39]

Finally, the various types (and permutations) of costs orders discussed earlier can come in particularly handy when dealing with multiple parties. They provide flexibility. In the case of *McGlinn v Waltham Contractors* (No 5)[40] the claimants sued three defendants (D1, D2, D3) for £3.65 million. The claimant lost against D1 (who had offered to settle for £300,000!). The claimant did better against the other defendants, but only just. He was awarded just under £440,000 from D2, and just under £135,000 from D3, for a grand total of about £535,000 – less than 1/7th of his claim. The costs incurred by the claimant amounted to some £2.2. million. D1's costs were £880,000 and D2's were £1.2 million (D3's costs were put over to another hearing – no 6, probably!). The total costs so far were about £4 million. Issue-based costs were ordered on a percentage basis between the

---

38 This gets its name from *Sanderson v Blyth Theatre Co* [1903] 2 KB 533, CA.

39 This can happen when claims and counterclaims also get thrown into the mix. See especially *Bank American Finance Ltd v Nock* [1988] AC 1002, HL

40 [2007] EWHC 1419 (TCC). Any case with a (no 5) after it's name is going to be messy!

claimant and D2 in relation to liability and quantum. The claimant was ordered to pay D1's costs, the judge declining to make a Sanderson or Bullock order. On this aspect alone, the claimant was already out of pocket, even before taking into account the fact that he would have to pay his own costs of pursuing D1. Ouch!

(b) Claim and counterclaim

Where a counterclaim amounts to a total set-off (one that completely extinguishes the claimant's claim), then the defendant will have been successful and costs will (all other things being equal) follow the event. Where, however, a defendant's set-off is less than the claimant's (and there is no other answer to C's claim), the defendant should make a Part 36 offer on the 'balance' to protect himself on costs because, unless the set-off fails, the claimant can never 'beat' the offer.

Otherwise, where *both* claim and counterclaim succeed or fail, the traditional rule has been that there should be two judgments and two separate orders as to costs.[41] This is known as the rule in *Medway Oil,* which also said that in such a situation, a defendant is only entitled to costs 'exclusively referable' to the counterclaim. But this can cause hardship where much of what is referable to the counterclaim is also referable to the main claim (and so is not 'exclusive' to the counterclaim). This will happen where there is a high degree of interconnection between the actions, including a set-off claim which does not entirely extinguish that of the claimant. For a long time now, where the rule in *Medway Oil* would cause hardship, the court has been able to make a 'special order' on costs, either a single order or no order as to costs.[42] The court's options in this regard are now reinforced by the breadth of discretion in the CPR, and in particular by the use of percentage and other orders, as described above.

---

41 *Medway Oil and Storage Co Ltd v Continental Contractors Ltd* [1929] AC 88

42 *Chell Engineering Ltd v Unit Tool and Engineering Co Ltd* [1950] 1 ALL ER 378

revision tips

- Do not drown in the detail. Get a good grasp of the basics.

- Make your own table of the possible orders which the court might make on an *interim* application and their meaning. Rank these interim costs orders from best for claimant through to best for defendant.

- Be able to recognise the common situations or circumstances where costs may not 'follow the event.' But bear in mind that every case is different.

- Be aware of the effect of public funding on costs outcomes.

- Know the range of costs orders available to the court at the end of a trial, includinge percentage or time specific orders, as alternatives (or adjuncts) to straight issue-based orders.

It is worth reading ...

The judgment of Dyson LJ (as he then was) in *Halsey v Milton Keynes General NHS* [2004] EWCA Civ 576; [2004] 1 WLR 3002 (don't worry about the *Steel v Joy* component). I think you are ready for this case now, having come something of a full circle from the one I suggested you read at the end of Chapter 2 (which gets a mention here, you will notice). This is a straightforward case, and the judgment reads a bit like a mystery thriller – you will be asking yourself: "What will the claimant suggest next?!"

CHAPTER 19

Judgment and beyond

Most litigants assume that once judgment is given in a case, it is all over. They would particularly like to think so if they have just been successful. But they would be wrong. In particular, the loser may want to appeal, or the winner may have to enforce the judgment. These are two particularly important aspects of the litigation process, which are discussed briefly below.

Final judgments and orders

We have seen over these pages the various *orders* which the court might make on interim applications; at the end of a trial, what is handed down is a final *judgment* on the issues in dispute.[1]

After final judgment is pronounced, it must be drawn up. In the Queen's Bench Division, this is normally the responsibility of the parties; in the County Courts and the Chancery division, the court will take charge of this, unless it prefers, and so orders, some other alternative.

Most judgments (and orders) must state the name and judicial title of the person who made it.[2] They take effect from the date they are *given,* not the time they are drawn up, sealed and served.[3] A judgment for the payment of money (including costs) must be complied with within 14 days of the order, unless the

---

1 This is the typical nomenclature. The distinction is more rooted in the old rules than the new, and can be a bit fluid. In terms of enforcement, there is little practical difference between an 'order' and a 'judgment': CPR, r 40.1 and WB

2 Exceptions include default judgments and consent judgments: CPR, r 40.2

commentary.

3 Although the court can order otherwise: CPR, r 40.7

court orders otherwise.[4]

Many judgments or orders are made 'by consent'. A 'true' consent order is a record of a contractual agreement between the parties, and (once perfected) can only be varied or set aside on grounds rendering the contract void or voidable (e.g. fraud or misrepresentation). 'Tomlin orders'[5] are a special kind of consent order, used when complex terms are agreed, or the terms go beyond the original issues in dispute, which in any case are secreted away into a 'schedule'. Thus such orders are typically worded:

> And, the [claimant and defendant] having agreed to the terms set forth in the schedule hereto, it is ordered that all further proceedings in this claim be stayed, except for the purpose of carrying such terms into effect. Liberty to apply[6] as to carrying such terms into effect.

Sometimes the court hands down a judgment on terms to which both parties are agreeable (indeed they may have suggested the terms to the court). This is not a true consent order in the contractual sense,[7] and will be enforced like any other court order or judgment.

1. APPEALS

Litigants will want to know whether they can appeal a case they have lost – sometimes even before it has started! So it is important to have a working knowledge of the appeals structure. For examination purposes, the best way to learn the basics is by creating your own diagram (a pyramid, perhaps) incorporating the following: (1) where the appeal lies, (2) whether permission is or is not required and (3) whether

---

4   CPR, r 40.11. The court can order payment by instalments, for example. In personal injuries cases, the judgement will set out the amounts awarded under each head of loss, and the amounts which are to be 'diverted' to the state to repay relevant benefits pursuant to the Social Security (Recovery of Benefits) Act 1997.

5   Named after Tomlin J. See Practice Note [1927] WN 290

6   This part of the order allows parties to return to court if there are problems implementing the order and/or to enforce compliance. It does not signify an ability to come back to change the order.

7   See e.g. *Siebe Gorman and Co Ltd v Pneupac Ltd* [1982] 1 ALL ER 377.

grounds must be shown or the appeal dealt with by way of re-hearing. PD 52 has a table you can work from, as does BCP, figure 71.1.[8]

If the appeal is a first appeal, you will need to note especially what *track* the case is on and *distinguish between interim and final decisions* – this affects *where* the appeal lies, and, in particular, when appeal lies directly from the County Court to the Court of Appeal. An appeal from a *final* decision in the County Court (even a District Judge) in a *multi-track* case will go directly to the Court of Appeal rather than a High Court judge.[9] A decision is final if it is determinative of the entire proceedings. Clearly this includes a judgment on the merits of a claim. But it can also include a decision following a hearing of a preliminary matter, if it would have the same effect. An obvious example might be a decision on the question of whether an action is time-barred. Orders to strike out or grant summary judgment, on the other hand, are *not* final (although they might feel a bit that way to the parties). They are classic interim remedies.[10] *Most case management decisions are, in the nature of things, interim decisions.*

As regards *leave* to appeal, generally speaking, permission to appeal is needed *unless* the liberty of the individual appealing is at stake (not common in civil cases).[11] Permission can be sought 'from both ends', as it were, asking the court below first.

The appellant must, within 21 days of the lower court's decision,[12] file an appeal notice to initiate an appeal.[13] This must set out the grounds on which it is alleged the judge went wrong. If permission to appeal is required, the request (even though made orally to the court below) must be re-iterated in the appeal notice,[14] which must be served on the other side within seven days of being filed.[15] The appeal court can give permission to appeal on the paperwork alone, although the matter can be reconsidered at an oral hearing if requested by the appellant.[16]

It is also necessary to *distinguish between first and second* appeals[17]. The latter *always* go to the Court of Appeal. Furthermore, it is easier to get permission to appeal if it is

---

8   BCP's checklists 33 and 34 are useful too.

9   Destination of Appeals Order, art 5

10 This aspect of the rules can get complicated, as even the WB admits at para.52.0.12. Do not get bogged down here – an exam will test you by using obvious examples of interim versus final orders.

11 CPR, r 52.3(1)

12 CPR, r 52.4(2)

13 This can be done electronically: PD 52, para.15.1B

14 CPR, r 52.4(1)

15 CPR, r 52.4(3)

16 See generally PD 52, para.4

17 'Second appeals', perhaps rather obviously, are those where the issue has been dealt with once already on a first 'rung' of the appeal ladder.

your first time: the test is 'real prospect of success' or some 'other compelling reason' why the appeal should be heard.[18] This should sound familiar – it is the same test that is applied in summary judgment hearings when deciding whether the defendant ought to be allowed to go to trial with his defence.[19] Not surprisingly, the test is more stringent for second appeals, which after all have already been considered once. Permission for a second appeal will only be granted where it raises an important point of law or principle, or there is some other compelling reason to have the Court of Appeal hear it.[20]

Finally, most appeals involve a *review* of the decision of the court below, not a re-hearing.[21] They are won or lost on the question of whether the lower court's decision was plainly 'wrong' or otherwise unjust because of some procedural or other irregularity. For this reason, the appellate court (unless it orders otherwise) will not receive new evidence which was not before the lower court. It would be illogical to criticise the lower court's decision on the basis of evidence it had not even heard.[22] Thus fresh evidence will only rarely be permitted on appeal – for example where credible evidence was simply not available at trial, but its impact would have been very important to the outcome. If the courts are not pretty strict about this, all appeals would be very susceptible to becoming re-hearings.[23]

JUDICIAL REVIEW

Judicial Review is a vast subject and beyond the scope of this book. It is important, however, to distinguish it from the appeals system. Judicial review describes the process by which the courts exercise a *supervisory* jurisdiction over the acts and omissions of public bodies (including the courts), to ensure that they are lawful.

Permission to apply for judicial review is always required, and the time limit for making the application is very short – three months. There is now a pre-action

---

18 CPR, r 52.3(6)
19 See Ch. 5
20 CPR, r 52.13(2).
    And see BCP, para.71.15
21 CPR, r 52.11(1)

22 CPR, r 52.11(2). This is
    why it is important to get all
    relevant evidence in front of
    the court hearing the case.

23 See e.g. *Hamilton v Al
    Fayed* [2001] EMLR 15
    and discussion at WB
    para.52.11.2

protocol for judicial review cases.

The typical orders sought by way of judicial rule are:

(i) A mandatory order (an order that the public body in question carry out its public duty);

and/or

(ii) A prohibitory order (an order restraining the public body in question from acting outside its jurisdiction or otherwise unlawfully);

and/or

(iii) A quashing order (an order in effect setting aside the order of the inferior court or public body in question);

and/or

(iv) A declaration or injunction (which can be ordered alongside one of the others above, if applicable).

For detail, as necessary, consult CPR, Part 54. Practitioner commentary is extensive, both in the WB and BCP, which also has a useful Checklist 35 worth consulting.

2. ENFORCEMENT OF JUDGMENTS

Parties who get judgment in their favour do not automatically obtain their remedy. The other side must do as the judgment or order says; in the case of money, this would be payment within a certain time (usually 14 days). Most people abide by court orders, but not all. Many a winning claimant has been distressed to find that the defendant cannot or will not obey the court's order.

'Cannot' is more of a problem than 'will not'. If, say, a money judgment has been made against someone with no money or assets, then it is probably not worth the paper it is written on. Legal advisors should be alert to such possibilities from the outset.

'Will not' leads to consideration of the powers of the court to enforce compliance with its orders, which are extensive. Enforcement of judgments is a solicitor's area of expertise, and so will figure most prominently on their professional examination syllabus. The BPTC requires an outline knowledge of the subject only. Whatever the level of detailed knowledge required, start with a basic understanding of the different kinds of enforcement order and marry them up with the type of asset or circumstance to which they relate. If, for example, a judgment debtor[24] has no earnings, it would be silly to seek to extract money from him by applying for an attachment of earnings order.

Let us consider a money judgment. If too little is known about the judgment debtor's financial circumstances, then it will be necessary to obtain this information, either informally or by means of a court order.[25] Armed with such knowledge, it is then possible to consider the most appropriate method of enforcement. In particular, have a look at the following:

(a) Execution against goods

Such orders are available in both the County Courts[26] (for judgments under £5,000) and in the High Court.[27] Armed with such an order, the relevant officer of the court will call on the judgment debtor's premises. No forced entry is allowed. Once inside named goods can be seized,[28] and (failing payment of the judgment debt) sold to satisfy the debt. Be aware that certain goods are exempt for these purposes, e.g. basic domestic needs, tools of the debtor's trade and so forth. Watch out too for

---

24 A 'judgment creditor' is a person who has obtained judgment for the payment of money. The person against whom such an order is obtained is called the 'judgment debtor.'

25 CPR, r 71.2

26 By means of 'warrant of execution'

27 The mechanism for doing this in the High Court sounds like something to do with football (the writ of fi.fa., short for fieri facias), but it is not (although it might help you remember its name).

28 It is possible to take 'walking possession' which is in effect a form of earmarking (but not then removing) certain goods for seizure if the debt is not paid.

goods belonging to someone else (especially hire-purchase goods), which may not be seized. You might be surprised how many things a judgment debtor has which do not belong to him!

(b) Charging orders (execution against an interest in *property*)

It may be possible to get a charge against property owned by the judgment debtor – this might be a good idea if he has a house.[29] But take care that there is some equity or beneficial interest in the property – it is no good if it is mortgaged to the hilt! Applying for such orders is a two-stage process; only the second stage involves a hearing and gives interested parties the opportunity to make submissions as to why an interim order made earlier should not be made final.[30] Getting the charging order may be easy enough – converting the charge to actual cash, however, can be difficult because in order for that to happen the property must be sold, which is yet another step in the process.

(c) Third party *debt* orders

This is useful if someone owes money to the judgment debtor. A typical example is a bank account in the name of the judgement debtor which is *in credit*. In effect, this form of order requires the person owing the debtor money, to pay the money directly to the judgment creditor. It is no good, however, if the bank account is overdrawn – in such a case the debtor owes the bank money, not the other way around! Like the charging order, the third party debt order follows a similar two-stage process.[31]

(d) Attachment of *earnings*

This may be the only option if the judgment debtor has no assets other than a salary. It is in effect an order directed to the debtor's employer requiring the latter to deduct,

---

29 It needn't be real property – shares or other securities qualify: Charging Orders Act 1979, s 2.

30 See generally CPR, r 73

31 See generally CPR, r 72

and pay to the court, a named amount from the employee's salary. These orders can only be made in the County Court following an order for payment by installments which has fallen into arrears. The amount deducted is limited by a formula which is intended to ensure that a judgment debtor is left with enough to live on.[32]

This is just a taster of the possibilities; if you need more detail, consult a practitioner text, which can point you to the myriad of sources for the various enforcement options.[33] If the new provisions under the Tribunals, Courts and Enforcement Act 2007 ever get brought into force it will make life a lot easier by gathering the options, insofar as they relate to money judgments, together under one procedural roof, as it were, which will make a nice change.[34]

---

32 See generally Attachment of Earnings Act 1971, s 24

33 The WB's Practice Guide 9 (in Part D Vol 1) is useful

34 See commentary in WB to CPR Part 70

revision tips

- Do not run out of steam and be tempted to leave out enforcement altogether – it is usually worth a fairly simple question or two.

- Make your own table on the appeals structure, from whatever source you choose (BCP has a useful table at 71.1). Do not just mindlessly copy the information – create your own representation. The idea is to get the knowledge into your head, not merely transmit it from one piece of paper to another!

- Do not get bogged down in too much complexity. For example, an exam will use obvious examples of interim versus final decisions when testing your knowledge of where an appeal lies.

It is worth re-visiting ...

Two cases:

- The judgment in *R (Lawer) v Restormel Borough Council* [2007] EWHC 2299 (admin), which I mentioned at the end of Chapter 4, for its discussion on the function and limitations of judicial review, and a warning against the over-enthusiastic making of such applications.

- The judgment in *Charlesworth v Relay Roads Ltd* (2) [2000] 1 WLR 230, which I mentioned at the end of Chapter 11, where judgment had been prounced, but not drawn up – an interesting reminder that the opera is never over until the big lady sings!

CHAPTER 20

Approaching the exams

As the time for your assessments approaches, you will need to think about a revision plan. You want to go into the examination hall alert and in a good frame of mind, knowing what sorts of questions you will find on the paper. It is important to remember that examinations are designed to allow you to show off what you know and the extent to which you know it – they are not designed to make you fail. If you are well prepared, there should be a part of you (possibly a very small part) which is looking forward to the test.

1. REVISION

Revision is a very personal thing – some people make lists, some people use index cards, some people like mind maps. Viva la difference. Having said that, there is some general guidance which is worth imparting. The first thing is to ensure that you are very clear about what is on your syllabus and how it will be tested. Take any mock exams which your course provides, both for the experience and to highlight any weaknesses in your understanding of the subject.

Secondly, I believe it is important to revise 'little and often' and in sensible chunks, giving yourself breaks and rewards for what you have accomplished. For example, you might spend a couple of hours in the morning revising default and summary judgment (they go well together) and then go out to lunch or watch a movie or go for a run. Take a break, in other words, if only a short one. My own view is that the brain (well, certainly mine) can only take in so much in one sitting and it helps to let what you have covered 'marinate' for a while before going on to the next item on the list. Studying just before falling asleep is supposed to be good – maybe because what you have just been working on marinates all night!

In any event, whenever you do it, *always* make sure that you really *understand* what you are revising.

When reading judgments as part of your revision, note the gist of the case and highlight the one or two sentences or paragraphs which encapsulate the reasoning and principle in the decision. If you find that all you are doing is colouring the entire document with highlighting pen, then you are not being discriminating enough – you may have just changed it from white to yellow! You must extract the essence.

Indeed, as your revision progresses, aim towards reducing to one page (or a few index cards) the basics of each area you are revising. Not only will this help you distil the subject, but as you approach the exam date you will have a handful, rather than a file full, of revision notes for a last minute run-through.

Do not enter the exam room sleep deprived. My own view is that a good night's sleep the night before the exam is a good thing – what you do not know by 10 pm that night is either not worth knowing, or it is too late. Having said that, I appreciate that many people get exam fever and are too excited to sleep. If you are one of these people, it is especially important that you get plenty of sleep as you approach the exam dates. Do not stay up two nights in a row. Besides a pen and pencil, all you are taking into the exam is your brain, and you want that working to full capacity.

For similar reasons, make sure you enter that exam room appropriately fed – you don't want to be faint from hunger or so full it makes you sleepy. Have a reasonably hearty and healthy breakfast (or lunch as the case may be). This would not be a good time for a bag of crisps and a Coke.

B. EXAM QUESTIONS

It is increasingly common for civil litigation and evidence to be tested by a combination of multiple choice questions ('MCQs') and short answer questions ('SAQs'). If you have not taken a multiple choice test recently, or if you are used to exams where you can get marks for telling the assessor something you know, even if you were not asked, then you will want to familiarise yourself with both of these formats for testing knowledge.

No doubt you have been given a lot of information about the assessments from your tutors and course directors. Make sure you take it on board. Remember that you need to be as good at SAQs as at MCQs because (for the BPTC at least) you must get a minimum mark in both halves of the paper. If you only pass one half, the whole test is failed and the whole paper needs to be taken again. You do not have many re-sit opportunities anymore, so make the most of this one.

SAQs and MCQs are designed to test for a general level of knowledge, understanding, and application that can be expected of a newly qualified lawyer about to embark on a pupillage, training contract or other form of internship. The questions are not directed at abstruse or historical points of law which a practitioner might need to research. Nor do they test minutiæ such as form numbers or precisely what documents go into a trial bundle. Similarly, the principles and rules are more important than the rule numbers. The latter may be referred to in a question, but as part of the description, not something to be tested.

Mock exams will help you become familiar with the nature of the questions and level of knowledge which is required. It is important to take them, so far as is possible, in *exam conditions*. In particular, do the mock test to time and with no access to materials – these are closed book assessments!

Finally, the MCQ and SAQ formats are very different. Half of the exam will be taken up answering some 40 MCQs, and the other half, some five SAQs. In other words you will spend (on average) some two minutes on each MCQ, but nearly ten times that (about 18 minutes) on each SAQ. So they demand different exam-taking skills:

A. THE MCQS

The typical MCQ will have a paragraph or two setting out a particular scenario. There will then be a sentence posing a question, followed by four answers: [A], [B], [C], [D]. You are required to select one answer, which you record on a separate sheet of paper. All four possible answers will be credible (to a greater or lesser degree, obviously), but only one will be the appropriate answer to the question. If you choose that answer you get one mark. You get no marks for choosing any other answers, and no marks are deducted for wrong answers.

My advice when tackling the MCQs is:

(a)   Read the factual scenario carefully ...

Note things like who the parties are, whom you are advising, are you a claimant or defendant and so forth. As you are reading you should be able to identify what aspect of procedure or evidence the question is testing.

(b)   ... and read the sentence which poses the question carefully too

Sometimes this asks for the **WRONG** statement or asks you to identify which proposition is **INCORRECT**. If you are not attentive to this, it can be surprisingly easy to get the wrong answer on a question like this, because you have identified a correct procedural or legal proposition but that is not what the question has asked you to do.

(c)   Read *all* four possible answers

This is so even if the first one seems like the right one. It might well be the right one, but you *must* double check that there is not a better one below it. Sometimes one choice is only partly correct, or another choice is more accurately worded.

(d)   The process of elimination can work to get
you to the correct answer

This is often an effective way of answering a question. You can be a bit doubtful about what is correct, but more confident about what is wrong. Also, what often happens is that you can fairly easily narrow down the field to a choice between two of the answers, but the difference between those two can be quite subtle sometimes. Eliminating the wrong answer will again give you the correct one.

(e)   Treat the examiner as infallible

If your initial reaction when you read a particular question is that there is no correct answer or there are two correct answers or it is impossible to give a correct answer, read it again. If you still feel that way, swallow your pride and choose the best answer you can in the circumstances. You can complain later. The questions have been scrutinised very carefully and while it is not completely unheard of for a mistake to slip in, this is very exceptional. In any case, if there is an error, it can be taken into account when the questions and answers are all analysed after the examination.

(f) Keep the momentum going

In particular, do not let a question stop you in your tracks. Obviously some questions will take you a bit longer than others – the two minutes or so for each question is an average. But do not linger too long over any one question or let a question de-rail you so that you cannot do your best on the rest of the test.

(g) If necessary make an intelligent guess

You do not lose marks for a wrong answer, so it is always worth guessing if all else fails. Narrow down the field as much as you can, make a sensible choice and move on. Remember to think laterally and apply basic principles when guessing – it should be as informed a choice as possible.

B. THE SAQS

These are a very different sort of question. It may be worth just giving yourself a few deep breaths and a bit of a stretch before going on. Change your pencil (used for MCQs) for a pen.

A typical SAQ will set out a case study in several paragraphs, followed by two to five sub-questions based on that case study. There are 10 marks allotted to the whole of the question, although these will not necessarily be distributed evenly between the sub-questions, each of which will indicate in brackets how many points it is worth. A variation is that a single SAQ may have two 5 mark case studies (one might follow on from the other), each with a number of sub-questions. Again the total is 10 marks available for the entire SAQ.

Marks are not transferable from one sub-question to another; you cannot get any more credit for the answer to a sub-question than it is worth. Remember the SATS tests you did in school, where you could see how many marks each question was worth. It's the same idea here. The exam may be harder than "Ahmed has planted some bean seeds. What do they need to grow? (*2 marks*)" – or not, as the case may be – but you still make your distribution of energy commensurate with the marks the sub-questions attract.

SAQs are rather more nuanced and so can be more challenging than MCQs. They require more active participation and a greater degree of concentrated analysis. Not only do you have to know the relevant principles, but you have to answer a specific question about a particular aspect of that area of procedure. There is nothing (except the case study) to 'suggest' or 'trigger' the answer. In short, you have to do more of the work.

Again, it is important to take any and all mock SAQs on offer during your course. In addition, here are a few suggestions about tackling these:

(a) **Do not write too much**

It is called a short answer question, not a long answer question and it means what it says. Typically *one or two lines* will be what is required for *each* of the 10 marks in a SAQ. So if, say, there are *(4 marks)* allotted to a sub-question, it may well be advisable to use four bullet points for your answer, although if in any doubt make some additional points for insurance purposes. It is worth remembering that if, say, 4 marks is allotted to a sub-question, this does not mean you could not make, say, six sensible points. But it does mean that however many sensible points you make, your maximum mark for that question will be 4. Especially beware writing a PhD dissertation for a 2 mark sub-question and not leaving time to do justice to a sub-question worth more. Be careful, too, not to make silly points which detract from a sensible one which you have already made. Know when to stop.

(b) **Do not write too little**

You might write a few words which identify the correct principle, but fail to indicate the relevance or application to the case study. A slightly fuller or more specific response might attract more marks. Make sure that you actually *answer* the question. Even a 1 mark sub-question needs to be answered in an intelligible and complete way. Remember that a correct answer plus a correct reason can get you 2 marks if they are on offer.

(c) **Do not write too soon**

This is very important. You have about 18 minutes per SAQ and you want to use the time wisely. Remember two things: you cannot formulate answers until you think about the case-study and questions posed *and* you want each answer to each sub-question to pack a punch (and not meander all over the shop). So my advice is to *read and give the entire SAQ some thought,* before writing down your answers to the individual sub-questions. Jot down a few things as you do so (on a separate piece of paper), even as you read the case study and begin to appreciate what information the examiner looking for. It is a bit like being in a firing range – you want to gather your thoughts, take steady aim and fire so as to hit the target each time. So, you might well spend half the 18 minutes thinking and formulating points for the entire SAQ, and the other half writing out the short answers to each sub-question, carefully and methodically. Distribute your answers sensibly. Double-check that you made the appropriate number of points (or more) for each sub-question. Do not dawdle over one sub-question at the expense of another, although, as a matter of common sense (and assuming you can answer both) give a 4 pointer some priority over a 1 pointer.

Finally, as I tell my students before their exams, remember:

P repare sensibly (little and often)
A pply basic principles when in doubt (think analogously)
S leep beforehand
S ustinence beforehand

This is known as the PASSword. Many of you, I am sure, will do even better than that. Now go show them what you can do!